Merry Xmas Sa... ♡
from David xxx

DANCE OF
THE FOUR WINDS

DANCE OF THE FOUR WINDS

Secrets of the Inca Medicine Wheel

ALBERTO VILLOLDO

AND

ERIK JENDRESEN

Destiny Books
Rochester, Vermont

Destiny Books
One Park Street
Rochester, Vermont 05767
www.InnerTraditions.com

Destiny Books is a division of Inner Traditions International

LIBRARY OF CONGRESS CATALOGING-IN-PUBLICATION DATA
Villoldo, Alberto.
    [Four winds]
    Dance of the four winds : secrets of the Inca medicine wheel / Alberto
Villoldo and Erik Jendresen.
            p.   cm.
    Originally published: The four winds. San Francisco : Harper & Row,
c1990.
    Includes bibliographical references and index.
    ISBN 978-089281514-2
    1. Shamanism—Peru. 2. Hallucinogenic durgs and religious experience.
    3. Villoldo, Alberto. 4. Peru—Description and travel. 5. Ayahuasca.
    6. Quechua Indians—Drug use. 7. Quechua Indians—Religion. I. Jendresen,
Erik. II. Title
    [BF1622.P4V55 1995]
    299'.833–dc20   99–34600
                                                                 CIP

Printed and bound in the United States

20 19 18 17 16 15 14 13 12 11

For Candi
Lover, sister, wife, friend.

Contents

Preface

In 1973 I embarked upon a journey that has no end. It began as a romantic quest to experience the effects of a legendary potion. It was inspired by youthful idealism and a Ph.D. dangling like a carrot in front of my nose. I traveled to Peru, into the Amazon, and found what I was looking for. That was the easy part.

Sixteen years, three books, and many lifetimes later, I am compelled to tell the story of my journey, the story of those years.

Every mystical tradition, from the Jewish cabala to the Upanishads of the Hindus, recognizes the existence of things that can be known but not told. There are certain qualities of sense experience that seem to defy description. Frequently our most vivid and important experiences are the very ones that confound us in the telling; it is easier to abandon the effort than to relate them poorly. Such is the nature of my adventures, and two years ago I was in a dilemma. I needed to relate my story, to communicate what I knew, yet I was confounded as to how to tell it.

Many years ago a half-blind soothsayer told me that there are two kinds of people in this world: those who are being dreamed and those who are dreamers. I needed someone to dream with, someone whom I could trust, someone who believed in the things that could be known but not told—and was willing to write about them nevertheless.

Erik Jendresen and I met in 1979. In 1982 he moved to Mexico to write, and although we were more or less aware of each other's lives, we did not see each other again until the spring of 1987. In the meantime I had continued my work in Peru, and Erik had written for the stage and the screen.

In April of 1987 we traveled to Brazil together, and spent three weeks talking, reading my journals, and wandering the beaches of Rio de Janeiro.

The Four Winds is the result of our friendship and collaboration. It is my story, in his words, and it is true.

Alberto Villoldo
January 1, 1990
Palo Alto, California

DANCE OF THE FOUR WINDS

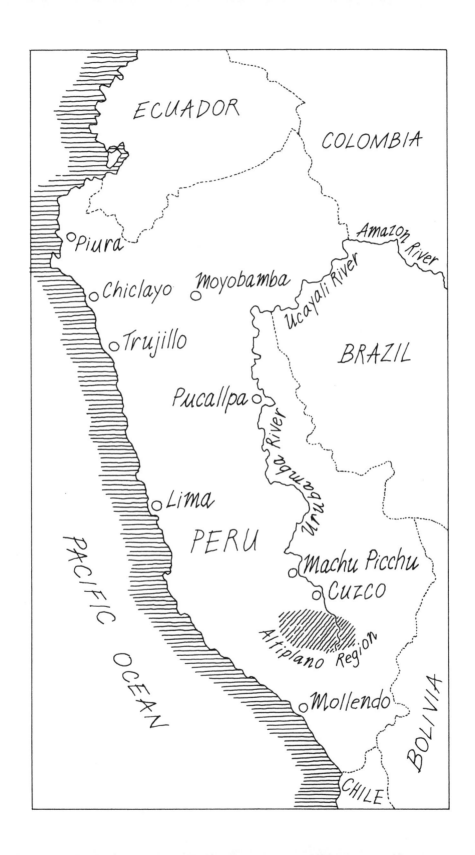

Prologue

I am moving. And breathing.

I move through a many-layered collage of wet leaves, hanging vines, reds, yellows, greens washed gray by moonlight. My head hangs low to the ground. Faster, I pant. The ground yields slightly beneath the pads of my . . . hands and feet? They move in cadence with the throbbing in my chest. My breath is hot and humid; my heart beats too fast, and I can smell myself beyond the moist tangle of the jungle.

There is the clearing and there am I, sitting cross-legged, naked, and shining wet in the moonlight. My head is thrown back and my throat is taut, exposed. Arms thrown out lax to my sides, hands palm up on the soil.

I watch myself from the edge of the jungle. Still but for my breathing. Behind me the jungle stirs sleeplessly.

I move with the lithesomeness of a shadow, following the contours of the clearing's edge to circle my prey.

Soundlessly. Closer.

Now we are breathing together. My head falls forward. My chin touches my chest. I raise my head, open my eyes to stare into yellow cat eyes, my eyes, animal eyes. A half-breath catches in my throat, and I reach out to touch the face of the jungle cat.

October 28, 1975

Third day back in the jungle. Three days waiting while Ramón prepares the *ayahuasca*. There was a full moon last night and he placed the fetid brew in the hollowed-out trunk of a tree that sits by the lagoon behind his thatched hut.

Tonight I will take the *ayahuasca* and Ramón will guide me through the ritual, take me to meet death. This time, I am prepared. Antonio saw to it, and Ramón knows, somehow, that I have done my work, completed my work of the South since—was it two years ago? Yes. That the *medico americano,* the gringo psychologist, showed up in the middle of the Amazon jungle with a taste for "the vine of the dead."

The jungle overwhelms me. The air is thick, more than a tropical density. Oxygen-rich, fragrant, humid, yes, but it feels like energy. The force of the jungle. I have become more sensitive to this sort of thing. . . .

It certainly exerts a force on my perspective of this world. Eden. The Earth's garden. I can imagine the Amazon as bottomless, a crack in the world from which spilled the living soul of the planet. A life of its own, conscious, greater than the sum of its parts.

Last night in that full moon, I wandered far from Ramón's and, in a little clearing beside an overgrown temple ruin, sat down to meditate upon this force.

I do not know if I "left my body" and . . . *became* the jaguar that was stalking me. Though my pragmatism has been shaken by my adventures, enough of it is still intact that I must qualify such experiences.

I do know that I met some part of myself last night and my heart beats faster even as I write this.

This afternoon I fasted in preparation for this evening. I made my way to the bend in the river, and, on my small, sandy patch of shore, remembered all that has brought me here and that tonight will mark the halfway point along this Medicine Wheel. When I reflect upon the events of the past two years, I realize that I do not have the power of imagination to anticipate what lies beyond tonight's "work of the West."

Can it be any more extraordinary than what has come before?

South

1

No mind is much employed upon the present; recollection and anticipation fill up almost all our moments.

—*Samuel Johnson*

I left California in February 1973. It was winter in San Francisco when I boarded the jetliner, and the middle of summer when I unfastened my seatbelt in Lima, Peru. I mention this because it served then to remind me that I had made a passage through time as well as a trip through space.

As I look back on that departure and the events that led me to it, I know that any one of them could be construed as the beginning of this chronicle. It is easy to assign significance to the moments of one's past, to see fate in history.

So this story could easily begin with my adventures among the Huichol Indians of northern Mexico, or my work with doña Pachita, the notorious healer and surgeon of Mexico City, or even my research into the spiritist practices of Brazil.

Were I to go back even further, I could cite the influence of doña Rosa, the one-eyed black fortune-teller who lived on the outskirts of San Juan, Puerto Rico, and warned me of my preoccupation with death and the uncommon realms of consciousness. I am even tempted to begin with my nanny, an Afro-American third-generation Cuban, who performed weird and wonderful rituals to summon the spirits in her little room at the end of a hall in our house in San Juan.

Or, further still, I could describe the sensations of a near-death, out-of-body experience during a blood transfusion at the age of two and a half. And I could foreshadow my predisposition to study the mind/body relationship by claiming a grandfather who became chief of surgery at a New

York City hospital at the turn of the century and returned to his native Cuba to build a hospital in the city of Havana.

But this is not an autobiography, and I have documented much of the above elsewhere. I will begin simply by saying that I had reached a critical point in my studies and the fulfillment of my doctorate in psychology at the Humanistic Psychology Institute. After three years of behavioral science, learning theory, clinical psychology, theoretical systems, and neuroanatomy, a year of clinical therapy at a community health care clinic, and a few brief forays into North and Latin American Indian healing traditions, I was restless, eager to do something different.

Something different from the antiseptic theories of Western psychology. Something different from the atrophied healing traditions of the North American Indian reservations, where the old myths and legends survive as quaint folklore.

Like many of my contemporaries, I was unimpressed with the traditional Western model of psychology. In my youthful arrogance I found it convenient to regard the practice of psychology as a patchwork process in which therapists seek to understand a person's problems by dissecting and rationalizing his or her condition, symptom by symptom, making an inevitable connection to inadequate parenting or a traumatic childhood experience. Ironically, the process itself substantiates, even reinforces, the pathology. Neuroses are cultivated for harvest during therapy.

Again and again I had found myself taking a patient by the hand and hacking a pathway through his or her tangled conscious and subconscious to the revelatory meadow of the unconscious mind.

I saw contemporary psychologists as dowdy, bespectacled paleontologists, and the fears, preoccupations, behavioral traits, or other symptoms that they sought to treat in therapy were bone fragments stuck in the surface of the psyche. They labored to collect these fossils and, piece by piece, reconstruct the skeleton of the beast within. Meanwhile, somewhere on the terrain of the unconscious, the fully fleshed-out creature wreaked its havoc.

And, in the laboratory, neurologists were slicing and staining the human brain and attempting to map neural pathways in hopes of finding the human mind and the nature of consciousness.

It was in this tradition that I had been trained. I knew how to work with the mind from the outside in, and I craved to be inside looking out. I was cynical, arrogant, impatient with the system, and judgmental of the complacency with which so many stuck a Ph.D. at the end of their name and hung up a shingle.

I was not alone. My attitude and ideology were by no means unique. On the contrary, questions regarding the nature of consciousness and the definition of mind had been posed with elegant simplicity for millennia. They are questions which remain unsolved. I would not indulge in this elaboration were it not for the nature of the adventure that lay ahead. I outline my disposition merely as a point of reference, an intellectual pre-flight checklist.

In my dissatisfaction I turned backward in time and tradition, turned my attention from the clinical psychology and neurology of the modern human to the clinical mythology and folklore of the primitive human. After all, mental and physical health are issues of equal importance, whether one is a Chama Indian of the Upper Amazon or an investment banker of the Upper East Side.

I had been able to design my doctoral thesis to support a study of traditional healing practices in the Americas and was fortunate to draw as my thesis adviser one of the world's foremost researchers in states of consciousness. Dr. Stanley Krippner was a pioneer in the study of paranormal phenomena. As director of the Maimonides Medical Center's dream laboratory, he had helped to bring dream research out of the basements and into the laboratories of universities across the country.

From San Francisco, the most accessible examples of primitive culture are in the American Indian reservations of the Southwestern United States. After I had studied the Navaho Indian tradition for a few months, it became clear to me that the displacement and acculturation of the tribes had resulted in the displacement of their tradition. My attempt to study the healing practices of the Plains Indian had been like trying to study the eating habits of a culture by examining a museum display of native basket weaving.

After that I had logged a few months in Mexico City and been fortunate enough to develop a close relationship with urban healers, who dispensed herbal remedies and practiced a variety of esoteric healing techniques, including psychic surgery. I had witnessed much sleight of hand and some spontaneous healing. This was controversial stuff, but a step in the right direction.

As so often happens, the critical instant, the decisive moment that would change the focus of my studies and the course of my life, came when

I least expected it, in a room at the end of an echo-tiled hallway at the University of California.

Brian Woodruff was an old friend, a first-year medical student at the University of California, San Francisco. I was fulfilling a graduate program requirement at the in-patient ward at a mental health care clinic north of the city, and Brian was hustling to complete his first-year requisites when he called me to suggest a late-night dinner in the city. I was to meet him at the medical school, room 601. It was after 10 P.M. when I stumbled out into the mental ward parking lot and headed south through the fog and into San Francisco.

The double door to the University of California Medical School anatomy laboratory was ponderous, institutional gray. The sound of its bar lock ricocheted off cold linoleum.

The room was the size of a small warehouse and blue-gray bright with fluorescent light. There were four rows of bakelite-topped tables upon which vague shapes were draped with black rubberized sheets. The stench of formalin wrinkled my nose. Brian set a stainless steel hacksaw beside a bucket of Kentucky Fried Chicken and an empty beer bottle, and slid off the tall stool at the head of his table.

"Hey, man! Pull up a stool. The chicken's getting cold."

Brian's cadaver was that of a young woman. The rubber sheet had been folded back to expose her upper chest, neck, and head. Her skin was like calf's hide, her complexion gray and tinged with olive drab.

"This is Jennifer," Brian said. "We've been together all semester." He lifted the surgical saw. "She's taught me more about the human body than I knew there was to learn. I'll never forget her."

"Brian . . ."

"Tonight she's going to lose her head for me, and I wanted you to be here."

"Thanks."

His eyes held mine in a matter-of-fact stare.

"You don't get to see a decapitation these days without a hundred-grand student loan and a year's worth of medical school. I thought you'd be interested."

"Why?"

"Psychologist."

"Yeah," I said. "When people lose their heads, they come to me."

He stared at me for a second, trying to gauge my tone of voice.

"You don't have to do this if you don't want to," he said. "I just thought—I mean, if you're uncomfortable . . ."

"It's all right," I said.

"If you'd rather . . ."

I looked at the bucket of chicken. "I'm just trying to stay away from fried foods," I said. I wasn't prepared to admit that I was strangely revolted, yet irresistably fascinated by the body on the table. He handed me a beer.

"Eat afterward?" he said.

"If we can."

"Incredible, huh? Just down the hall there's a lab where they conduct the foremost research in recombinant DNA. One floor down, neurologists are teaming up with biochemists and computer gurus to simulate the neural pathways of simple brain functions. But here we are cutting up dead people just like Leonardo da Vinci did five hundred years ago." He looked around the room at all the black-draped figures.

"We start on the back because it takes a while to get used to what you're doing, and it's easier if you don't have to look at the face—as if they can really look back at you and make you feel guilty for violating them with a scalpel."

He reached down and cupped the cadaver's chin in the palm of his hand. Her head moved back slightly.

Decisively, he placed the serrated blade of the saw on a wedge of cartilage between the exposed vertebrae of her neck. I couldn't take my eyes from it. When the head was free from the body, he held it in both hands.

"You wouldn't believe some of the more creative things that anatomy students think of to do with other people's body parts." He placed her head on the table, wiped his hands down the front of his smock, and handed me a drumstick from the bucket and took one for himself.

"Here's to science," he said.

"Extra crispy," I said.

We ate the drumsticks and I watched him suck the bone clean. We talked about our plans for the future: he was committed to a four-year graduate program. The discipline was imposed, sink or swim. Mine was self-imposed and lacked direction. While we talked he took what looked like a large dental drill from a drawer, plugged it into an electrical socket, and selected a bit, a round, disklike blade about two inches in diameter.

"They save the best for last," he said, and the handpiece whirred. "Hold her for me, will you?"

I took the head in my hands and positioned it for him, and he brought the spinning blade down on the forehead. When he was through, when he had rotated the head a full 360 degrees, he switched off the little saw. The whine of the blade still rang in my ears. There was a curious smell in the air, and a fine powder of bone dust lay on the face and clung to its eyelashes. He leaned over and gently blew it away.

"Imagine," he said. "No human being has ever seen Jennifer's brain. You and I are the first. Drum roll, Maestro."

And he pulled the calavarium away from the skull. I had seen a human brain. I had seen many, floating in formalin-filled lab jars. But that moment will always live for me.

Aristotle thought that the brain cooled the blood, that thinking was a function of the heart. René Descartes described the brain as the pump of a nerve fountain. It has been compared to a clock, a telephone switchboard, a computer, yet the mechanics of the brain are far more intricate than any analog. Theorist Lyall Watson wrote that if the brain were so simple that we could understand it, we would be so simple that we couldn't. And the source of all this theory and speculation was the walnut-shaped, fleshy, gray mass of tissue before me.

Brian looked at me and nodded his head toward Jennifer's. Once again I placed a hand on either side of her face, and Brian eased the brain from her head. He stood weighing it in his hands for a moment, then handed it to me. It was heavy.

Brian interrupted the silence.

"I don't believe it either," he said.

I smiled back at him, placed the thing on the table, sat on my stool, and folded my arms. It was easy to make the distinction between Jennifer and the 110 pounds of flesh on the dissecting table before me. It took no great leap of my imagination to accept that her body had ceased to function when her heart had stopped forcing oxygen and nutrient-rich blood through her tissues, and that this brain had regulated all of the systems that had animated it.

But the body does not define the person. Jennifer had lived for forty years. Fifteen thousand days of consciousness. Twenty-one million minutes of being Jennifer. One billion three hundred million instants of experience unique to her and to no other living being, for none other than Jennifer had inhabited her space and experienced her perspective. At the time of her death, each of those moments, the totality of what it had been to be Jennifer, lived as memories. Just as Brian and I were seeing her brain, she had undoubtedly seen things that no one else had seen. She had experienced emotion, intuition, and flashes of creativity. She had felt joy and anguish as only Jennifer could feel them. It was hard to believe that all that had been Jennifer was lost because this thing in front of me wasn't working anymore.

Jennifer had been conscious. What had happened to her conscious*ness*? Where had it gone? I could not help but resist the notion that it had simply ceased to be, that all that had been Jennifer was lost forever.

"What's next?" I asked.

Brian poked his nose back into the bucket of chicken. He grimaced and chose a powdery roll. "Neurology," he said. "The brain gets dissected in neurology class. Slice, stain, study its structure." He glanced down at the three pieces of Jennifer's head. "There's still some work to do on her face, but I'll get to it later." He stuck the roll in his mouth, unplugged the electric saw, and removed the bit from the handpiece.

"Aren't you supposed to have a partner?"

He nodded, wrapped the cord around the handpiece, and gave it to me. "Yeah. It's strictly one corpse per couple. I wasn't here the day we chose our co-cutters, so I got Stephanie. That goes in the drawer."

I slid open the drawer, put away the saw. "Where is she?"

"Safe in bed. Toes all tucked up. She wanted to miss this part."

I lifted a copy of the *International Journal of Social Psychiatry* from the drawer and held it up.

"Uh-huh." He nodded at the magazine. "She wants to do her resi-cency in psychiatry. You'd think she wouldn't have missed this. Stephanie would rather medicate people with personality disorders than heal them. And she has a . . . problem with the human body."

I laughed at him. The sound echoed eerily. "Very bitter," I said. "So you're in love. How long has this been going on?"

"Three months. She's going to change her specialty, settle down into a monogamous relationship, and we'll live happily ever after."

He pointed with his scalpel at the magazine in my hands. "She thinks someone should go down into the Amazon and find the folks who dispense the 'vine of the dead.' "

"What?"

"Page 256." He grinned broadly. "It would take a psychiatrist, someone who speaks Spanish. Of course you're 'just a psychologist. . . .' "

The literature on the *ayahuasca,* also known as "the great medicine," the "visionary vine," and the "rope of the dead," was scarce and confused. The most significant research in its use had been conducted by anthropologist Marlene Dobkin de Rios, the author of the article that I took home with me that evening. Dr. Dobkin de Rios's studies had been carried out on the outskirts of the jungle town of Iquitos, and focused on the use of *ayahuasca* in folk healing and religious and magical rituals. The source of the *yagé,* the broth made from the visionary bark of the *ayahuasca,* was the *ayahuascero,* the jungle shaman or medicine man to whom the methods of its preparation and the attendant rituals had been passed down for generations.

The first Western record of *ayahuasca* use was made by British botanist Richard Spruce in 1851. Spruce identified the vine as *Banisteriopsis caapi,* a climbing vine or liana that used jungle trees for support. Subsequently a handful of early twentieth-century explorers and traders of the Upper Amazon referred to the *yagé* as a potion made from the bark of the vine and the leaves of select jungle plants.

I read of reports of the specificity and recurrence of archetypal images and visions shared by two, three, or more people under the influence of the *yagé,* telepathic experiences, and the use of the vine for psychiatric purposes, a sort of jungle psychotherapy led by the *ayahuascero.* The plant was referred to as the "vine or rope of the dead" because it reportedly "took one to the portals of death and back again." Based on the richness of the mythology and on depictions of the visionary vine on ceramics, and in rock and cave paintings, the use of the plant and ritual for visionary purposes seemed to be rooted in the prehistory of South America.

This was the adventure for which I yearned. I would go to Peru, not just to sample the psychoactive effects of an obscure jungle vine, but to study the psychological traditions and altered states of consciousness of the medicine men and women, the shamans of the Amazon. Peru: the only country in the Americas where the Indian outnumbered the white man.

The two weeks following my dinner with Brian were spent searching for references to the vine and reviewing all that I knew about shamanism. One of the most definitive sources on the subject was the authoritative, if prosaic *Le Chamanisme et les techniques archaïques de l'extase* by Mircea Eliade. Eliade's study described shamanism as a religious phenomenon occurring throughout Asia, Oceania, the Americas, and among the ancient Indo-European peoples. Throughout this vast area the magico-religious life of society centered on the shaman, "at once magician and medicine man, miracle doer, priest, mystic, and poet." To Eliade, shamanism was a "technique of ecstasy."

I pored over anthropological and ethnological journals and texts. By the end of that second week I knew little more than when I started. Shamanism was a tradition found in virtually every primitive society, in every forgotten corner of the globe. In general, the shaman was a "person of knowledge," a "man or woman of vision," a mediator between the natural and supernatural forces of nature. Because these were the forces that the shaman held responsible for health and disease, the shaman was a healer. And, although ignorant of modern medicine, the shaman was said to be able intuitively to diagnose disease and, through ritual, could effect a positive change in a patient's health.

Legend held that the shaman acquired his or her extraordinary abilities through arduous study and ritual-laden exercise and by journeying into other realms of consciousness.

The concept of this primitive person as a traveler within the domains of consciousness fired my imagination. Was it possible to witness the nonconscious workings of the human mind? Must we rely on the vaguely recalled images and visions of our dreams as our only contact with the unconscious? Or are there ways to access the unconscious mind consciously?

By the time the check came from the student loan office, I had been packed for two days. I was holding a brand new passport and a reservation on the next flight to Miami and a connecting flight to Lima. It would be the last time for many years that I would be fully prepared for anything.

I called Brian, invited him and Stephanie to dinner, and spent the last of my loose change on fresh pasta, vegetables, salad greens, and a bottle of 1968 California cabernet sauvignon.

I also bought a journal, a small, leatherbound volume of 250 blank pages.

"Can I have your car?" Brian helped himself to another plateful of salad.

"My car?"

"Yeah. In case you don't come back."

Stephanie frowned, but her eyes were smiling. "Brian!"

He shrugged. "Anything can happen. He's going into the Amazon, and we're talking about a 1964 Porsche, Stephanie. A convertible. Needs body work and new seats, but I could handle that."

"Is it dangerous?" she asked casually. Stephanie was a handful. She was tall and athletic, with a straight nose, strong chin, auburn hair, and blue eyes. Effortlessly beautiful, she worked at being tough. Medical school does that to some people.

"I don't know," I said. "I haven't been there yet."

"You'll probably be captured by Oogly Boogly Indians and inculcated into their tribe," Brian said. "All they'll find is a soiled diary with 'February thirteenth. Heading upriver' scrawled in pencil on the last page."

I smiled down at the gift Brian had brought, an authentic Bowie knife with a nine-inch steel blade in an oiled black leather sheath.

"Or," said Stephanie, "you'll find refuge in the altered state of some jungle brew and never come back to reality."

"You don't think much of all this, do you?"

She smiled into her wine glass. "Psychedelic drug therapy was researched to death in the fifties and sixties. Albert Hofman, Grof, Leary, Metzner. . . ."

"LSD wasn't researched to death," I said. "It was condemned to death, federally. I'm not interested in LSD, and I'm not talking about clinical research in psychedelics."

In 1943 Dr. Albert Hofman had synthesized lysergic acid diethylamine, a substance two thousand times as strong as mescaline, the most powerful psychoactive then known. A decade of subsequent clinical research was followed by unprecedented social experimentation. By the time the substance was federally banned, it was estimated that between one and two million Americans had experienced life-altering, or at least consciousness-altering, experiences. Much of the research of the 1950s, 1960s, and early 1970s was funded by the U.S. government. I had gotten tapped, and so had my thesis adviser, by the Army Chemical Corps and the Technical Services branch of the CIA to join a couple of hundred others investigating mind-altering substances for the government and the Chemical Warfare Service. Their programs included both animal and human experimentation. There was a lot of money in it, and many academics opted to participate. The government research opportunities were unlimited. We had turned them down.

I watched Stephanie sip her wine, and leaned toward her over the table between us. "We're neophytes, Stephanie. Whether we're wearing white lab coats, administering drugs to mice and Japanese fighting fish, or interviewing tripping schizophrenics." I lifted the bottle of cabernet and filled her glass. "I'm not interested in that. It's a blade of grass."

"A blade of grass?"

I nodded. I knew what was coming would provoke her. "Claude Lévi-Strauss, the anthropologist, said that the civilized man needs to understand the workings of a blade of grass before he can comprehend the universe. The primitive seeks to know the nature of the universe so that he can appreciate the dynamic beauty of a blade of grass." She looked at Brian as though she were expecting him to say something about all this. I drained the wine bottle into his glass.

"I'm interested in folks who have entered and explored nonordinary states of consciousness for hundreds or maybe thousands of years. They're not students, they're masters, and if they know how to enter other realms of consciousness, access heightened states of awareness, healing states, then they know something that I want to know."

Her eyes narrowed. "And you expect to hack your way through the jungle and find some medicine man who's willing to share his mythology and his ritual with you."

"Yes," I said. "I do."

"Here's to it," said Brian.

He raised his glass and so did I. Stephanie smiled and lifted hers. The glasses chimed over the center of the table. Hers seemed to hold its note longer than ours, but it could have been my imagination.

When they had gone and the plates had been scraped, I dug my unopened journal from my duffel bag, cracked it open, and folded back the first page.

Emerson said that those who write to themselves write to an eternal public, and my first lines were necessarily melodramatic.

February 7, 1973

If the unconscious mind communicates with us through the imagery of dreams, draws from a lexicon of images to talk to us, can we not learn its vocabulary and talk back to it? Communicate consciously with the unconscious? Enter it? Alter it?

Are there states of consciousness in which we can disinhibit the body's latent healing capabilities?

Let us begin with the states of consciousness.

The only way to *study* consciousness is to experience its states directly.

2

*all ignorance toboggans into know
and trudges up to ignorance again.*

—e. e. cummings

You can fly into Cuzco only in the morning. The capital of the ancient Inca empire lies in an Andean valley at eleven thousand feet above sea level. The afternoon updrafts make the approach to the airfield unnavigable.

The captain muttered something through the crackling distortion of the cabin loudspeakers. The "Fasten Seatbelts" sign blinked erratically in red, and the thirdhand DC–8 banked sharply to the left, winged through a narrow gap in the overgrown mountain range, and entered the valley of Cuzco, the oldest continuously inhabited city on the continent.

Scarcely eight hours before, sometime around 2 A.M., the ten-hour flight from Miami had ended in Lima. The night was humid and starless. My senses had been deadened by the all-night flight, neutralized by the fluorescent lights and the conditioned air of the cabin, and I was struck, as I always was, by the smell of a foreign city. Lima was diesel fuel, pork rinds frying in old oil, exhaust fumes, industrial stench, and a barely discernable tang of sea air.

An *aduana* official with brilliantined hair squinted up at me, stamped my passport, and granted me ninety days in his country. I made a nest of my duffel bags and backpack, settled into a corner of the concrete-and-tile terminal, and waited for my connecting flight to Cuzco.

I feel like averting my eyes, denying the ugliness of the city that I will see when the sun rises. It's the romantic in me.

Lima. Another capital of another third world country.

Four hundred years ago, the Spanish conquerors leveled a pine forest that stretched to the sea, and Lima is a desert city. Once the hub of colonial South America, now conquered by the twentieth century. The industries have been nationalized, the republic is governed by a military junta, and a third of the country's fifteen million have come here to live in the squalor of the *pueblos jovenes* on the outskirts of town, to find work to buy bread or cornmeal or beans.

I don't want to see this.

I did see it, of course. Although I would return to Lima, pass through it many times during the next decade, come to know its museums, colonial hotels, and other charms, I shall always think of the city as I saw it that morning from the air, when the sun hovered above the horizon like a perfect orange ball, its rays filtered out by the *garúa*, the coastal fog that mingled with the smog and blanketed the capital of Peru in mist the color of wet ashes.

Cuzco was breathtaking—literally. The high-altitude air was cool, bright, sparkling fresh, and, like anything worth having, hard to get. I shielded my eyes from the sun, the sharp contrasts of light and shadow patterning the mountain faces and Spanish tile roofs. I hailed a taxi and headed downtown.

There is a legend that tells of Manco Capac, the first Inca, the "son of the Sun," born in the waters of Lake Titicaca, sovereign ruler of the Quechua Indians, who, when he had come of age, assembled his brothers and set out "toward the hill over which the Sun rose." He carried with him a golden rod. When he reached this valley surrounded by four great snow-capped peaks, he plunged the rod into the Earth and it disappeared. The sacred spot was Cuzco, "the Earth's navel," and here he founded his capital sometime around A.D. 1200.

His successors conquered most of Peru and Bolivia. The ninth Inca, Pachacuti, expanded his territory north to Ecuador and south to Argentina, and, by the time the Spanish arrived, the Inca Empire was the greatest kingdom the Western hemisphere had ever known.

And Cuzco was the seat of this empire, the largest city in the Americas, a wondrous metropolis built in the shape of a jaguar, where the Sapphi and Tullumayo rivers were diverted to flow beside stone-flagged streets criss-crossing the city. It was a place of great temples and fortresses, engineering and architectural achievements without parallel in American antiquity, nested between the terraced hillsides of this remote Andean valley.

Captain Francisco Pizarro marched into Cuzco in 1533. By that time the Europeans had "discovered" their New World, and smallpox and the common cold were spreading faster than the epidemic conquest. Pizarro installed a young nobleman named Manco as a puppet ruler, but Manco fled from the capital to raise an army of a hundred thousand to lay seige to the Spaniards in Cuzco. The last great battle of the Spanish conquest of Peru was fought at Sacsayhuaman, at the "head" of the jaguar-shaped city, and armor-plated men on horseback swinging steel swords and wielding firearms won out over men with clubs, spears, slingshots, and arrows. Finally the empire, its millions of subjects and unimaginable wealth, fell to a relatively small company of Spanish soldiers, and Manco fled high into the Andes, where none could follow, to a hidden sanctuary fortress called Vilcapampa.

February 11

Spent the day knocking around Cuzco. Now at a little desk by the open window in my room at the hotel—a cozy little place with a colonnaded courtyard, fountain, bougainvillea, the works. Colonial Latin America.

There's a fiesta on somewhere, I can hear the music on the cool night air. This is a magical city. A real monument to the history of Latin America.

For instance, the Plaza de Armas. Wonderful. Flags flying.

This was the heart of the Inca city. Now a classical Spanish plaza surrounded by colonial arcades. There is the cathedral, the churches of Jesus Maria and El Triunfo, and La Compañia. All built on foundations made from the great stone blocks of Inca temples and palaces torn apart by the Spaniards to support their places of Catholic worship. An Inca wall, a wall of the palace of the great Pachacutec, is now a wall in the Café Roma. I ate there.

The base of the church of Santo Domingo is the Corinacha, the "golden courtyard," an Inca temple whose perfectly fitted walls were once covered with gold. Astonishing.

Funny how the United States seems light years from this place. Thinking changes. If you let it. If you have no tour schedule to maintain, if your agenda is specific to being here rather than getting to the next place you're going to. . . .

Different time. Life moves at a different tempo. Time to digest.

Cloistered, protected. Not from the world, for the earth is in evidence here, nature is everywhere, from the whitewashed adobe and red clay tiles and rough-hewn beams, to the fruits and vegetables still dirty with soil, to the cobblestones, to the vista of the mountains that surround the place. Terraced hillsides and snow-capped peaks.

Nature in evidence subtly in the hats the men and women wear to shade their eyes from a sun that beats down upon them, shines directly upon their city, unfiltered by the by-products of civilization. Remarkable, really. Very real. Essentially a place on Earth inhabited by man rather than a complex built on a framework of concrete, steel, and asphalt. A city that lives in nature, but hasn't replaced it.

I'm here because the Andes are the Himalayas of South America, and Cuzco is its Katmandu—the travel hub. From here I can head for the jungle, but I'd rather go knowing something. Could go to Iquitos, where Marlene Dobkin de Rios did her research, but would rather not. In Mexico I found that there was a subculture of *curanderos,* a network of hearsay, so I'll start in the market, ask a few questions.

Tomorrow.

The market was set up along an Inca wall that stretched between two of Cuzco's 360 churches. Latin American markets are more or less the same, from Mexico to Chile. Cobbled walkways lead you through a maze shaded by umbrellas or stretched *manta* cloth on stilts, where the most vibrant colors of nature are arranged in pyramids or overflowing from wooden crates worn smooth from years of handling. Reds: tomatoes, apples, sides of beef and rosy pork, sliced watermelon, peppers, chiles. Yellows: papayas, squash blossoms, lemons and grapefruit brought from the lowlands, bananas, peppers, chiles. Oranges: squash and pumpkins, mangoes, carrots, chiles. Purple eggplant and cabbage. Dappled breadfruit and grenada fruits spotted yellow-brown like a leopard. There are the grays of salted fish and sacks of grain. Little mounds of canihua and quinoa seeds, corn, wheat, and barley, arranged on burlap blankets or palm-mesh mats on the flag-stoned sidewalks, and, at your feet, dogs and chickens, household goods and utensils, both wooden and tin, nylon net *bolsas*—pastel shopping bags with plastic handles, ceramic bowls, and Inca artifacts reproduced in shopworn clay.

The vendors, proud and passionate, sing, shout, exclaim the praises of their produce, entice the people with the ripeness, heartiness, tenderness, freshness of their fruits, vegetables, meats, and poultry. What will you have? Here! Look at what I have brought for you! Look at the colors, feel the texture, smell the ripeness, taste the succulence! How many? And the pan of the crusty metal scale jerks and the needle swings wildly. *¡Medio kilo!* Only two *soles!*

I purchased a rainbow-colored *bolsa* and maneuvered my way through the throng of housewives, cooks, hungry Indians, wide-eyed schoolchildren. I bought a fresh-baked roll of sweet bread here, a banana there. Drank a blended mango and papaya drink at a linoleum juice counter.

On the edge of the market, a thick-skinned, shriveled old woman sat, legs folded beside her, on a woven mat near the sidewalk. She was an herbalist, the native druggist. Strips of bark, bits of dried seaweed, withered leaves, tiny mounds of sulphur, quinine, and other powders and grains were arranged in tidy little piles before her. Bottles of oils, sun-dried snakeskins, jars of animal organs, tiny packets—twists of paper. Her eyes were like craters, and she had the devilish look that goes with the trade.

"¿Tutacama ninacha?"

What did she say? I smiled into her eyes. *"¿Perdón, señora?"*

"¿Tutacama? ¿Munacquicho fortunacquata?"

Quechua. The language of the Indians. I had heard its curious clipped and guttural rhythms in the market, but most of the vendors spoke Spanish. The old woman reached down into the folds of her woven skirt and held three leaves in the palm of her hand. Even the palm was wrinkled.

"¿Fortunacquata?"

"She is asking if you wish to have your fortune told."

Spanish. The voice came from my right shoulder. I turned and looked down. A young man, possibly eighteen or twenty. A white shirt and navy blue trousers, a stack of books under his arm. He had a flat Indian face and a nose that started high on his forehead and curved down, dividing his face into two halves. He smiled up at me. "She does not speak Spanish, only Quechua. Do you wish your fortune?"

"Yes. Thanks."

He grinned and gave her the go-ahead, and she blew on the leaves and let them fall to the mat. A quick glance was all it took before she peered up at me and rattled off something in Quechua.

"Hmmm." The young man touched the end of his nose with his forefinger. "You are on a quest," he translated, "looking for something that will save your life."

She nodded, then added the punch line.

He grinned again. "And it will kill you if you do not find it, and it might kill you if you do."

I liked that.

"You are looking for something?" he asked.

"I'm looking for a healer, a good *curandero*," I said.

"You are sick?"

"No. But I would like to meet one. A good one. Do you think she knows of one?"

"She will tell you that she is one."

"If she were a good one, she wouldn't be selling her medications in the market."

"That's true," he said. "I think there are some healers. . . . But if you are not sick. . . . You are a tourist?"

"No. I'm from a university in the United States." I dug a few *soles* from my pocket and handed them to the old woman with a smile and a nod.

"A university! You are a student?"

"Well, a teacher, actually. Psychology."

He wagged his head up and down as though he now understood something profound. "We have a university. I am a student. You should see Professor Morales!"

The Universidad Nacional de San Antonio Abad del Cuzco lay in a mountain cul-de-sac near the edge of town. It was an unimpressive complex of two-story, weathered concrete buildings ventilated by louvered windows that had been modern in 1940; the university had been founded in 1692. My young friend of the market had neglected to mention that the school was on strike and the place was more or less deserted, though it was, I think, a Monday.

The philosophy department was at the end of a dreary gray corridor. A pink three-by-five card taped to the door told me that Professor Morales's class would be meeting in the cafeteria.

Why the cafeteria was open and functioning during a strike, I'll never know. I chalked it up as one of the mysteries of Latin America, where things are seldom as they seem and rarely as they should be.

Professor Morales's students were already filing out by the time I found the cafeteria in the basement of the main building. The man I sought stood near a table in the center of the room. His hands were buried deep in the pockets of his trousers, and his head was bowed as he listened, nodding, to a young Indian student at his side.

He was a small man, no more than five feet six, but not slight. He had a durable and compact shape, but it was mostly hidden in a pin-striped suit that was out of fashion in 1945 and had lost its shape soon after. His hair was gray and straight, parted in the middle and brushed back from his forehead, but his eyebrows were black and hooded his eyes.

He withdrew a hand from his pocket and placed it reassuringly on the student's shoulder, said something, and the young face brightened. The student made an awkward little bow and joined a girl waiting for him at the door.

"Professor Morales?"

"Yes?"

I introduced myself. His eyebrows arched as I listed my credentials, not exceptional by U.S. standards, but he looked around the room and back, as if to wonder what this university could possibly have to offer me.

I mentioned my experiences with Mexican healers, my desire to study the use of the *ayahuasca* and explore the primitive healing traditions of the Peruvian shaman. I needed advice, I said.

"I am merely a philosophy teacher," he said. "You should go to Lima. There is a museum of anthropology there."

This was going to be a dead end. "I have heard of it," I lied. "But I'm a psychologist, a therapist. I want to find an *ayahuascero* and experience his form of therapy firsthand. I want to write about it."

"Write about it?"

"For my doctoral thesis."

His eyes moved down from my face, down my shirt front, down the strap of my shoulder bag, stopped on the bag, and continued on down my trousers to my hiking boots. Then he lifted his eyes to a spot somewhere on my forehead. His eyes reminded me of someone, but I couldn't place it.

"What brings you to me?"

"I was told that you knew something."

His face brightened into a handsome smile. "And where did you hear this?"

"In the market."

"In the market! There I am known only for my ability to bargain with the fruit vendors." He frowned. There was a trace of suspicion in his voice. "Do you speak Quechua?"

"No. I was trying to communicate with an herb seller. A young man intervened on my behalf. It was he who mentioned your name. He said that you knew something about the *curanderos*."

He nodded his understanding. "One of my students, no doubt. Very polite to help a traveling stranger."

He pushed back the shirt cuff protruding from the sleeve of his jacket and looked at his watch, an old Timex. "Would you like a little coffee?"

3

Experience is the name everyone gives to their mistakes.

—*Oscar Wilde*

"So." Professor Morales lifted the lid from a sugar bowl and dipped his spoon into the mound of coarse, unrefined sugar. "Do you seek to have an experience, or to serve an experience?"

"Pardon?"

"With the *ayahuasca*."

"I don't understand."

"How will I explain. . . ." He held the spoonful of sugar just above the oil-spotted surface of his coffee. "Have you ever taken the Sacrament?"

"Professor?"

"The Eucharist. The consecrated bread and wine of the Catholic faith. The body and the blood of Christ. Have you tasted it?"

"Yes."

"You are Catholic?"

"No." I looked down at the spoon, hovering motionless.

"But you have knelt before the altar."

"Yes."

He nodded. "You have taken the wafer on your tongue, and it stuck to the roof of your mouth and tasted like cardboard, and the wine was cheap and sweet."

I laughed. "Yes."

"You have done this, yet you are not Catholic. You have had an experience of the Holy Communion, but you have not communed." Carefully, he lowered the spoon onto the surface of the coffee. The liquid seeped into the sugar from the edges of the spoon, and the little mound was saturated crystal by crystal. "*Experience* rather than experience served." He tipped the spoon and the thick sugar syrup oozed into the coffee. "The ritual did not serve you, for you did not serve the ritual. It is a question of intent."

I smiled at this and said: "My intentions are strictly honorable."

"You intend to study the use of the *ayahuasca* by the Peruvian shaman?"

"Well. . . . Yes."

"*That* is your intention. What is your purpose?"

I took a deep breath and let it go. Professor Morales reached his hand across the table. The cuffs of his white shirt were slightly soiled. He touched my forearm with a gently weathered hand. "You are growing impatient with my . . . semantics."

"Not at all," I lied.

"You are Latin, yes?"

"I was born in Cuba."

He nodded and stirred his coffee. I studied his brow, the bridge of his nose, the sculpture of his cheekbones, his hair. Indian. The head of the department of philosophy of the Universidad Nacional de San Antonio Abad was an Indian. A Quechua Indian. His ancestory was pure, unviolated by the Spanish conquest. But not untouched.

And I had the sudden conviction that he knew a great deal, that his wisdom was profound and his eccentricity genuine. For some reason, by some fluke of association, I thought of Merlin. As I did so, he reached into the pocket of his jacket and withdrew a tiny bird's nest. He made a sort of "hmmm" sound and produced a pair of ivory dice, a couple of kernels of corn, and a small Mexican God's eye: a cross formed by two straight twigs woven together with white and red yarn, forming a diamond-shaped bull's-eye. Tassels of green yarn dangled from the ends of the twigs. He placed this in the center of the table, returned the other objects to his pockets, and sipped from his coffee.

"The *ayahuasca* has been studied, has been written about in scholarly journals."

"Marlene Dobkin de Rios. Yes. I have read her papers. She is an anthropologist," I said.

"And you are a psychologist. You have read these accounts and are curious about the effects of this folkloric plant on the human psyche and the . . . unconscious mind."

He blinked and his eyes moved from mine, shifted to the left and seemed to focus on a point somewhere over my right shoulder. I turned my head to follow his gaze. An empty table in the corner near the door to the cafeteria. When I turned back he was smiling at me. His eyes were younger than his face; walnut brown iris and ebony black pupil stood out in sharp definition against veinless whites.

"You want to taste the *yagé,* and you are drawn to it by a fascination with death." He sipped again from his cup.

"It's true, then?"

He raised his eyebrows for a question.

"The *ayahuasca* takes you to meet death?"

"That is the claim, yes. *Aya* is Quechua for "death." *Huasca* is "rope" or "vine." The "rope of the dead." It is one of the sacred medicines of the shamans of the Amazon jungle, and that is where you must go to find it. But if you do this, if you work with an *ayahuascero.* . . ." He cocked his head, grinned. "And if you survive, and if you write about your experience and speculate on its effects, who will read it?"

"Professors at my university. Psychologists."

"And this will win for you a doctorate?"

"Yes. This and my work with healers in Mexico."

"I am surprised that any scientist in the United States would be interested in such subjective experiences."

"Psychology is still a young science. It is not yet even fully accepted *as* a science, and I am capable of reporting objectively on my experiences."

His eyebrows arched. "Is any man able to be objective about his *own* experience?"

"Perhaps not, but I can document the psychological effects I experience just as I have documented the physical effects of traditional healings that I have witnessed."

"Undoubtedly. But which is more important, the cause of healing and the cause of a psychological experience, or the effect—the end result?"

I thought about this and framed my answer carefully. "They are of equal importance, but one must judge the effect before investigating the cause."

"That is a Western answer. It is rational. But you are on the brink of a realm in which cause and effect cannot be separated. If you enter this realm it will become important to understand this relationship." He leaned forward over his cup. "*Your* cause must be clear, for it will determine the effect. Your experience will be affected by what you bring to it, how you approach

. . . the . . . the *ayahuasca* ritual, for example. The realm of the shaman requires one to be impeccable of intent. It is quite a challenge."

"You know a great deal about this."

He shrugged. "I teach philosophy. I am an Indian, the only one here." A graceful sweep of his hand included the whole university. "An Indian, and an old one at that, so I must be wise." He laughed at this and said: "There are ancient traditions in my country. It is a very rich culture, and I grew up with its myths and have studied its legends. Shamans are the masters of the myths and often the makers of the legends. Men and women of knowledge, the physicians, psychologists . . ." He nodded. "Yes . . . and the storytellers of a community. They understand the forces of Nature and use those forces to maintain the health and well-being of their people." He drained his cup, set it on the saucer, and pushed them to one side. "They are the caretakers of the Earth. An intriguing notion when understood. On the surface, very quaint."

"How should I proceed?"

"Follow your instincts. They have brought you this far."

"Yes, but where will I find a shaman who is willing to work with me?"

"The villages of the *altiplano,* the high desert plateau. You will find healers, perhaps a self-styled sorcerer or two. You do not speak Quechua and you will need to hire the services of a translator. But you are interested in the *ayahuasca,* the medicine of the jungle. Do you have a piece of paper?"

I nodded quickly and dug into my pockets. Coins, my hotel room key. I reached for my shoulder bag. At last I was going to get something concrete. I pulled my journal from the bag.

"There is a custom," said Professor Morales, staring at the unworn binding, the unfingered pages, "that a shaman will share his or her knowledge with all who seek it if they present themselves with impeccable intent, purity of purpose. That is how you will know a *hatun laika,* a master shaman, from a simple healer. If you wish to enter the other world, the world of the shaman, if you wish to journey through the Medicine Wheel, then you will need to find a *hatun laika,* and you will need to be prepared to approach him or her as a student, as a beginner, not as a . . . psychologist." He produced an old-fashioned fountain pen from the breast pocket of his jacket. "If you wish simply to taste and to study the use of the *ayahuasca* you will need only to meet one who is skilled in its preparation and the rituals of the jaguar path. I have heard of a man . . . No, no! Do not tear it!"

He reached across the table and placed a hand on the page that I was set to rip from the journal. He smiled and pulled the open volume toward him. He unscrewed the cap from the pen and wrote something in the upper right corner of one page.

"The jaguar path?"

"The journey West. The second cardinal point on the Medicine Wheel." He blew gently on the ink and closed the journal, and his eyes rose to meet my curious gaze.

"The Medicine Wheel," he said again.

I shook my head.

"The Medicine Wheel, the fourfold path of knowledge. It is also called the journey of the Four Winds. It is the legendary journey that an initiate undertakes to become a person of knowledge." He lifted the God's eye from the table.

"Yes?"

"Yes. The Medicine Wheel is the mandala of the Inca shaman, although there exists no real symbol for it, just as there are no writings, no figure of worship, no human prophet, or son of a deity. None are needed. The journey through the Medicine Wheel is a journey undertaken to awaken vision and to discover and embrace the Divine within oneself, to reestablish one's connection with Nature and the mystery of the cosmos, to acquire skills and the wisdom to use them." He turned the God's eye by twisting its base between his finger and thumb.

"The Four Winds are marked out like the cardinal points of a compass." He pointed to the base of the God's eye. "It begins in the South, the serpent path, where one goes to shed the past, just as the serpent sheds its skin. The jaguar path in the West," he pointed to the left point on the cross, "is where one loses fear and faces death. In the North one takes the dragon path to discover the wisdom of the ancients and to create a union with the Divine. Finally," he pointed to the tip of the right arm of the cross, "the eagle path of the East—the flight to the Sun and the journey back to one's home to exercise one's vision in the context of one's life and work. The legends claim that this is the most difficult journey the shaman undertakes."

He replaced the God's eye in a jacket pocket. "It is said that few complete this journey of initiation. There are few true shamans, few true persons of knowledge. Many who tread this path stop along the way and are content to be healers and medicine men. They become masters of their own direction. And then there are those who become trapped by power." He made a fist. "Lost along the way. It is a journey that can take a lifetime." He relaxed his grip. "But it is a charming program, don't you think? And so much less complicated than the sephiroth of the Jewish cabala or the Buddhist pathways to nirvana."

He pushed my journal back across the table. "But you are concerned with the *ayahuasca,* which is said to aid one along the path of the West. I have heard of a man, an *ayahuascero* in the jungle near Pucallpa. I have written his name and rough directions in your book. You can fly there from here."

"You have met this man?" I asked.

"No. One of my students is from the area and has told me of him. He has quite a reputation. I have often thought of taking myself there, but I have not found the time." He looked again at his watch. "I must leave you now. I am meeting a class at the ruins of Tambo Machay. If you return to Cuzco, I would be greatly pleased if you would be my guest to lecture to them about Western psychotherapy. They would be most interested." He smiled. "And so would I."

He looked about him, patted his pockets, and stood. I jumped to my feet and offered my hand. "Thank you, Professor Morales, for your time and patience. I was fortunate to find you." He waved it off. "And I *will* return," I said. "It would be an honor to lecture to your students."

Again, the professor's attention was drawn to something over my shoulder. I turned and this time there was something to see. Two young Indians stood dripping wet at the doorway to the cafeteria. Their straight black hair was matted to their foreheads and their clothes were sopping. They were barefoot, clutching their shoes to their stomachs. They stared wide-eyed and expectantly at the professor.

"Why do you carry your shoes, *jovenes?*"

"It is raining, maestro."

"Yes," said the professor, patiently. "I guessed that. We will have our class here in the cafeteria. But why do you go barefoot?"

They looked down at the floor. "We do not want to get our shoes wet."

Professor Morales sighed and placed a hand on my shoulder. "Yes," he said in careful English. "It would be an honor to lecture to them."

Experience and experience served.

I sit in my window seat in this trembling relic of an airplane that was probably overhauled sometime during the Eisenhower administration. Outside the twin propellers tear the air to shreds and pull me closer to some jungle airstrip, and I am reminded of a similar flight three summers ago.

Oaxaca, Mexico. The Huichol Indians. Experience? Or experience served?

In 1969, at the end of my senior year of college, with a bachelor's degree in inter-American studies, I was accepted to the master's program at the new Humanistic Psychology Institute. To make ends meet during my senior year, I had been teaching summer school Spanish to a small private high school class, and when word came of my acceptance into the master's program, I decided to celebrate by organizing a four-week field trip to Mexico. It was a toss-up whether the students or their parents were more eager for the kids to disappear for the summer.

After a month of touring Mexico City and, southeast, to the Yucatán Peninsula and the home of the Mayas, I packed the students back to San Francisco, their suitcases crammed with dirty clothes, heads filled with colloquial Spanish, eyes widened by their first experience of the third world. I stayed on, flew to Tepic, on the west coast of Mexico, and hired a pilot and his single engine Cessna to take me to Mesa del Nayar, in the state of Oaxaca.

We were forced to buzz the narrow mountain airstrip twice to clear the runway of livestock: wandering pigs, sheep, skeletal cows, all shepherded by a little boy dressed in white. His name was Gerardo and I hired one of his burros to take me into the mountains above the mesa, to a village that proved to be his own.

I stayed with the Huichols for three weeks. I lived in their village, dazzled their children with maps of the world drawn in the sand, learned something of their isolated culture and the significance of the brightly colored yarn paintings for which the tribe was famous. A painting, made by pressing naturally dyed yarn onto a beeswax-covered board, was used to portray the psychodynamic of a person in a pictograph, a "spirit catcher." The artist was a sort of psychologist who carefully designed a painting to tell the story of a client's condition. The decisive moment in this form of therapy was the moment when the soul was captured in the picture. The artist/healer would then alter the picture subtly and thereby effect a change in the client's condition.

Tourism is now the principal source of revenue for the Republic of Mexico, and the paintings have become popular curiosities, colorful souvenirs; Day-Glo synthetic yarn has replaced natural color and fiber, and the art form has all but lost its meaning.

But there, in that remote mountain village, on a stool in the doorway of her adobe *casita,* Gerardo's grandmother, doña Juanita, worked the yarn with deeply stained, callused fingers. She attributed much of her skill and insight to *hikuli,* peyote, the sacred cactus of the rural Indian tribes of Mexico.

Had I had the time and means to stay with the Huichols for more than a few weeks, I might have accompanied the members of the village on their annual pilgrimage to the northeastern desert to gather peyote on the slopes of the sacred mountain of Wirikuta. I might even have "learned to think as a Huichol" by ingesting the cactus in their company.

Instead, at the end of the second week, Juanita suggested that I "go be" with the peyote. She pointed to the crest of a mountain some two miles from the village, and instructed me to go there and meditate for two afternoons, to eat nothing, to clear my mind. So I spent two afternoons sitting cross-legged on a scorched mountaintop, trying to think of something to think about, falling asleep in the warmth of the Mexican sun.

On the evening of the second day, I returned to find Juanita standing on the outskirts of the village.

"You have the same problem a deer has," she said. "You always come down a mountain the same way you went up."

I had read accounts of the psychedelic effects of peyote, the beatific visions, the voices of whispered wisdom, the experiences of time without sequence, and my empty stomach fluttered with adrenaline as she pressed five peyote buttons into my hand and told me call upon the spirit of the plant, to chew them carefully, to imagine that I was chewing the flesh of the Earth.

Dutifully, I hiked back to my mountaintop perch and took the peyote buttons one after the other. They tasted like twice-puked puke. Their vile bitterness set me trembling, and I spent an hour retching over a manzanita bush.

Then my stomach relaxed, the spasms were gone, and I felt alone. The manzanita bush shimmered in the white heat of the sun, and I was sitting on a world of sharp contrast, an Earth that I was not part of, but apart from.

Displaced, an alien who did not belong, dispossessed by the rocks, the twigs, the dirt, the radiant manzanita, the vista of Nature before me, I was forsaken.

I touched the brown dirt with the palm of my hand and felt its warmth, and it stuck to the sweat that oozed from my pores, and I brought the palm to my face, touched it, and the dirt smeared across my cheek and mixed with the drool at the corner of my mouth.

And the whiteness of the sunlight turned to a glowing yellow, then a radiant orange as I smeared my face with mud of dirt and sweat and saliva.

I stripped off my shirt and painted myself with russet earth, camouflaged myself, slathered my chest, arms, and neck and felt myself collapsing. As the mud dried and cracked, I knew that I was of the Earth and that it was to the Earth that I would return. This mother would care for me, cradle me, love me, although all I had done was walk upon her, unmindful of her, seeking my own pleasure, living my own melodrama.

The sun was setting and I stared at it with dilated pupils. I sucked it in through my eyes and felt its glow saturate my tissues from the inside out, held in by the shell of dried, caked-on mud. A planetary poultice.

I remember becoming aware of my breath. I breathed with the sun. I could set the sun with my breath, perceived myself setting the sun, lower with each exhalation. I remember marveling at the discovery, testing the depth of my breathing against the progress of the sun toward the horizon. A deep breath, two lungs full, a long sigh, and it was gone. And I slept.

I woke up sometime after midnight and made my way down the mountain, taking care to return to the village by a different route. Juanita was waiting for me. She eyed me suspiciously and I embraced her, let her lead me to my bed.

Ten hours later I awoke to the stink of my body, stumbled into the late morning sunlight, and washed in the cool waters of the river that ran down from the mountains and beside the town. Downstream there was a widening in the river, a sort of pool, where I floated on my back and stared at the mountain-blue sky. A bolus of peyote and earth swallowed the day before rushed from my lower intestines in a sudden diarrheal evacuation. I moved upstream and washed myself, climbed out of the river, felt chastised. I sat on the bank and realized that no matter how much earth I smeared on myself, I was still a white man who shits in the waters from which others drink. I learned more about ecology from that one incident than from all of the books and articles I have read since.

I returned to California dressed like a Huichol: white pants, white shirt, colorful woven sash at my waist.

But I was in my early twenties then, and was convinced that the profoundness of my experience gave me the right to such an affectation. The right to advertise.

February 13
Later

We've dropped to a thousand feet. The green density of the jungle below has taken on definition, botanical detail.

A wide turn to the right, and we're . . . circling the airstrip—a gray scar—no, a tear in the woven fabric of the jungle, the deep green mantle of the Earth.

I suspect that my time with the Huichols, my communion on the mountaintop, was merely an experience. Perhaps as superficial as my reaction to it. Counterfeit spirituality. Wearing another's costume does not make one kin.

Shitting in the river may have been the most genuine act of that particular journey.

I did not serve the peyote experience (I did not know how to), yet the experience served me, continues to serve me, as I question my level of preparation for what may lie ahead and below in some invisible clearing in this jungle.

Professor Morales hinted that I was not prepared for the jungle, for the "jaguar path of the West." First comes the "South," something about shedding the past. . . . Interesting how my past is with me now. The Huichols. . . . Anxiety. Morales's words have gotten under my skin.

Two hundred, one hundred feet above the airstrip, and we are level with the trees! Chihuahuaco trees that would dwarf a redwood and set the standard scale of the Amazon jungle. Primeval. The land of giants.

A blast of heat that carried with it the smell of the jungle greeted my arrival in Pucallpa. The airport was everything it should have been. Sturdy pillars held up a thick thatched roof gray with age and airplane exhaust. Tattered mosquito netting, here and there a corrugated metal wall, a rusted tin Coca-Cola sign, worn benches, mosquitoes. On the edge of the airstrip, a bus with a makeshift wooden roof, a couple of battered pick-up trucks.

The fifty-meter walk from the plane to the shady door beside the Coca-Cola sign had me fighting for breath, my cotton shirt sticking unpleasantly to my back. A bead of sweat broke free from my chest, and I felt it course down my belly as I stood before an old Westinghouse fan, leaned against the counter of the bar.

I waited while a little woman, an Indian, filled her nylon net bag with dripping wet soda bottles and counted out her *soles* for the barman, a fat, fresh-faced native. The transaction completed, she lifted a burlap-wrapped parcel onto her head, and, balancing it there, hefted the shopping bag by its plastic handles and headed out, into the heat. I looked after her a moment, realized that she was bare-breasted, pictured a *National Geographic* cover photo, and turned to the proprietor.

"*Cerveza, por favor.*"

"*¡Sí, señor!*"

The little man smiled broadly, reached into a washtub crammed with beer bottles and soda bottles in ice water, drew out an Amazonas. He wiped it off with a damp towel, popped off the cap, and set it before me with a flourish. "*Una cerveza fría para el . . . español.*"

"Not Spanish," I said. "*Gringo, americano.*"

"But your accent . . ."

"Cuban."

His eyes widened. "Truly?"

"Before the revolution." I grinned and raised the bottle. *"Salud."*

"Salud, señor." He leaned over the bar and looked down at my backpack. "Engineer?"

I shook my head. He gave me the eye. "Oil," he said.

"No."

His lower lip came up to lap the upper. "You are not an American rancher. . . ." He brought his hand down on the counter with a soft slap. "A consultant!"

I laughed. "Psychologist," I said.

He frowned.

I said, "Doctor."

His face cleared. "Ah!" He thought about it for a second or two and said: "No. You are too young."

"You are right," I said. "Perhaps the heat will make me grow older."

"Do not mind it," he said. "Soon your body will slow down. Your heart will beat slower and you will stop sweating. You will adjust. Another beer?"

"No, thank you. I need to go down the highway. Is there a bus or taxi?"

"No. The bus is gone. How far?"

I brought my journal out of my bag and found Professor Morales's notation.

Don Ramón Silva
From Pucallpa airport south on Trans-Amazon Highway to
kilometer 64. Follow path to the left two kilometers.

He peered down at the page with the earnest look of someone who cannot read.

"An hour," I said. "South."

He squinted and pointed out the door to a boy of twelve dragging a dirty canvas bag across the pavement. "Jorge. He takes mail to a plantation. He can take you." He rubbed together the forefinger and thumb of his right hand.

The Trans-Amazon Highway is a decaying two-lane pathway through the jungle. Tropical rains and sweltering heat have cracked and pitted the roadway, and here and there thick lianas creep up the shallow embankments and slither far across the pockmarked pavement from both sides, as though to close the wound. Natives are forever keeping the jungle at bay, hacking away the groping fingers of Nature with worn-out machetes.

Jorge and I bounced along on the rusted springs of the cracked vinyl seat of his pick-up. A plastic virgin of Guadalupe hanging from the rear-view mirror jerked like a puppet at the end of its string. We talked about baseball, about the U.S. restaurant companies burning down the jungle to raise cattle, about the rubber plantation three hundred kilometers away.

I got out at the white wooden post marking kilometer 64. There seemed to be no break in the foliage left or right until Jorge jumped down from behind the wheel and pointed to a delicate banana palm standing knee high among the giants.

"Trail," he said.

We stood in the middle of the road, looked at each other for a moment, and he shrugged, shoved his hands in his pockets.

I slapped a mosquito on my cheek.

It had rained here the night before, and steam was rising from the roadway. All around, the cicadas droned and the jungle hissed. The air was thick with pungent mist and the grumble of the old pick-up's engine was lost in the steady, breathless hum of the Amazon.

"Why do you go in there?" he asked.

"To see a man."

He nodded and gazed down the road.

"Stay on the path," he said, without looking at me. "If you step off you get lost, never find it again."

"Thanks," I said.

"*De nada.*" He climbed back up into the cab, jerked the door closed. I dug into my pocket and came up with a handful of *soles*. He rested his arm on the door, looked down at the money in my hand, squinted over my shoulder to the tangle of trees, vines, dripping leaves, and then smiled into my eyes. The smile was much too wise for his twelve-year-old face. He shook his head at the money and revved the engine. It backfired with a percussive clap. And something screamed.

"*Los monos,*" he said. Monkeys.

"Thanks for the ride," I said.

"*Buena suerte,*" he said. Good luck.

I stood in the middle of the Trans-Amazon Highway and watched the truck rattle away, distort, waver in the shimmering heat waves, disappear like a mirage.

February 13
Later

Following the path. Four feet wide, hard to distinguish. Here everything is overgrown, exaggerated, tangled and wet. The jungle floor is pulpy. An overwhelming sense of the Earth as a living thing, walking on its flesh. . . .

I've been following it for an hour. It. Shit. I think this is the path. Not sure. Senses on the alert. Catching the movement of light and shadow, eyes fixed to jungle floor, peripheral threats . . . jungle noise like white noise, steady sshhhhhhhhh, but it's background to the rustle and squish of my footfalls, moist snaps of old vines and branches, the slap of leaves . . . sinuses filled with the pungent sweetness of decay that smells like life, like a shut-up greenhouse . . . the touch of fronds and vines, vines that stretch, reach across my way and waver, brush my face . . . the taste of anxiety.

I've stopped by this tree because I've been moving too fast. My heart is beating too fast. I'm breathing too fast. Thinking too fast. I would like to know that Don Ramón Silva lives at the end of this path. Let's hope so, 'cause it's a long way back to Pucallpa. I've stopped here to rest and reassure myself.

Am I afraid?

No. Can't define this feeling. It comes in through my pores. Energized. But I could sleep here and now. Stimulated. But my pencil moves thoughtfully across the paper. Very alive. I've never felt Nature like this. It knows I'm here. I can *feel* it and I know it can feel me and I feel that it knows I am here. My God, what a powerful thing this is!

My back to the tree, my legs stretched out before me, crossed at the ankles, I closed my journal around the pencil, shoved it into my pack. I closed my eyes and listened to the jungle sing. I don't know how long I listened. I felt myself winding down, my metabolism slowing, comfort growing within and around.

Was something slithering?

I jerked awake, hands to the ground, and pushed myself back hard against the tree. Nothing. No movement. No snakes. Just a change in the light, about a half-hour's worth: a shift in the dappled patterns, the chunks of light cut up by the tangled ceiling of leaves and branches and vines.

What startled me so?

I moved to get up. There was resistance, a gentle tug, and I looked down at my body. Here and there, on my legs, at my side, by my arms, creepers, long delicate feelers touched me, had begun to bend to coil around me. I didn't mind.

The clearing was thirty meters away, a hundred feet from where I had stopped.

No one's home.

The house sits in its clearing like the archetype of the primitive jungle paradise. A thatched roof over an L-shaped platform, walls of palm-frond mesh. Chickens, a pig tethered to a banana palm.

Out back (though it's hard to tell front from back), the jungle floor gives way to sand on the bank of a little lagoon. Ducks or mud hens with brown and green feathers. The lagoon is surrounded by the fringe of the jungle. An old, cracked dugout canoe is overturned on the bank, stern end in the water, covered with algae slime.

There is a dead chihuahuaco tree, a twisted, hollowed-out trunk on the edge of the clearing, and near this, a fire. A couple of tin cans—oil cans—filled with a dappled reddish-brown, purple, and orange liquid. The colors don't quite mix. A clay pot is hanging from a wooden brazier over the fire, and a broth is bubbling inside—a funny, sour smell.

Sit and wait. Using the thick exposed roots of the chihuahuaco tree as the arms of a chair.

"You are here!"

I struggled to my feet, got tangled in the roots of the tree. He'd come from behind the tree, from out of the jungle. He stood about five feet four inches, a body that had been toughened by the jungle. He had a soft, square Indian face, large hooked nose, and long upper eyelids that gave his eyes an Asian slant. His hair was silver-gray and thick, brushed back from a deeply wrinkled forehead. Deep creases ran down either side of his nose to the corners of his mouth. His lips were brown, the same color as his skin.

"Don Ramón Silva?"

"Ramón," he said, and grinned, and I shook his hand. Short, thick fingers, large, maybe arthritic knuckles. He cocked his head and looked up at me out of the corner of his eye.

"*Bienvenido*," he said.

Later

He knew I was coming. He expected me. He saw me in a dream.

But he did not expect me to be so tall.

I told him I was a psychologist. He nodded.

I told him that I had heard of him in Cuzco. He smiled.

I told him that Professor Antonio Morales Baca had told me where to find him. His face showed no recognition. Then he looked past me. His eyes widened as though with surprise, then he grinned, nodded as though he understood something.

"We will have a *toma*," he said.

"A *toma*?"

"Yes." He pointed to the brazier. "*La soga.*" The rope.

"An *ayahuasca* ceremony?" I asked.

He nodded. "Have you eaten?"

Food! I hadn't even thought about it. I remembered swallowing down a plateful of scrambled eggs at six o'clock in the morning. The airport in Cuzco. I looked at my watch. It was quarter to six. Twelve hours. I was ravenous.

"No," I said. "I'm very hungry."

"*Bueno*," he said. "Then you will have a good appetite in the morning."

Fifty meters from the clearing there is a bend in the little river. The water of the lagoon is clear but almost stagnant; here it flows lazily away into the jungle, into the Amazon.

I've stripped and bathed, wrung the sweat and dust out of my clothes. I feel refreshed but achingly hungry. I am to return to the clearing after the sun sets.

So here I sit, cross-legged on a wet, sandy shore and wait for another experience. I don't know how to serve this one, either. I'm either going about this all wrong, as Professor Morales hinted, or the experience will speak for itself. Don Ramón seemed to accept me without hesitation, so I've either managed to present myself impeccably (I can't imagine how) or there are no prerequisites for this work (Ramón does not strike me as indiscriminate). It can't be the wool poncho I brought as a gift from Cuzco—he'll never use it anyway, it's so bloody hot. So I don't know what to think about this. It's almost like a set-up and that's unreasonable, illogical, and presumptuous.

Morales said something about cause and effect being indistinguishable. Maybe I should stop thinking about it.

This will be my last entry before tonight's ceremony. Before I take the *yagé*.

This is for you, Brian:

February thirteenth. Heading upriver.

4

And Jehovah God also laid this command upon the man: "From every tree of the garden you may eat to satisfaction. But as for the tree of the knowledge of good and evil you must not eat from it, for in the day you eat from it you will positively die."

—Genesis 2:16–17

I sat on a *petate,* a mat of woven palm fronds in the center of a room. The room was large, taking up the whole of the short leg of the L, and barren. Vertical rough-hewn wooden poles, the criss-cross pattern of palm frond walls, and, above, the underside of the thatchwork roof resting on an open framework.

One wall was open to the lagoon, and moonlight reflected off its surface and into the room. Four crude candles had been placed at the four corners of the *petate,* and they burned with tall unwavering ribbons of orange flame.

I sat cross-legged, wrists resting on my knees, and looked down at two objects glowing in the candlelight: a tall hardwood pipe carved in the figure of an Indian holding a cup, like an offering in the palms of his hands, a serpent coiled at his feet. Loosely packed tobacco hung over the edge of the cup. Beside this was a harp, a simple, hollowed-out length of hardwood, a thin wire stretched taut between its ends.

The sound of the jungle was different at night. The steady, sweltering hiss of tropical day had resolved itself into the rhythmic chant of a million insects. Somewhere a deep, resonant hum was matching its tempo, and I looked out to see Ramón silhouetted against the glistening path of moonlight on the lagoon. The murmur of his chant was measured to the cadence of the jungle. His hands held something: a bowl? He raised the thing to the sky.

I could not make out the words of his song, but the refrain was steady, and the verse changed four times as he turned and faced each of the four directions.

It was a bowl, a wooden bowl, that he set between us, and it was filled with the broth I had seen by the fire. A thick liquid the color of mushroom soup, beet juice, and carrot juice, it gave off a pungent tang. I thought of my tissues, starved for food, anxious to absorb anything. The *yagé* looked potent and dangerous.

"You are thinking about death," he said.

I met his eyes and nodded.

His eyes moved smoothly left and right, rested on a point above my head. "It is a fungus that grows inside us."

He raised the pipe, pulled a twig from the pocket of his shirt, caught a flame from one of the candles, and held it over the tobacco. He puffed long and hard on the mouthpiece, and the tobacco crackled, sparked, and glowed. One strand, a tiny tobacco ember, broke free and fell to the floor and died. He took the smoke deep into his lungs, exhaled a long, steady stream of acrid fumes, then puffed and blew smoke over the *yagé*. The smoke hung in the motionless air, hovered over the surface of the liquid, and curled around the lip of the vessel. Then he leaned back and puffed heartily. The tobacco glowed red hot within the thick wooden walls of the pipe, and he leaned forward toward me, blowing smoke on my chest, down my arms, around my head, into my lap. Then he handed me the pipe.

The tobacco was stronger than any I had tasted. It caught in my throat and burned my lungs and I gagged, coughed, blinked away my tears, and drew deeply. Ramón was humming again, eyes closed, rocking gently back and forth, a weird melody of mumbled words with no refrain. A slight breeze set the candles wavering and played across the hairs at the back of my neck.

Then he opened his eyes and they shifted to the left. Focused. I turned my head to look, but he reached out and stopped me, his hand on my cheek. I met his eyes. He lowered his hand and took the pipe.

"You are fortunate to have such a power stalking you."

"What power is that?"

"A cat, my young friend! A jaguar black as the night. A most powerful ally, but you have much work to do before you can claim it as yours." He nodded. "The spirit of the *ayahuasca* is also a jaguar. When you have met death, it will take you across the back of the rainbow and into the next world." He nodded his approval. "Call upon your jaguar now. Summon it to help you on your journey."

Call upon it? I closed my eyes and imagined myself standing at the end of the path to Ramón's house, whistling for the cat. Here, kitty! I couldn't help myself.

But it took an effort to keep my eyes shut. My eyelids were fluttering and my heart was beating fast with anticipation. The jitters.

I took inventory. The woody taste of the jungle tobacco, palms damp, neck and shoulders held rigid. Nervous energy, anxiety. I took a deep breath and tried to release it slowly, evenly, lowered my shoulders. A jaguar. Stalking me. All right. How shall I call upon it? Visualize it. Conjure up a picture. A sleek panther, black like polished . . . ebony. Pitch black. I imagined it moving fluidly, stealthily through the jungle, just like they're supposed to.

"*Así es mejor.*" That is better.

The voice came from somewhere above. I opened my eyes on nothing. Ramón was gone. A cloud had passed before the moon, and the room was darker, the blackness pierced only by the candle flames. Smoke. He was behind me, blowing smoke at my back.

He returned to sit before me. He set aside the pipe.

"Tonight we will bring the death out of you."

He hooked his thumb over the edge of the bowl and held it before me. "Drink."

A tremor went through my stomach as I took the bowl in both hands and lifted it to my lips. It smelled sour and my throat tightened as I took my first sip. Cold, like sour mushroom soup, an acid milkiness and bitter aftertaste. I felt it go down, coat my insides.

I nodded and offered him the bowl. He shook his head.

"All of it," he said.

He raised his hand and made a fist, and the muscles of his forearm contracted. *Poder.* Power. Strength. A universal symbol of vigor and fortitude.

What the hell. A deep breath and I opened the back of my throat and poured it down. Two convulsive swallows and it was in. I placed the empty bowl between us and sucked the residual broth from the inside of my mouth.

He approved. "Lie down now," he said.

I stretched out on the palm-frond mat, and stared up at the dark peak of the thatched roof. I closed my eyes and entertained a moment of perspective. I riffled through my memory and took stock of my situation. What was I bringing to the experience? My education. Where was my power? In years of theory; chalk diagrams; frayed spiral-bound pages of notes, volumes of them; textbooks; stories of psychosis and treatment, cause and effect, complexes, dreams, analysis, all of the imaginings of all of the men and women who had struggled to define the experience of ordinary consciousness and understand the influences upon it. Thinking about thinking. Psychology. The crackpot science based on nothing but theory, ideas about ideas, thoughts about thoughts. Of the frontiers of science, this was the first, and "civilized" man had only just gotten around to it.

Consciousness is like a body of water. Conscious mind and unconscious mind. The surface of the sea and its unseen depths. I ran with the metaphor. Modern psychology had taught me to study the depths, to speculate on the geography of the bottom, by observing the color of the water, the patterns of the waves, the stuff that floated up to the surface. Ask questions of a patient and get answers back. Like sonar. Send out a signal and listen to what bounces back and try to piece together what lies below.

But we hadn't learned how to dive in to see for ourselves. Afraid of getting wet? Watch the waves and see how they break and guess how deep is this ocean. . . .

Waves breaking on a sandy shore. Water sliding up the sand, sucked, saturated, sparkling crystals of wet sand shining, sunlit. Surf sounds. I open my eyes, and the sound swells and pinpoints of candlelight are rising from the four corners around me. Floating up toward the thatched roof. Neon red and pastel green luminous particles floating toward the peak and swirling . . . no . . . *coiling* . . . tightly . . . tighter. Ready to spring. The center cannot hold, is taking form and rushes, plummets toward me from the ceiling. A thundering roar and the light has jaws; I shudder at its impact.

A hand falls on my face. I flinch, but I can feel the hand and I can feel my face, so it must be my hand. What's feeling what? My mouth is open and I can feel my tongue with the tips of my fingers, but I do not feel my fingers with the tip of my tongue. Numb. Face like putty. Lump of tongue.

A sound with a texture, a colored vibration . . . a green resonance, the color of the jungle reverberates through my body, from my ears to my feet.

The room shifts, rotates upward, because I've lifted my head. Ramón, eyes closed, holds the one-stringed harp to his mouth and plucks the wire and his head vibrates with green neon and he shapes the sound with his lips and I watch it coil down the hollow of the harp. His eyelids part and his eyes take mine and lead them left to where the shadow moves, slinking around the perimeter of the room. A shadow with depth, 3-D. Follow it. The shadow stops, and the walls move left, and the room spins on Ramón's axis.

Dizzy and diseased. Oh, the smell! Fumes rising with my breath from corrupted innards. Guts withering in the vapors of decay. Spoiled tissues moldering inside. I shudder at Ramón's touch. I look down. Hand on my arm. I can see the rot inside, under my skin. He points to the jungle.

"Purgate."

Beyond the end of his finger the sand is iridescent, and my feet sink and slide in its glow. The jungle is alive with light. Spinning ultraviolet orbs that I know are elemental forces of Nature—the trees, the plants, shimmer. Drawn to the chihuahuaco, my palms on its warm bark, my body arched, vomiting fungus. *Purgate,* purge yourself uncontrollably, cathartically, from the soles of your feet. What is this toxic stuff? My stomach is like a bulb contracting, sucking the rot from intestines and expelling it with each wrenching contraction.

The tree moves, the bark shifts beneath my hands, and I fall away, backward to the sand, and watch this snake, this water boa, unwind its thick, thick brown, black, and yellow shining body from around the trunk of the tree. The size . . . unspeakable . . . Satchamama . . . serpent . . . guardian of the Amazon opens its mouth to me, webbed pink tissue, a clucking, croaking sound, and a sharp breath draws in the sweet night air, and still the body moves in layers from around the tree. No end to it. Then its tail thuds to the sand. Its head at the water's edge, cleaving its path, a sparkling wake across the mirror surface of the lagoon and away, through a black gap in the phosphorescence of the jungle.

My belly moans, movement. Scramble to my feet. Urgent. In the bushes holding onto a vine, pants bunched around my feet, holding my ankles down, evacuating my bowels, wiping myself with leaves at hand. Clean, scoured out, I stand and look, and lose myself in the beauty of the jungle. It has revealed itself to me. It *does* have a spirit.

The vine pulls at my hand. Vine? No. Ramón's arm.

He whispers: "Do not be overpowered by the *ayahuasca*. Do not be seduced. Attend to the ritual."

The ritual? I thought this *was* the ritual!

He leads me to the water's edge. I am submissive. Trust. Must give myself to his care, because I fear the pull of the jungle and the influences of the night on my fresh self. I see the lagoon, the crispness of its liquid surface.

"Can you go in?" he asks softly, mother to child.

Oh, I . . . wonder . . . shattering the surface . . . the shards could cut me and I could fall into the blackness below . . . tumble, bleeding through the blackness.

His lyric song brings me back to the water's edge, standing in the sand. Hallucinating wildly. Again. Can I go in? Let me see. I look down at the liquid mirror. I want to touch its . . .

Reflections. . . . My face, shining brightly, particles of light skittering away from its edges, skipping across the glassy surface. . . . The moon. Three-quarter moon. Stars shining through pinpricks on the water's surface. A shadow moves across the field of reflected sky, and I twist my head to look up. Something in the air. Well. . . .

Ripples of concern wave across my brow. Face looking up at me from the surface, so smooth. I lean over and it grows, smiling back at me. I am relieved. I reach out and my fingers touch the water and the reflection floating there wavers gently. Fingers move through water to its edge.

I pinch its edge between thumb and forefinger and lift it, lift my reflection from the surface of the lagoon. Like the skin or film that forms on a cup of cocoa, it has no weight. Limp, sodden reflection hanging, dripping from the ends of my fingers, twisting, writhing into a liquid stringiness, bits and pieces of face falling in colorful drops, drip . . . drip to the sand. Sand at my feet.

Bird!

A bird the size of a dog, all black and gray, wrinkled pink neck stretched from a flouncy ruffled collar and a hard, battered beak, pecks at the pieces. Stabbing at the sand.

Jab . . . jab . . . jab, jab.

Stop it!

Feathers bristle, its eyes roll, and it hops . . . awkward . . . grotesque step . . . back. Wings stretch eight feet, gray-tipped jungle size. Its screech echoes over the lagoon. . . .

"Condor."

Ramón's hand tightens on my arm. "You have much work to do, my friend. Come! Quickly. Before it returns . . ."

Back inside the hut, a world of shadows. I sit across from Ramón and stare at his face. He lifts the one-stringed harp to his mouth and plucks and the room vibrates to the chord. Green and red. Water music. Pillars are wet.

Again. Lower. An octave. His heavy lids lower. Drop of water from thatch above.

Again. Lower. An octave. Flowing down.

Again. Lower. Octaves of time. . . . His face sags and blanches, drawn and hollow-cheeked. The harp falls away with his old hand, and he opens his eyes to smile at me one last time. Death.

His head falls lifeless, lax, to one side, eyes clouded and mouth bent in a last grin and drooling . . . something . . . ooze. . . .

My hands cover my eyes, hide them from the sight. Falling, like falling in a dream. Feel the sickening thrill in my loins, the flutter of falling. Through . . . layers, one by one. Intricate lacework, architecture . . . planes of time . . . and space! Possibilities and choices. No hand-hold. Sliding too fast to see what lies between them, knowing they are important. Vastly important.

Light below. Tunnel vision.

Tunnel? Light?

If I move my legs out of the way, I could see better, but it's hard to move. Legs asleep. Arms? Tightening, not responding. Neck hardening and cool spreading down. Rigor . . . setting. Mortis . . . coming surely. Inside tissues not giving, and my heart thumps slower against hard walls, rigid, bloodless cavity.

Light growing, glowing white. Last nausea swelling, a final bolus thickening, rising, hardening in my throat, and I . . .

Can't . . . breathe. Oh . . . no. . . .

There's smoke coming from Ramón's mouth. The pipe again. Sweet, woody smells. Blowing it onto my chest and it's swirling. Look at that little vortex—that smoke swirling on my chest! The room is singing, a gentle, lilting hum. The sound of breathing. Long, deep breaths. Hot breath. That's mine. Taste the air and feel the tears swelling your eyes. You're back. I'm back. He's smiling, but shaking his head side to side, slowly.

"Come with me."

I rolled over and pushed myself up, trembling from the woven mat. On my knees, on my feet, I used him as a crutch. Let it be over.

An old woman with braided gray hair slept on a mattress in a room we passed. Ramón's wife. I lifted my watch to my face, but the dial just confused me. It was still dark and the sounds of the jungle were back.

There was a small mattress, made up with a single sheet and a pillow, in a room at the end of an open hall.

Yes. Let me sleep now and forget this and live to see another morning.

The darkness behind my eyelids was filled with laughter, colors still ricocheted inside, off the walls of my skull. I tossed and fretted, soiling the single sheet with my sweat. I struggled out of my pants and lay there, fighting to dull my awakened senses, feeling every fiber of the sheet against my naked skin, tasting the acid of my saliva. There was a lingering smell of candle wax and the essence of tobacco smoke, and the whir and hiss of insects echoed intricately in my head. The laughter mocked me. Shadows mixed and mingled. I reached under the sheet and felt my belly, the muscles there, found that I could contract and relax them, each one of them, separately, at will. And there was something else. An emptiness, a hollowness inside, where I fancied that the jungle breeze, the gentle wind that moved the leaves, moved inside of me, in the empty spaces in my gut, emptied of . . . what? Memories?

I never saw her come into the room, never saw her at any distance allowing a full description. I only know what she felt like, lying next to me in the darkness, the textures of her body and her clean smell, the closeness of her Indian face, shining eyes, black hair cushioning the weight of her head on my shoulder. So simple. I need not bear this night alone and sleep without comfort. This daughter of . . . the jungle was here to reassure me, to hold me, to hold.

I held her close. Nothing had ever been so effortless, so natural, so easy.

My footfall crashes onto the moist soil, sound is magnified a thousandfold, and I flinch from disturbing the peace and harmony of the jungle . . . this perfect garden.

No need to step on it, I can float through it and up, away from the Earth and into the blackness between the stars, an exultation of freedom and purity. Very fast I can travel along the note that Ramón plays, that I have heard before. The tone of a crystal wine glass, a thread of sound that I follow as it synthesizes into an electric hum and numbers glow red in the darkness. 6:00. Her hand reaches out clumsily and bats at the bedside table, cluttered with tippable things, and the sound is a constant, whining buzz.

Stephanie! Sits upright, terrified, covers her breasts with a bunched white sheet, looks for me. I feel you, Stephanie. Deeply. Do you feel me. There? Startled? Don't be alarmed. I know you can't see me, because I'm too black and I move too perfectly. Just a breathless shadow, but I'm strong enough to take you. Now.

I woke up, all of a sudden, alone. The sun was flooding the little room with tropical heat. I hate waking to sunlight. It always gives me a headache.

I pushed myself back up against the wall, scooted my butt up the mattress, rubbed my face awake. Where was she? Wait. Stephanie or that girl? I yanked aside the sheet, and there was the evidence of our loving.

I pulled on my trousers. Shirt? In the other room. I stood and threw out a hand for support, and it almost went through the palm mesh wall. I found a vertical post, leaned against it, and tried to clear my head.

There was no one home. In the large room around the corner, on the central mat, was my shirt, neatly folded, My pack. Beside them, a bowl of fruit.

I squatted there and fed myself. The fruits—I think there were mangoes, papayas, bananas—were exquisite, succulent, and their juices saturated my starved tissues.

No one was home. I looked for Ramón by the lagoon, beyond the chihuahuaco tree, and down the path to the bend in the little river. I bathed there, soaked in the warm water of the shallow stream, and returned to the deserted house feeling alive, but less than human.

February 14

Brain dead.

This pencil feels funny on the paper. Scraping, scratching at words that can't possibly express my feelings. Scrape scrape. Scratch scratch. Stupid to write with a pencil anyway.

There. Found a pen. Now this is no good either. Too slippery. Make an effort, now, because in a few days your head is going to clear and you'll get serious again and you shouldn't waste paper, anyway. See? There you go.

Why am I talking to myself? Why? Because there's NO ONE HERE TO TALK TO. Feel like screaming. Go off into the jungle and start screaming.

I might just as well have survived a car accident, a near-death experience. Yes, I'm glad to be alive and everything does look different, better, brighter, take a breath, think about it, resolve never again to take respiration for granted.

Let's get this straight. I almost died. I *know* it. If Ramón hadn't breathed smoke into me—God! those spinning vortices—I'd have plunged into that light or slipped and slid through and between those . . . those . . . planes of ~~reality~~ (think twice, three or four times before using that word again) and gone away.

Jennifer on a slab.

So I feel the relief, yes it's great to be alive, and I think (though I'm in no condition) that I experienced myself, my consciousness, or let's say my thinking awareness, as separate from my body, and of much more importance than this flesh.

But goddamn it! The fear was consuming, paralyzing. What's *really* scary is what was behind the visions, on the *other side* of the shadows, *between* all those planes and layers, *under the surface* of this pretty little lagoon.

I missed it all because I was dying and too fucking scared.

There's more to this, and I've missed it. I was a guest at my own funeral and I missed it.

I'll wait here at the foot of the *chihuahuaco,* where the serpent was. I'll wait here and feel the ecstasy of each breath, the rapture of the jungle and my living presence.

But I know there's more to be had, more to being human than this, and I'm not at peace, and won't be until I understand what it is that I've missed. Again.

I'll sit and wait for Ramón.

Ramón never came.

Sometime around noon I headed back down the path to the highway. It was hotter than the day before and I shone with sweat. A mosquito got stuck on my arm. Its wings plastered to my wet skin.

I waited for two hours, sitting on my pack, and it took no effort at all to think of absolutely nothing. I caught a ride on a wagon, a shallow, flatbed wooden wagon, a pallet attached to a truck axle and a couple of worn-out tires, pulled by a burro led by a hunchbacked Indian.

We got to Pucallpa eight hours later.

In 1967, as a philosophy student at the University of Puerto Rico, I had heard a lecture by Dr. Stanley Krippner, the director of the Maimonides Medical Center's dream laboratory. Afterward, at the reception, he met my enthusiasm for his topic with a challenge. Puerto Rico had a rich spiritist tradition; why not study the dreams of the soothsayers and spirit mediums of San Juan?

And I had found doña Rosa, a one-eyed black fortune-teller living in a tiny apartment on the bottom floor of an urban housing development on the edge of San Juan. She was a fierce old woman with a patch over her bad eye, a leaf held in place by a strip of palm. The good eye was like a precious stone in a hideous setting, and the full range of her expressions were reflected in the facets of that eye, and she read my fortune by gazing with it into a fishbowl. We became friends.

"There is a power stalking you," she said. "You have great things to do, but you will do nothing of any importance until you stop running and turn to meet it face to face."

She told me to drive to El Yunque, the rainforest mountain outside of San Juan. Go there and wait, she said.

I did so. I parked off the road among the banana trees and tropical scrub. I sat cross-legged on the hood of my car and waited.

I don't remember falling asleep, but you never do. I do remember leaning back against the windshield and closing my eyes on the dusk.

A twig snapped. My back arched and I was on the ground on all fours, hands and feet, scrambling in pitch blackness, crashing through the bushes, rolling to my left, something clammy touching my cheek. I clawed at the banana palm leaf sticking to my face and stopped breathing, and as my eyes adjusted to the night I saw my car and the lights of San Juan. My pants were torn and my knee was bleeding through a dirty gash. I'd sprained my wrist, and when I breathed again I limped back to my car.

Things that murmur, creak, wheeze, go bump in the night. I could not bring myself to tell Rosa. I was too embarrassed. But when I visited her a week later, she looked me in the eye and frowned. "You failed," she said.

"I fell asleep," I said. "And something startled me."

"You lost an opportunity," she said.

February 14
Much later

Nightime, Pucallpa riverfront hotel. Huddled in bed. Writing by flashlight. River-boat sounds. Old cargo steamers, outboard-powered dugouts headed downriver.

Just a couple of questions. For the record.

The cat, the jaguar. What is it?

The colors and lights of the jungle.

The serpent. Satchamama. How did I know that word?

The condor and my face. My God! I know that happened, I can still feel its sticky wetness on the tips of my fingers.

The architecture.

The spinning smoke.

That girl. Ramón's daughter? I might have really blown it there.

Stephanie. Of all people. What I felt for her.

Bothered by the girl. How tender that scene and how erotic! But, Jesus! What if she came to me for comfort? To nurse me through the night? What if Ramón gave her to me to hold. Only. I can see that. Woman, my complement. Fill me out with your femaleness and we'll travel into sleep, into the night, into the garden.

So what do I do? She is there for me completely and I kiss her, I love her, I take advantage of her, I do what every man would do. I collapse the intimacy of the moment into a sexual encounter.

Should I have stayed until Ramón returned? Or was he waiting for me to leave?

I stayed in Pucallpa for five days, explored the piers and cargo boats that had ventured there, to the last navigable port in the Amazon, thirty-five hundred miles from the Atlantic. I visited Lake Yarinacocha, swam with the pink-bellied dolphins, and sunbathed on its gray sand beaches. The more I wrote the closer I came to explaining my experience with Ramón—and the further I strayed from understanding it.

5

Much learning does not teach understanding.

—*Heraclitus*

Back in Cuzco the strike was over. Students hustled through the halls with an earnestness peculiar to Latin American schools. Here higher education was a privilege, not a right, and not likely to be taken for granted.

I had been directed to a classroom at the end of a hall. I stood looking through the little window set into the door and watched the faces of Professor Morales's students as the professor, looking distinguished despite the silliness of his suit, walked among them.

I counted sixteen students, only two women. They were mostly Indian, Quechua, but then so was Peru. Unlike the Mixtec and Aztecs of Mexico, who had mixed with the Spanish conquerors to form the mestizo Mexican, the Peruvian Indian had maintained the bloodline, although Spanish and other whites still ruled the military and the government and held most of the republic's wealth. Few Indians held university professorships.

There was movement at my elbow, and I looked down to see the Indian student the professor had been counseling in the cafeteria the week before. He had a harried, sheepish look. Late to class.

"Disculpeme, señor."

I stood aside and he pulled open the door. Professor Morales looked up and smiled at me, and the student slid into an empty seat. I stepped into the room and stood close to the wall.

"The English prelate and scholar William Ralph Inge said that the whole of nature is a conjugation of the verb *to eat*. What do you think he meant by this?"

A hand went up. A red-haired, freckled boy.

"Fernando?"

"What is a prelate, *maestro?*"

"A high-ranking member of the clergy, such as a bishop or an abbot. But, Fernando, what do you think he meant by his words?"

Fernando looked down at the spiral notebook on his desk.

A girl with light brown hair and a crimson scarf raised her hand.

"Yes, Francesca?"

She dropped her hand and smiled. "You are what you eat?"

Professor Morales shook his head. "That is just another proverb. Come now! 'The whole of nature is a conjugation of the verb *to eat.*' " He reached into one of his bulging jacket pockets and withdrew an apple. He placed one hand on the tardy student's desk, leaned toward him, and took a bite out of the apple. "Juan Ignacio," he said around a mouthful of the fruit, "what is the primary function of life?"

The young man slowly raised his deep brown eyes. "Eating, *maestro?*"

"Eating! Say it with confidence, Juan Ignacio, for you know it is true!" He pushed himself back from the student's desk and moved to the front of the class. "Eating. This is Nature's constant. Life depends on eating other life. Think about it! Eating, consuming, digesting. It is not the primary function? The driving force? Chickens pecking at the sand, llamas grazing on the hillsides. In the forests and the jungles and the deserts of the Earth, Nature is engaged in feeding. Eating and being eaten. Primary. Primal, is it not? Yes, Francesca, you *are* what you eat and you will be eaten. Here in this simple fact is an elegant example of the inseparability of life and death. Life itself lives by killing and eating life."

He set aside the apple, went to the blackboard, and, with a stump of chalk from his pocket, drew a circle open at the top and then filled in the details. The *uroboros,* the serpent eating its own tail. He stepped back from his drawing.

"Life as an immortal force, perpetuating itself. And here is a symbol. The serpent eating its own tail. The serpent, so simple a creature, so primal. A traveling digestive system, that is all. A creature that sheds its skin and renews its life, sheds its past and wriggles forth. And here," he tapped the board with the chalk, "here is the serpent eating its own tail, a circle, an unbroken, unending path. Immortality. The life force itself. Life is immortal and lives by killing and eating life itself.

"And we will find the serpent as a symbol in the philosophies and religions of humanity, from the Old and New Testaments to the Upanishads of the Hindu to the traditions of your Indian ancestors. The serpent is a universal symbol. It represents an elementary idea, an idea common to the consciousness of us all. And these symbols are what Carl Jung called the 'archetypes of the unconscious.' They are powerful forces of Nature and myth."

He dropped the chalk into a pocket and looked at his watch. "Tomorrow we will have a special surprise: a psychologist from the United States, who will tell us how the human brain works. Do not be late for our guest." He grinned over their heads at me, and they all turned to look, and I felt the blood rush to my head. I nodded awkwardly. I had hardly expected him to put me on the spot, but I was just beginning to know Antonio Morales Baca.

Books thumped, papers shuffled, zippers zipped; the class collected itself and headed out into the hall. The professor asked Juan Ignacio to stay for a moment, and the young Indian shuffled up to him, head bowed. "Excuse me for being late, Professor . . ."

"Juan Ignacio Peralta Villar. Always look into another's eyes. No matter who they are. Men will receive your gaze as a sign of confidence and strength. Women find it irresistible."

"Yes, sir."

"How is your mother?"

"She cannot breathe, *maestro*."

Morales looked up, either to make sure I was still there or as a sign for me to leave. I was feeling a little put out, so I held my ground. The professor lowered his voice.

"Did you take her to see Dr. Barrera?"

"Yes, *maestro*, thank you. He said she was allergic, that it would be this way always, and the medication . . ."

"Is very expensive, isn't it?"

"Yes, sir."

"Well. . . ." He looked up at me again. "There is a man named Gomez," he said, and mentioned an address. "Perhaps you should take your mother to see him. He practices a different kind of medicine."

My introduction to Maximo Gomez and the healings that he performed would be documented in *Realms of Healing*. I would spend two weeks living with Maximo and his wife, Anita. Two weeks that would culminate in an incident that would have a profound effect on my education, on my understanding of the realms that I was destined to explore.

At Professor Morales's suggestion I accompanied Juan Ignacio and his mother to a simple whitewashed apartment house on the outskirts of town. Señora Peralta clearly suffered from acute asthma. Every breath required conscious effort, and her face was drawn and hollow from sleeplessness. Walking across town was out of the question, so I hired a taxi.

A teen-aged Indian girl was helping an ancient man down the front steps when we arrived at the address. She supported him with one hand, and, I noticed as I paid our driver, carried his cane in the other.

A tall, delicately boned woman stood smiling at the top of the steps. One hand rested on her pregnant belly, the other held open the door.

"Brother Maximo is treating someone, but he will be with you soon," she said. She led us to the kitchen: wooden floor, counter, and sink. The room was filled with plants, green and thriving in pots and tin cans, dead and drying, hanging from the open beams and the top of the windowsill. We sat around a brightly colored oilcloth-covered table. There was a light green parakeet, a *lorito,* in a tin-and-wire cage by the window.

Brother Maximo. *Brother.* Professor Morales had told me that Gomez was an "esoteric healer" recently in Cuzco from Lima, that the local medical association was pressing a lawsuit against him for practicing medicine without a license, that here was an opportunity to observe his practice.

"You did not mention him before," I said.

He shrugged. "You wanted to meet an *ayahuascero.*" He smiled into my eyes and continued. "And by the look of you, you succeeded."

"Does it show?"

"You look like you've seen a ghost."

"I'd like to talk to you about that. . . ."

"Certainly. Tomorrow. After your lecture." He had patted me on the shoulder and Juan Ignacio and I had gone off to fetch his mother.

Now, the woman who had met us at the door poured strong Peruvian coffee from a tin pot. I introduced myself.

"Yes," she said. "Brother Maximo is expecting you." She smiled, and placed a demitasse cup before me. "I am Anita, Brother Maximo's wife. You are welcome here." I thanked her for the coffee and wondered who'd foretold my itinerary and sent it around to everybody. So far no one had seemed much surprised at or interested in my presence. I passed it off as an egotistical fancy, added sugar to the bitter coffee, smelled the smell of all the herbs, listened to Señora Peralta wheeze, and studied Anita's face. There was something almost ethereal in her presence, something careworn around her eyes, a sense of resignation, maybe.

Maximo was a mestizo; he had a light Indian face and a scraggly Spanish beard that only partially covered the craterlike scars of smallpox. An attention getter. Short and stocky, energetic. He obviously thought quite a lot of himself. He exchanged a few whispered words with Anita and glanced sideways at Juan Ignacio and his mother. Then his face broke into a crooked smile, and he left Anita and put out his hand to me.

"Welcome, my brother! And you have brought your cat, your owl, and your deer with you!"

I shook his hand. "Well, I hope they're housebroken," I said.

He frowned, more confused than annoyed. He turned to Juan Ignacio's mother. "Come," he said, and gestured toward the open door.

I followed, but reluctantly. How many times in Mexico had I been used to endorse the status of the healers I had visited? How many times had I seen patients reassured by the presence of the *"doctor Americano,"* the important scientist who had traveled from the United States to meet the great healer?

The living room was Maximo's clinic. It was a cramped, simple room with a bare wood floor, some chairs, a table covered with herbs and oils, a small cot in the center. There was a window with a view of Salcantay, the highest of the four snow-capped peaks of Cuzco. There were candles everywhere: stumps of beeswax, red Christmas candles, votive candles of dark yellow wax poured into small glass tumblers. But none of these were lit. The whitewashed room was naturally bright, and electrical fixtures on the cracked walls and an incandescent bulb hanging on a wire from the ceiling diffused the shadows cast by the late afternoon sunlight streaming through the window.

Juan Ignacio was asked to wait in the kitchen and, after Maximo explained that I was an "important medical man from the United States," Señora Peralta removed her blouse and lay face down on the cot. She was at least fifty pounds overweight, and this position proved too much for her lungs, so Maximo instructed her to sit up, which she did, clutching her blouse to her chest. Maximo walked around the cot, circling her, watching her out of the corners of his eyes.

"Breathe deeply," he said, and she made a self-conscious effort to do so. Then he stopped at her back and, eyelids fluttering half-closed, placed his hands on either side of her spine. He traced an invisible line with the forefinger of his right hand, stopped, and pushed his fingertip deep into her fatty flesh. She sighed and flinched and he told her to relax, continuing to trace lines down her back, applying pressure at various points, sometimes twisting his thumb or forefinger and leaning into it. She grunted with pain and I saw that his fingers were leaving red blotches and deep fingernail marks along her back.

He removed her shoes and touched a point on her left foot. Then he lifted her long black skirt and zeroed in on acupressure targets on her veined calves and puckered thighs. Then he walked away, leaving her there, shoeless, her skirt bunched at her hips. Eyes closed, she held her blouse to her chest and rocked back and forth, still breathing with a mucousy wheeze. He went to Anita and she handed him a short twig covered with coffee-colored bark and still bearing one dried leaf.

"You can go now," he said to his wife and turned abruptly back to the señora.

"Get dressed."

She opened her eyes and managed to slip into her blouse without exposing the front of her brassiere.

"Take this branch," he commanded. "I have blessed it. Boil it in water from Tambo Machay and drink the tea three times a day. Come back to me in two days. That is all."

So he used acupressure, worked along the meridians that the ancient Chinese had charted two to three thousand years ago. He prescribed herb teas, acted pompous, and told her to come back for another treatment. I had witnessed this scene a dozen times among the urban healers of Mexico. And I had watched doña Pachita slice people open with a hunting knife and remove tumors; had even held aside the intestines of a "bladder transplant" patient in the candlelit back room of her Mexico City home. I wasn't much impressed with Brother Maximo.

"I'll find a taxi," I said.

Maximo shook his head. "No. You will not find one in this poor part of town. And I want her to walk. Please stay and eat with us."

I said my goodbyes to Juan Ignacio and his mother, and Maximo ordered Anita to go out and buy some food. His tone was infuriating. We sat at the kitchen table.

"You are here for long?"

I told him that my stay in Peru depended on my success in finding and working with traditional healers.

"You are from a university in the United States?"

"California," I said.

He repeated the word slowly, emphasizing the four syllables. "I have heard of it," he said. I told him of my interest in healing traditions, mentioned that I had spent time in Mexico and was eager to study and write about the psychology of healing. He seemed impressed. He filled two glasses with a clear liquid from a bottle out of the cupboard.

"You have heard of me," he said.

"Professor Morales, at the university here, suggested I meet you."

"Oh." His eyes grew slightly rounder and then he nodded quickly. "Yes. He has been to see me also."

"For treatment?"

"No. Just to meet me. *Salud!*"

"*Salud.*" I raised the glass, sipped the liquor, and shuddered. It was like sweet gin and burned on the way down.

"*Pisco,*" he said.

I nodded and took another sip. The second one was easier. "You use acupressure," I said.

He raised his brows. "Eh?"

"With Señora Peralta. You followed the Chinese acupuncture meridians. Where did you study this?"

Maximo shook his head and suspicion clouded his face. "I am sorry. I do not know of this. What is it?

I explained to him the concept of the Chinese tradition, the two thousand–odd points located along vertical meridians of *ch'i* energy running through the body, but it just seemed to confuse him. Finally he laughed it off. "No, no! I do not do any such thing. It is much simpler. I look at the rivers of light and follow them. Where there is a blockage, I clear it."

This was new.

"Rivers of light? What do they look like?"

"Oh . . ." He stuck out his lower lip in the effort to describe them. "They are . . . light . . . blueish sometimes . . . like streams of energy. They flow through the aura. I can see them," he reached out and held his finger half an inch from the skin on my arm, "there. . . ."

"You can see them now?"

"Yes. If I look."

Maybe it was the *pisco*. Maybe it was the altitude. It was probably the combination of the two. In any case, five minutes later I was standing on a chair, stripped down to my shorts, and Maximo Gomez was drawing the "rivers of light" on my body with a tube of Anita's lipstick. I gave him my camera, curious to compare the "rivers" with an acupuncture chart when I got back to San Francisco, and he was snapping away when Anita came home with a *bolsa* full of groceries. She dropped the bag, burst into tears, and ran from the room. It was her only tube.

February 23

Need a plan. Maximo has invited me to stay. "Stay with us and learn." Learn what? More about esoteric urban healers? Well, sure.

What I *could* do is stay here for a while and study Maximo's practice.

What I *want* to do is follow up the *hatun laika*, master shaman, rural wizard angle.

What I *need* to do is sort out what happened to me in the jungle.

Got a letter. From Stephanie. Of all people. Must've mailed it the day I left. Thanking me for the dinner, apologizing for her "attitude."

I think she likes me.

Perfect. I'll unlock the secrets of the human mind. My laboratory will be the jungles, high forest plains, and desert wildernesses of the world. I'll experience the states of consciousness and realms of healing of primitive, skilled mystics, glean their wisdom and translate it into a workable Western form. With her help. A classically trained Western psychiatrist, a rationalist. Yin to my yang. Left brain to my right. We'll bridge the gap between the instinctual wisdom of the ancients and the pragmatic, hard-won "facts" of modern, civilized man. Hand in hand, perfect balance. Right.

Why must I see a mate in every beautiful woman I meet? There's a limbic function for you. Reduce everything to sex.

Limbic brain. Talk about that tomorrow. Lecture to Morales's students. Knock 'em cold with some brain theory.

But there's no denying that I . . . felt her that night in the jungle. I wonder what her bedroom really looks like.

I'll send her a postcard. Something like:

"Ramon's daughter was beautiful. Wish you were her."

Note: Buy lipstick for Anita.

She's the more genuine of the pair. Maximo talks a good line, but she has a look. . . . Maybe it's the pregnancy. Wholesomeness. Innocence. Power. He treats her like a dog on a choke chain.

The next day at four o'clock Professor Morales introduced me to his class as a young doctor of psychology from the United States. It had been evident that Morales was unique within the university, and not only because he was an Indian. During the strike I had not seen a soul save for a janitor, the cafeteria staff, and the old professor's loyal students. I had heard the tail end of his lecture, and I knew that Morales was a rare breed, an educator rather than a simple teacher, that he had created a learning environment for his students, had won their respect, had personally engaged them in the learning process, and, I was sure, had taught them more than the university catalogue promised. Now it was my turn.

I started off with Lyall Watson's line: "If the human brain were so simple that we could understand it, we would be so simple that we couldn't," and proceeded to outline the basics of the tribrain theory.

The tribrain theory, I explained, is closely tied to the evolution of *Homo sapiens.* It describes the human brain in terms of three "subbrains," which developed separately and independently: the ancient reptilian brain, the limbic brain, and the more recent neocortex.

The first, the reptilian brain, is not much different from the primitive brain that powered the dinosaurs. This brain regulates and maintains the machinery of the human body, including growth and tissue regeneration, movement, circulation, respiration, and other physical systems. It is the brain of habit, an indispensable survival tool for the ancient reptiles, who lacked the ability to evaluate their decisions once they were made, to change their minds.

What the dinosaurs lacked in intelligence they compensated for with brute strength, plowing through life rather than steering a course through it. The great reptiles lacked any predators to challenge their supremacy, and the complexity of their brains was in direct proportion to the simplicity of their lives.

With the extinction of the dinosaurs and the rise of the mammals, the requisites for survival became more complex. The demands of the environment on the warm-blooded, more vulnerable mammals were such that their brains developed to nearly one hundred times the size of the cold-blooded reptile brain (in proportion to body weight). In early humans the instincts of the reptilian brain were complemented by a new neurocomputer, the limbic brain.

Whereas the reptilian brain of both the dinosaur and the human was programmed with an unfaltering obedience to instincts, the limbic brain was programmed with a new language: the emotions. Over time the limbic brain became the prime driver of human experience with its four emotionally laden response programs: the "four F's:" fear, feeding, fighting, and sex. These four drives have controlled human behavior since the birth of our species.

The limbic brain is responsible for fence building and territorial thinking, for raiding and plundering neighbors' villages, and for branding as enemies those whose skin color or features are unlike our own.

Guided by the emotionally volatile, nonrational, acutely intuitive limbic brain, early humans began to form hunter/gatherer tribes and villages and to develop social rituals and laws that would regulate and temper the impulses of the limbic brain.

One hundred thousand years ago, in a curious and as yet unexplained evolutionary quantum leap, the brain of *Homo sapiens* nearly doubled in size. In one fell swoop Nature endowed our ancestors with a powerful neurocomputer they would not learn to use for thousands of years. The neocortex provided a logical, rational thinking cap for the superstitions and ritualistic thinking of the limbic brain.

The left and right hemispheres of the neocortex are associated with mathematical, spatial, and abstract thinking. Its frontal lobes are a center of higher brain function we know little about, but they almost certainly house the faculty of foresight. The ability to see the tool or weapon hidden in a length of bone, to see the sculpture inside the stone, to look ahead, to plan the seeding and harvesting of crops, to imagine, and to dream set humans apart from the other animals and allowed them to forge their own destiny.

With a simple tool, a digging stick that would become a rudimentary lever, and then a plow, humans began to take control of their environment. The hand of Nature was joined by the hand of humanity.

The emergence of the neocortex was the dawn of what is called mind, for with it came the ability of the brain to reflect upon itself. Early man could now encounter his reflection in a forest pond and, rather than running away or throwing a stone at the apparition, could stand entranced by the image of himself, could begin to see and understand himself. Until this point in history, early man had been able to perceive the environment that surrounded him. Now, he could perceive something else—his own reflection in Nature. He could reflect on himself, on life, on destiny, on God.

The neocortex is also the brain of language. Language allows us to define and communicate the experience of our senses and our inner life. The limbic brain lacks the power of speech, communicating instead through body language, gesture, symbols, and music. Now sight, sound, smell, taste, touch, and emotions—all of the stimuli that the limbic and reptilian brains would simply record and react to—could be expressed with words.

The reptilian brain served the self-sufficient creature (the dinosaur), and the limbic brain flourished among the members of a small tribe or hunting band. The neocortex required a larger social unit to create the culture necessary for it to explore its potential, to create science, music, art, and architecture.

Intelligence was augmented by increasing the number of intelligent brains linked together in a society whose beliefs, traditions, folklore, and knowledge formed a society of mind, a community of consciousness greater than the sum of its parts. Soon towns developed links with other towns through commerce. Eventually the Earth was enveloped in a global network of trade and communication. But the four F's of the primitive limbic brain had to be restrained before individuals could coexist in large numbers. Religious dictates, commandments, and common law acted to restrain the emotional and often aggressive instincts of the limbic brain.

This was all pretty dry stuff, but Professor Morales's students ate it up. I could have talked about the ten billion neurons of the human brain and the hundred trillion bits of information they processed. I could have rambled on about neural networks, holographic memory and localized brain function theory, neurotransmitters, synaptic gaps, and receptor sites, and they would have struggled gamely to understand it all. As it happened, they got a simple evolutionary model: a body brain, a feeling brain, and a thinking brain.

Fernando, the red-haired Spanish boy, raised his hand.

"*¿Disculpeme, doctor, pero que es la conciencia?*" What is consciousness. I took a deep breath and said:

"I don't know. Like God or love, it seems impossible to define accurately. We all know we have one, although we do not know exactly what it is.

"It has been defined as the component of waking awareness perceptible by an individual at any given moment. But that's not good enough. Consciousness is our awareness of the experiences of our senses, and that awareness cannot be limited to our waking state. After all, we see, hear, smell, taste, and feel when we dream. We need to explore the limits of our perception, conscious and unconscious, before we can begin to define consciousness, or mind.

"In laboratories in the United States, we dissect the brain and examine its tissues. But just as the wetness of water cannot be described by H_2O, by the properties of hydrogen or oxygen, the properties of consciousness cannot be derived from the neurology of the human brain." I erased my simple schematic chalk drawing of the brain.

"But the fact that you are able to ask that question, that we are here wrestling with these concepts, is a celebration of our new brain," I tapped my forehead, "this neocortex. I know I haven't answered your question. It is a good question, but, ultimately, one you will have to answer for yourself."

"The wetness of water . . . ," said Professor Morales when the lecture was over and the students had thanked me. "Very intriguing," he said.

"John Stuart Mill," I said. "It's an old metaphor."

"You have accumulated a great deal of knowledge," he said, glancing at the clock on the wall above the chalkboard. The clock read 3:15. It had not moved since I had gotten there. It had probably read 3:15 for years.

"I suppose I have," I said. "But it's not much good unless I can understand it. You can accumulate knowledge until you're blue in the face, but you don't necessarily end up any the wiser. I suppose wisdom comes when you take all that information," I swept my hand across the room, the empty desks, "and use it to discover something new about yourself. To self-reflect." I turned to the professor. "That's what you meant about the difference between having an experience and serving an experience, isn't it?"

He nodded. "More or less," he said. "What was your experience in the jungle?"

I told him about finding Ramón, the jaguar, the psychedelic qualities of the *ayahuasca*, the serpent, Satchamama, my reflection on the lagoon, and the condor, the feeling that I was dying. All of it. I told the part about the young woman as though it were another hallucination. I tried to explain the sensation of being in Stephanie's bedroom.

Professor Morales listened carefully, poker-faced. When I was through he turned to me and said: "What do you think it all meant?"

"I don't know," I said. That made twice in one day. "My overwhelming feeling was fear. It got in my way. My clearest sense is that I could have gone further, that there was something more to . . ." I stopped again. "Like the lagoon. Standing on the brink but too scared to jump in. Limbic response. Fear."

"Mythically," said Morales, "the *ayahuasca* takes you to meet death. The place of the West on the Medicine Wheel is where one confronts death and is taken by it."

"Resurrection? Rebirth?"

"In a mythical sense, yes. The shaman is one who has already died. He has overcome our greatest fear and is free from it. Death can no longer claim him. He casts no shadow."

"But I didn't die. Ramón brought me back."

"Because you were not ready for the experience. The *ayahuasca*, like any sacred medicine, is a signpost where a path diverges: it helps you along the way, yet is useless and misleading unless you are on the path to begin with. Don Ramón was guiding your ritual and must have sensed that you were not prepared."

"How?"

Morales just looked at me and raised his eyebrows. Dumb question.

"What do you think would have happened if he had not brought me back?"

"You are better qualified to answer that than I am," he said. "Perhaps a dangerous psychotic episode? But then, Westerners have generally associated the shamanic experience with psychosis, have they not?"

"Uh-huh. From the Western perspective of reality, the world of spirits and such things is the world of the psychotic. Abnormal."

"Leave it to the Western culture to define normality," he said.

"What is Satchamama?" I asked.

"The spirit of the Amazon. The great serpent."

"An archetype?"

"Let's say an archetypal spirit."

"I thought it was real."

"Well, of course you did. And it was. How can you distinguish be-tween the reality of a serpent you meet in waking consciousness and one encountered in, for instance, a dream state?"

"That's an old question," I said. "The only difference is that in the one instance your eyes are open and in the other they are closed."

"A shaman would say that if you see with your heart and feel with your head, the position of your eyelids is of no consequence."

"Where will I find a shaman who will show me that?"

"What do you think of Maximo?" he asked.

I told him what I thought. That he seemed to be like other urban healers that I had encountered, that he was congenial, pompous, and had invited me to stay and learn with him, but I was more interested in the concept of the *hatun laika,* the master shaman/sorcerer that Morales had mentioned.

"In two weeks we will be in recess," he said. "A two-week vacation. I was planning on taking a little walking tour, following parts of the Urubamba River along the *altiplano.*"

"I was thinking of going there myself," I said, watching him closely. "Hiring a translator."

Professor Morales scooped the chalk from the desk and into his pocket. He grinned. "I am not for hire, my young friend."

"I didn't mean to suggest . . ."

He waved a hand at me. "But if you know how to travel light and sleep outside, then you are welcome to accompany me. I would gain a companion, and you might learn some Quechua."

"Thank you. The fact is, I can't afford a translator. I can barely afford the hotel."

"Accept señor Gomez's offer," he said. "You will save the money you would otherwise spend at a comfortable hotel, and perhaps you will learn something new. In two weeks we will see what we can find in the country."

And so it was settled. We would set out into the high plateau, the *altiplano* of Peru, and search for a *hatun laika,* a master shaman. But first I would spend two weeks living with Maximo and Anita. "Stay with us and learn," Maximo had said and I did. I learned that Maximo was a talented clairvoyant, an enigmatic healer whose training included the cabala, the tarot, yoga, nutrition, herbology, and applied astrology—what he called cosmobiology.

Although Maximo's practice was a healthy one and served his patients well, it was unspectacular. His techniques included the laying on of hands, massage, water treatments, acupuncture, and herbal remedies. I learned that he employed the help of spirit guides, two of them, to help him in his diagnoses as well as during the healings themselves. Whatever his paranormal talents were, there were always a variety of possible psychological and physiological explanations for his results.

I also learned something of the willingness of people to put their faith in something new. Maximo was practical enough about his diagnoses to be able to distinguish between those cases requiring his herbal or paranormal intervention and those that were purely psychological. He began to refer the latter cases to me, and, within a week, I was known as *el médico americano*, the gringo healer. As was my custom, I took careful notes on Maximo's cases, a few of which would appear in *Realms of Healing*, for example, Paliza, the quadrapalegic Peruvian artist who would later dance at his own wedding.

Maximo was a great sensitive, I've no question about that. He exhibited wonderful visionary abilities, but although Maximo acted the part of the mystic to perfection and sought recognition as a privileged healer, his greatest secret was that his wife, Anita, was the better healer of the two. She was invariably present during every diagnosis, and his consultations with her were masked by the abruptness and scorn with which he treated her.

He never let down the mask, never yielded to her but once: at the end of my second week, when she told me that it was time for me to acquire vision.

6

The eye altering alters all.

— William Blake

Anita and I became friends. One morning in the middle of the second week of my stay, I accompanied her to the market. After an hour and a half of pressing avocados, dodging pigs, squeezing oranges, bartering for limes, sniffing cantaloupe, stepping over chickens, stripping corn husks, tripping over dogs, knocking on watermelons, colliding with housewives and children, with two *bolsas* full I steered us toward the center of town and into the Café Roma.

She protested, of course. I suspected that she had never been in a restaurant. I leaned the *bolsas* against the old Inca wall and ordered a couple of coffees and some pastry.

"Tell me about the . . . animals that Maximo sees," I said. I leaned across the table. "That you see."

Her eyes, roving the restaurant, stopped on mine, then dropped to the tablecloth. "The power animals," she said. "The elementals."

A white-jacketed waiter set our coffees and a plate of sugary breads before us, reached across, and drew the sugar bowl to the center of the table.

"They exist in nature," she said when he had gone. "They are nature energies that unite with you. The power animals serve you and you serve them. They are a part of you. They are bonded to us at each of the seven chakras." She watched me peel the thin foil from a pad of butter. "They are simple forms of energy, but powerful beings. Just as the spirit guides connect us with the spirit world, we connect the power animals with our world. And they connect us with nature."

"What do they look like?" I asked, struggling to understand.

"Animals," she said.

"So I have seven of these animals?"

She sipped her coffee and shook her head. "No. They do not always connect to each of your centers of energy, and sometimes they hide or are too young to look like anything. Of course, you can acquire more. Sometimes there are two at a chakra." She broke a piece of bread in half and offered one piece to me. I smiled and shook my head. I watched her eyes and wondered if they saw things I couldn't.

"How do you see them?"

"By not looking," she said. "It is difficult to explain."

"What are mine?" I asked. "What do you see?"

She took a moment, debating, and then said: "There is a cat, a jaguar. Here." She touched her pregnant belly. "But your relationship with it is confused. There is also a great black cat that is . . . following you, but they are one and the same. Because you have not received it, claimed it as a part of you. And it *is* a part of you. It is stalking you. It is very powerful. It is challenging you to meet it." Again, she placed her palm on her belly. "This is the center of all life, where my child is growing within me, where you were tied to your mother and fed in her belly. This cat is your mother seeking to nurture you with a gift of power. Not your biological mother, of course. I am speaking of the Earth."

"The Earth?"

She nodded. "Pachamama, the great mother, gives us the gift of luminescent energies, life forces that we represent as power animals. They are with us until the day when we return our physical bodies back to her, back to the Earth. This jaguar is your principal power in nature. Your coffee is cold."

"Hmm?" She pushed the cup and saucer toward me. I lifted the cup and drained it. "What else?"

She set aside her pastry and swept the crumbs from the tablecloth and onto her napkin. "There is a deer." She touched the base of her throat and smiled. "A stag with wonderful antlers. An owl rides with it, perched on one of the antlers. These are at your throat chakra, your center of expression and communication. There is great dignity and wisdom. This is very beautiful."

"Is that all?"

"They are the most fully formed." She frowned and looked at the tablecloth.

"Yes?"

She shook her head. "Tell me," I said.

"There is something else. It is not yours. I spoke with Maximo about it. . . . It is from somewhere else."

"What is it?" I confess, she had my attention.

"A bird. Like an eagle. It too is following you. It is . . . tracking you."

"What does it want?"

"I don't know," she said. "And you will not know unless you encounter these forces."

"How do I do that?"

"There are many ways," she nodded. "You must learn how to see." She folded her hands in her lap and nodded again. "Yes," she said, "I will speak to Maximo. I think it is time you learn to see."

March 10, 1973

Maximo and Anita have something in store for me. My "apprenticeship" with them is drawing to a close. In three days the university goes into recess, and Professor Morales and I will set out trekking.

They have been very good to me. Maximo has provided me with some provocative material, and, all in all, I've benefited from living with them, observing a folk healing practice at its most practical and workmanlike. Living here, if even for a couple of weeks, has taught me something about faith. The faith in the eyes of the people who line up to this door every day. The poor, the middle class, even a superior court judge. The other day, an enterprising old Indian woman set up her charcoal brazier in the street and fried dumplings for the gathering. People on crutches, paralyzed, depressed, skin-diseased, diabetic. . . . It's like something out of the Old Testament. Or the New Testament. Or the waiting room at San Francisco General. In any case, I'm anxious to get on with it. See what the countryside has in store.

Went to the *farmacia* today, spent about ten bucks on a selection of U.S. brand lipsticks for Anita.

Still trying to sort through her explanation of the power animals. I've tried to press her for more, but she's all but mute around Maximo, yields to his running commentary on things spiritual. Curious relationship. His abrasiveness, so distasteful to me at first, is,

I think, a kind of spiritual machismo. He's intimidated by Anita's grasp of all that he claims to be the master of. She lives what he talks, and he knows it. Macho response, knee-jerk chauvinism to cover his insecurity.

Pachamama/Mother Earth concept has me going. So much of my psychology, Western psychology, is rooted in problems with mom. Here is a way of setting her free. One need not go through life feeling abandoned, pushed away from a mother's breast, cast into a hostile world, kicked out of paradise. The Indian (through rites of passage?) bonds with the Great Mother, the Pachamama, the Earth that continues to feed us, house us, clothe us, and even receive us in death.

This afternoon Maximo asked to borrow my Bowie knife. He's been admiring it for over a week. I'll give it to him when he tries to return it. Sorry, Brian, but I'm sure you'd approve.

With past experience in mind, I've determined to devote myself to whatever ritual the Gomezes have planned, so I'll follow their simple prescription: Fasting (yet again), this time for three days. Eat only bee pollen, drink only lemon water and herb tea. Cleanse my *chakras* twice a day with the water at Tambo Machay.

I found my way to the temple on the afternoon of the day of my breakfast with Anita. I had eaten nothing since that morning, and remember thinking that I should have taken the half-pastry she'd offered me.

Tambo Machay is the "Temple of the Waters," a three-tiered spring built by Inca masons on the outskirts of Cuzco, three colossal steps of interlocking white granite set into the mossy banks of a hill. Its water flows from a central spout on the upper tier, branches into two on the riser of the second step, then converges again at the base of the temple.

The sun was setting behind Soiroccocha, at 18,197 feet, the lowest of four great mountains of the valley of Cuzco. I stripped to the waist, and, in the long cool shadows of late afternoon, placed my hands under the spout, shivered, and washed my chakras.

The concept of seven principal energy centers is common to most primitive cultures and religions, although it is generally associated with the yogic practices of the Hindus. Patanjali, the writer (or writers) that systematized the disciplines of yoga, described them in detail. The first is at the base of the spine, at the genitals; the second is slightly below the navel—the "belly of the Buddha"; the third is the pit of the stomach, at the solar plexus; the fourth is at the center of the chest, at the heart; the fifth is at the base of the throat; the sixth is above and between the eyebrows; and the seventh, the crown chakra, is at the top of the head. They have been described as spirals of energy, vortices of light, spinning clockwise, like the smoke I saw at my chest that night in the jungle. Appropriately enough, they all correspond to nerve bundles or plexuses along the spine and with the seven major endocrine glands.

As instructed, I washed them with wet fingertips, counterclockwise. I unzipped my pants and my skin tingled with the sensation of my light touch and the icy cold water.

For the next two days, at dawn and at dusk, fortified with bee pollen, lemon water, and weak herb tea, I made my way to the hillside and, as un-self-consciously as I could, went through the motions. I even tried to visualize the chakras as whirlpools of light, of energy.

I returned to the house after sunset on the third day. I felt empty, but satisfied with my attention to the regimen. I thought I was ready for anything.

I could smell the candlewax as soon as I entered the kitchen door. And something else: the pungent woodiness of burning sage. The lights were out in the kitchen, and a warm glow came from the living room door. It was cold, even in the house, and the light was inviting, and I went in.

It was quite a spectacle. The plain little room had been all but cleared of furniture. The cot, the sofa, the wooden table, were gone, and a haze of smoke hung low in the cold, smoke that caught and diffused the flame glow of each of the forty or fifty white candles there. The candles marked out a circle in the center of the room and, from there, covered the floor, filled the corners. Within the circle there were two bowls, one large candle, two straight-back wooden chairs ten or twelve feet apart. Anita, hands folded in her lap, sat on one of the chairs. There was a small bundle of bound sage smoldering in one bowl, flower water in the other, petals floating on the surface. Maximo stood, arms folded, within the circle.

I felt a sudden thrill of affection for these people, for their care and consideration. Even though I was skilled at concealing it, I suspected that they could always glimpse the flickering light of skepticism behind my eyes, the hem and haw of doubt in my voice when we discussed the esoterica of their belief system. Here they had made a considerable effort for me. For my own good. So that I might acquire their "vision."

"It's beautiful!" I said.

Anita smiled without looking at me. Maximo said, "Sit down, my friend."

I stepped carefully between the candles on the floor and sat on the chair opposite Anita. Her head was bowed and she was breathing with such regularity that had she not smiled, I would have thought her asleep.

"Take off your shirt and jacket," Maximo said, and, although I was still feeling the chill of the night, I did so, folded them, placed them under my chair. It was then that I noticed my Bowie knife, unsheathed beside the bowl of flower water in the center of the circle. I looked questioningly up at Maximo.

"It is time for you to acquire vision," he said. "Because you are particularly thickheaded, we must resort to unusual means."

I looked over at Anita. She had not moved.

"Close your eyes now and breathe deeply from your stomach. Calm yourself."

I closed my eyes and breathed deeply, and wondered what my razor-sharp hunting knife could possibly have to do with acquiring vision.

A sudden draft of night air reminded me somehow to attend to Maximo's instruction, and I tried to ignore the knife and concentrate on relaxing. I could hear Maximo softly murmuring, calling upon his spirit guides, the "brothers superior," to bless our circle of fire and let none enter uninvited. Then my name. He was calling upon my spirit, inviting my jaguar to enter the circle of light and curl itself at my feet. He invoked the Earth, the Pachamama, wind, water, and fire. He called upon the power animals to come and be fully present, to make themselves known to me, then lapsed into what I think was Quechua and I caught the names of the four *apus,* the four great peaks surrounding the city. It was quite splendid, but through the drama of it all, as I sensed the air clearing and the light slowly fading, I began to feel a vulnerability, an anxiety for what was to come. It was almost exhilarating.

I heard a window close, and Anita. "Open your eyes," she said.

The fresh night air had cleared the room of sage smoke; the smoldering sage bundle was gone, yet its tang still lingered in the air. The candles outside of the circle had been snuffed and all that was left was the central candle and the candles that defined the circle itself. Anita was staring at me, at my forehead, so I could not catch her eyes. Then she looked up at Maximo and handed him something. A tube of lipstick! She smiled at me and nodded, and Maximo crossed the circle to stand at my side. He squinted at my forehead and touched it with the lipstick.

"*Abajo*," Anita said. Lower. "Ah, ah, ah! *There!*"

The difference was no more than a quarter of an inch. Slowly he began to draw the lipstick down toward the bridge of my nose. He stopped between my eyebrows, then drew another line across the first. I imagined the lipstick cross on my forehead, realized that I was holding my breath, and Anita said: "Keep breathing."

I exhaled, inhaled evenly. Anita told Maximo that it was too low, and he drew his finger firmly across the space between my eyebrows, wiped it on his pants, and I saw the lipstick stain. Anita nodded and I felt him draw a circle around the cross. When he was through he stepped back, cocked his head to regard his work. Anita said that it was correct, and he capped the lipstick and handed it back to her.

Anita and I locked eyes. She took an exaggerated breath and blew it out through pursed lips; her eyes fixed on mine. She was inviting me to match her rhythm and I did so. As we breathed together across the inside of the candle-rimmed circle, Maximo knelt in its center. He lifted my knife and washed the blade with the flower water, then passed it once or twice over the candle flame in the merest gesture of sterilization.

Sterilization. I knew he was going to use the knife on me, or was he? Gesture. Ritual. Drama symbolizing an act. Were these not all part of the healer's repertoire? Of course they were.

"Do not be afraid," said Maximo, and Anita began to chant softly, lyrically in Quechua. "Stay with your breathing," he said. "Meditate upon the candle flame. This will not take long."

He rose from beside the candle and bowl, and, holding the knife before him, came to stand before me and slightly to the right. I could still see Anita staring at the target on my forehead. I dropped my eyes to the candle flame wavering seductively on the floor between us and wondered what I'd gotten myself into.

I confess that Anita's presence forced me to face it stoically. I am not particularly proud of this. It is a weakness of the human male to feel challenged to conceal such emotions as fear in the presence of a woman. There was even a moment, and this passed at the speed of light, when I wondered which I feared more: the touch of the blade or the fear itself. Then I felt the point of the knife touch my forehead, and, for an instant, became acutely aware of my flesh.

I was sweating in the cold of the room. My body was rigid, my fingers curled around the ends of the arms of the chair, like a death grip. Maximo placed his left hand on the top of my head and said: "Release your tension. Breathe out your fear. Follow Anita."

I exhaled, allowed my shoulders to drop, my fingers to go lax and Maximo pressed the tip of the knife into the skin high on my forehead and I flinched . . .

"Breathe."

. . . and a thin trickle of blood ran to the bridge of my nose, along its side to the crease beside my nostril and down my upper lip. I opened my mouth, felt the drop hanging there, and tasted it with the tip of my tongue. My blood. Familiar taste. Then Maximo, holding my head in place with his left hand, drew the knife blade down, down the center of my forehead and it hurt like hell and I felt the skin part, slashed, and the blood flowed freely, following the course laid down by the first trickle.

Shut off the pain, I told myself, but telling myself didn't do any good, so I closed my eyes and tried to control my breathing, although every breath was a series of rapid gasps and I closed my eyes and welled-up tears broke free and stuck to the sweat on my face.

I had no choice but to stay with it and fight the pain that made me tremble, and Maximo made short order of the second, horizontal cut, and the blood began to flow over my eyelids. Warm liquid flowing from my wounded head, scarred for life?

"Do not worry," I heard Anita say. "You will still be handsome. We are simply cutting through the psychic crust that hides vision from your third eye."

Then Maximo cut around the cross, cut a circle around the cross on my forehead and I felt the metal blade touch my skull, and a wave of nausea welled up from my stomach. The blood was flowing down to my chin and running down the sides of my neck and under my chin like drool and dripping to my chest. I lifted my lids and blinked reflexively at the blood and tears in the corners of my eyes, felt the blood on my cheeks, and saw it on my chest.

"All right now." Maximo's fingers gripped the top of my head and I knew that I was a fool and he took a corner, a flap of skin, between the blade and his thumb and pulled.

"Shit!"

"No, no, my friend. All is well. Calm yourself."

Anita: "Your vision will open like the blossoming of a rose."

I must have gone into mild shock at this point. I felt Maximo peel away the four sections of skin from my forehead, skin resisting, sticking, tearing, blood washing down my face and neck and chest. I disengaged from the pain, visualizing my nerve endings as cauterized, shriveled dead things that couldn't possibly send the signals of pain to my brain, and I stopped feeling the pain, only the pressure of the blade, the pulling at my flesh, the warm wetness of the blood. Savage . . . Disfigured . . .

"What do you see?"

"Huh?" I opened my eyes, but the lids were sticking with thickening, drying blood. "What?" They must have been closed for a while. . . .

"What do you see?"

I looked up at Maximo standing beside me, Anita seated across the room. She was leaning forward slightly.

"You." I said. "I see you. The room, the candles . . . " My breath caught in my throat all a lump and I sobbed. Anita, the candles, my vision, distorted as my eyes filled with tears, a confusion of blood and tears. I wiped at my eyes and my hand was trembling, tingling. I was hyperventilating. What had they done? What had I done?

"Do not worry. It will come. Prepare yourself. You must trust us and trust yourself, completely. Soon. Breathe."

And Maximo was at my forehead again. He scraped at the wound in my forehead and the pain was excruciating. I clamped my eyes against it and swallowed back a scream. My head was throbbing behind closed eyes. A dark redness behind my eyelids.

"What do you see?"

Again I opened my eyes. Anita in her chair. The room, the candles all hazy. I blinked away the haze.

"Here!" she said, and touched her forhead, her throat, her heart. . . . What was I going to see? I squinted back at her and shook my head.

I was beyond the pain now. It was medically not feasable, I knew, but the fear was gone and I was resigned to my condition. I felt detached somehow and the nausea had been replaced by a thrill in my stomach. Adrenaline. So when Maximo repeated the procedure a third time, I closed my eyes and felt nothing but the pressure, the scraping. And then there was a light, the kind of light that you see after staring at a light bulb or a fire and you close your eyes and blink, the light of an image burned briefly into your retina. That kind of light.

I opened my eyes and saw something. Anita was leaning forward in her chair, hands gripping the chair arms, and there was a strange radiance around her. There was a luminescence, a small hazy brightness at her forehead, throat, and her pregnant belly glowed, sort of. Fleeting, all of it. I blinked and looked again through a milky gauziness and saw color around her, green and red, like a rainbow fading in the mist.

"Now do you see?"

I blinked, wiped at the blood coagulating on my eyelids, tried to focus, and the colors and lights were gone.

"Look!" she said. "Not with your eyes! What do you see?"

My heart was pounding. I relaxed my focus, stopped trying, and there came a moment I will never forget.

Anita's forehead dissolved, just gave way to nothing, and I saw the head of a horse superimposed like a holographic image over her head. There for an instant, but vivid. I saw it. I held my breath and looked at her, softened my focus, and the aura of light around her became more distinct, brightly colored blue and violet, almost gaseous.

"What do you see?"

I started to laugh. "Colors," I said. "And a . . ." I hesitated. "A horse?"

"Yes!" She laughed and clapped her hands.

"That is it," said Maximo. He dropped his hand on my shoulder.

Anita asked if I saw her aura.

Her *aura*. Was it really?

"I think so," I said.

"What color is it?"

"Blue. Soft blue and . . . violet."

"That is right."

And there were other things, but they were vague and lacked shape. Lights like fireflies spinning on the outskirts of the circle. Hazy, luminous, amorphous shapes. If I looked too hard they were gone. There was a small cat—I don't know what kind—at her chest or in it, it was difficult to qualify its location, but I saw it there where the surface of her blouse gave way, became almost diaphanous.

"Look at me," she said. "Do not focus, look with your third eye. Look at my aura. Do you see it?"

I did. I couldn't help laughing.

"Close your eyes."

I closed them, and instead of blackness, the background was gray and the light and the colors lingered. I lost Anita, but what she called her aura remained, but different, yellow.

"What do you see?"

"Yellow."

"Yes!"

Then it was red, glowing like a stop light on a rainy day. "Is it red?" she asked.

I nodded. She could change the color. She was testing me.

Then I could see her. The aura shifted and I could see Anita. I remember raising my hand and touching my eyelids to make sure they were closed. She was coming closer. Her hand, faintly glowing blue and violet again, reached out toward me and I lifted my hand to touch hers.

I opened my eyes as we touched. She was there, standing before me, smiling. I began to cry. The trauma, the tension, the release, was too much, and I was overcome with emotion, just emotion. I laughed and cried and Maximo washed my face and chest with a damp cloth.

"You did well, my friend. Now you must work to keep your vision. It is a gift."

There was blood caked to my face and dried on my chest, and Anita brought a bowl of warm water from the kitchen and another bowl that smelled like tea. They washed me with the cloth and the water turned red and Anita drew a moist brown leaf from the second bowl and applied it to my forehead. It stung. There were three or four leaves altogether, I can't exactly remember, but they bound my head with a strip of some plant to hold them in place over the wound.

Maximo told me that it wasn't that bad, that I could not remove this poultice for three days. "Do not lift the leaves from their place," he said. "And do not exercise this new vision too hard." He told me to sleep, that my night would be filled with dreams.

Middle of the night, 2 A.M. I'm in the living room and having a hell of a time. I'm scared shitless and it's fabulous. Something has happened to my visual perception centers. I can't explain it, I'm almost scared to try because maybe it'll go away. I . . . don't know what to say here. Jesus God! I've submitted myself to a mutilation. If I'd known, I'd never have gone through with it and I'd have missed this, and the thought of missing it makes me anxious even now.

Slow down.

All right. In the living room. Anita and Maximo are asleep and the house is quiet except for the sound of Lorito in her little tin cage in the kitchen. Everything is as it was a couple of hours ago here except the candles are all out (I lit one to write this by) and I'm sitting on the floor, back against the wall looking at the circle of burned out candles and the two chairs. The scene of the crime.

It's very quiet. Wait a minute.

All right. I just went into the kitchen. Little Lorito on her perch. All the lights are off and when I shifted my focus, say instead of focusing on her, focus on a point half an inch or so in *front* of her, I can see this soft light, much like the Kirlian photographs I've see. Yes, it's what auras are supposed to look like—a soft hazy light and there are colors. Lorito's is sort of blue-green. I can't believe I'm writing this.

Back up. Classical ritual circle of fire, in this case, candles. Incantations and chanting. Anita, possibly in a hypersensitive state, guides Maximo in drawing a circle presumably around my sixth chakra, my "third eye." The son of a bitch cuts me, down and across and around the circle, peels off the sections, the four quarters of the "pie," and *scrapes* my forehead and I start seeing things.

I can't sleep. Went to my sleeping bag in the hallway and lay there until they had gone to bed and I couldn't get blackness when I closed my eyes. Light gray behind my eyelids. Went to the bathroom mirror. There are these leaves on my forehead and a headband of some long leaf like a palm leaf. I hesitated before looking.

Maximo cautioned me not to. Do I or don't I? I peeked. Lifted an edge of the leaf. The leaves are marinated or something because they're not stuck to the wound. I satisfied myself with a glimpse of a raw, inflamed redness under the leaf. I won't take it off for three days. I know I'll really look in the morning, though. Can't help it.

Went to the window and there's all sorts of madness! The trees and hillsides have a kind of soft iridescence in the night and there are lots of spinning lights like fireflies. Maybe they are fireflies.

March 14
Morning

Exhausted. Anxious. Fell asleep last night but might just as well have run a triathalon. The experience of the dream has buried itself somewhere deep in the flesh of my brain. Fading from recognition like a cloud that you watch because it looks like something. You look away then try again to find it, but it is gone—the cloud is still there but the shape is no longer recognizable—you've lost it. A watercolor dream. Abstract, light and shadow and glowing orbs and there was a cat. That's something. I knew it was the thing that scared me off the hood of my car at El Yunque, it was the thing that moved in shadow around the walls of Ramón's hut. And I knew it was the thing that Antonio saw over my shoulder. Like dogs do. You're sitting in the room with the dog. Reading or watching television and all of a sudden the animal's attention is drawn to something. It gets up, ears pricked, staring, fixated at something in the next room. What is it? You get up and look and there's nothing there. Nothing. Not a thing. You pat the dog reassuringly, he whines his anxiety and you chuckle and go back to your book. Like that. Some dream. It was a black cat, a jaguar and so very black that I could not even make out the contours of its body, but there was a sun shining and when the cat moved in its undulous way towards me, the sun glinted off its fur and it sparkled with gold.

Woke up and rolled over and felt the cool nylon of the sleeping bag on my cheek and the memory of last night came crashing down on me. Felt the stuff on my forehead, still miraculously in place, went to the mirror and lifted the leaves without even think-ing about it. There's a scab that's formed under the leaves. Scab. Around the perimeter of the circle. What has it been? Eight hours since Maximo cut into my head? And there's a scab. Formed on what looks like a very bad scratch. The skin around it is red and inflamed. A scab in eight hours. What did I expect? Well, with all the blood and pain, I expected to see bone. What the hell hap-pened to me?

Things look normal, not paranormal. Everything's got edges this morning. Back to normal including my rationality. The whole thing has the quality of a dream. Like I had this nightmare and brought back an organic head bandage as a souvenir.

I know that in cultures the world over a healer can create a "ritual space" like a circle of fire and do their dance and sing their incan-tations and create ceremony that will affect those who are condi-tioned to believe it will affect them. This is the creation of an altered state in a willing individual and let's not kid around, that stuff works. Works on a purely subjective level just like a placebo.

And here I am. Like Maximo said, "particularly thickheaded." In my normal operating state of consciousness, I perceive the world much in the same way that everybody else does. Let's accept the possibility that in a different state, an *altered* state of consciousness, my awareness, my *perceptions* might also be altered. All right. What's it going to take?

What drives "normal" people raised in a rational Western culture to behave *ab*normally? To behave *ir*rationally? When do we "lose our grip?" There's hunger. That can drive us to act out of desperation and, if it's bad enough, to hallucination. Then there's panic. Fear. The grip of terror. There's physical conflict. Violence and rage. There's love. Desire. The exultation of an orgasm. Jealousy. Jealous rage, temporary insanity.

Fear, feeding, fighting, sex. For the life of me I can't think of any others. Limbic response systems that can drive us over the edge. Into altered states. Naturally, without specific mind-altering sub-stances.

If, in the absence of drugs, it takes one of these, then surely fear was the operative element of my altered state, my altered perceptions. I was scared shitless. Acute stress.

I know that I'm pulling the rug out from under the experience. I am compelled to write it off to the power of suggestion on a mind bent by fear and pain. Surely a simplistic psychological interpretation is available: Maximo scraped the wound three times, scraped until I "saw" something. By "seeing" I could stop the torture.

Does that make Maximo and Anita craftsmen of suggestion? Manipulators of fear?

Such an explanation does not deny the fantastical quality of the state, does not deny the astonishing programmability of the human mind, yet fails to explain how I managed to pass Anita's aura color test.

Setting aside the cause of the state of mind, the question remains: Was I creating what I saw or was what I saw there to be seen? Did I project the images or were my visual perception centers reorganized, allowing me to perceive, to become visually sensitive to, things I'd never perceived before?

Can ask all the right questions, can objectify this 'til hell freezes over. I am left with the experience.

Maximo returned the knife to me that day. I shook my head.

"No. It is my gift to you," I said.

He grinned, nodded, took my hand, and placed the knife on my palm. "Thank you," he said, "but it has opened your vision to the real world, and it is for you to keep. It has been blessed. It was given to you by a friend, and it has been used by a friend. Keep it close to you, and cherish it as an object of power."

How he knew that it had been a gift, I don't know. As I said, he was an extraordinary clairvoyant.

We said goodbye the next day. I was to meet Professor Morales at the train station. Anita gave me a bandanna to cover the bandage on my forehead. I kissed her and thanked her for her kindness. Maximo gave me an *abrazo,* and told me to take care crossing the *altiplano,* to beware of the eagle that was following me.

A few years later I learned that Maximo had left Anita, that when he left his wife his healing powers began to fade. He relied on his clairvoyance and simple herbal cures to make a living among Lima's millions.

7

Why level downward to our dullest perception always and praise
that as common sense?

—Henry David Thoreau

Professor Morales was waiting for me at the train station. I did not recognize him at first. The baggy suit, bulging pockets, and frayed white *manta* shirt had given way to a pair of rough-woven wool trousers, sandals, a blousey shirt, a simple brown poncho with a cream-colored border, and a wide-brimmed slouch hat with a satin band. A cloth bag hung from a braided cord on his shoulder, and a small, colorfully woven pouch was attached to the thin leather belt that held up his pants. In jeans, hiking boots, cotton safari shirt, parka, and backpack, I thought I was ready for anything, but then, so was he.

March 15

We have left Cuzco and the Urubamba river valley for the *altiplano,* the high plateau of central Peru. We travel third class. Oh yes. The train station. I gave a handful of *intis,* about a dollar's worth, to a boy of twelve who seemed to be soliciting for a sightless woman who must have been his grandmother. I joined Morales at a small stand where he was purchasing bread and fruit.

"Do you feel better?" he asked.

"What do you mean? I feel fine."

"That *propina,* it made you feel better?"

"Yes," I admitted. "And I'm sure it helped . . . a little."

He placed the food in his shoulder bag.

"Yes. You Americans take care of the poor, don't you."

His sarcasm stunned me, but before I could reply, we were off, running for our train.

Wooden benches, many with no backs. Chickens, pigs, a small goat attached to its owner by a piece of nylon clothesline tied to a hind leg.

Straw. The smell of maize, corn cakes and tobacco and the *campesinos* themselves. Mostly Quechua, most speak Spanish, all are unspeakably poor. With his Indian features, his hat, his poncho, and shapeless trousers, Professor Morales could be one of them. I soon discover that the fruit and rolls are not for us as much as for them; his words are for their benefit, not mine.

His eyes are a magnet and soon we are sharing our food with a handful of peasants made not to feel grateful, who listen as the professor talks to me in simple Spanish about the grandeur of his heritage, the native Peruvian, the cultural legacy that was laid waste by the *conquistadores*. "We" (he includes our fellow passengers with a simple gesture) "domesticated over a hundred food products, including the potato, established a social security system; built paved roads up to three thousand miles long, suspension bridges and tunnels to join our empire. We charted the course of the Sun and the Moon, and when we traveled, we always brought seed as a gift to a new town. We carried kernels of corn." (He produces one from his trouser pocket.) "Corn, the gift of the Sun, the Sun in its center. We are truly a great people of the Earth."

We got off at a rural train station.

"The way to help the poor is by restoring their culture," he said. "We are a raped and beaten people. The source of their hunger is the loss of their past. The Indian needs bread, yes. But he also needs pride. And hope. Here, in his belly."

On the platform one of our small audience of farmers tugged at my shoulder, nodded toward Morales's retreating figure and pulled down his lower eyelid with a callused forefinger. A Latin gesture. *Mucho ojo.* Beware.

We set off from that train station, headed off across the barren plateau known as the *altiplano,* a rugged plain of granite-studded pastures and deep *arroyos,* jagged gullies through which the water ran in the rainy season. South southeast the Andes piled upon one another, rising high above the ten thousand–foot elevation of the plateau. The air was exquisitely fresh, crisp, exhilarating to both of us. Antonio moved with the gait of an antelope. He set the pace and we talked.

I realize now that I did most of the talking; although it seemed as though we were getting to know one another, somehow I was the one telling the story. I told him of my childhood in Cuba, the family's escape to Florida, my year at a university in Pennsylvania, and our subsequent move to Puerto Rico. I told him about doña Rosa and my return to the United States, traveling across the country with Victoria, my first long-term lover, and our breakup over infidelities and irreconcilable differences. I outlined my experience at the university, described my little one-room house on a hill in Sonoma, my work at the Latin American Counseling Center that I had founded in my senior year, my training in psychology, my impatience with the system, and the scorn with which the science was regarded. He seemed particularly interested in my accounts of the neuroses and psychoses that I had treated in therapy.

We stopped by the bank of a little creek. Morales dipped into his pouch and formed little balls of yucca paste and cornmeal. I had brought along some strips of dried beef, and we lunched on this simple food and water from the stream.

"It is fascinating, really, how a philosophical difference between two cultures can lead to such extreme differences in practical psychology," he said.

"Yes?"

"The Western world," he said, "the 'civilized' nations, what is called the 'first world' cultures, rule the Earth by right of their economic and military strength. And the philosophical foundation of the Western culture is based on a religion that teaches of the fall from grace, original sin, and the exodus from the Garden of Eden. This concept is fundamental to the mythology of the West, and it represents Nature as hostile and man as corrupt."

I dipped my collapsible camping cup into the stream and offered it to him.

"Adam and Eve eat of the fruit of the tree of the knowledge of good and bad," he said. He took a drink and handed back the cup. "And God said: 'Cursed is the ground on your account. In the sweat of your face you will eat bread until you return to the ground, for out of it you were taken. For dust you are and to dust you will return.' "

" 'And so,' " I quoted, " 'he drove them out and posted at the east of the Garden of Eden the cherubs and the flaming blade of a sword to guard the way to the tree of life.' "

"It is such a peculiar myth," he said, "The emphasis is not man's relationship to his environment, to Nature, to the Garden, but man's relationship to himself as an outcast, fending for himself, becoming self-conscious in a hostile world. The Westerner has accepted this tradition, has promoted this concept through art and literature and philosophy. Indeed, it has become ingrained and second nature, has it not?"

"I suppose it has," I agreed. "You can live your entire life in a city, for instance. It provides shelter, a controlled environment, and acts as a buffer between the individual and Nature. Even foods in supermarkets are treated before they are consumed, either artificially ripened, colored, or preserved, then packaged for consumption."

"So the Westerner," he said, "the outcast from the Garden, has turned inward, and, it is interesting that within such a culture, when the individuals experience a psychological crisis of some sort, a psychotic or neurotic episode, they will turn to religion or the psychiatrist or medication instead of to Nature to become well again. To become normal. Is this not so?"

I nodded. He offered me a ball of yucca and cornmeal.

"But," he continued, "you end up with an entirely different focus when the tradition of a culture is not founded on the fall from grace, where man was never banished from the Garden of Eden and lives close to Nature and Nature is a manifestation of the Divine. In those cultures a psychotic break or a schizophrenic episode is magical. The unconscious mind opens up, and, if the person is young, he or she is encouraged to dive into it, not pull back from the brink. They fall into their unconscious, into the realm of pure imagination, the realm of Jung's archetypes, into a world of spirit. They are allowed to experience other realms of their own minds and they are changed as a result. In many primitive cultures, they become the medicine people. They have experienced the Divine."

"So," I said, "you propose that psychotic episodes and schizophrenic crack-ups should be encouraged?"

"I propose nothing of the kind. It would be dangerous to promote such incidents within your culture, because your mythology is based on thousands of years of tradition that such episodes are not normal, are unnatural, are unhealthy. I am merely pointing out a difference. In primitive cultures the opening of the unconscious is a blessing. It is *unusual,* yes. But not unnatural. These are children of the Earth, the Garden, living in Nature, not banished from it. In such a culture everything is *of Nature.* Natural. Even a psychotic episode. It is safe, especially when guided by one who has had a similar experience."

"Madness is a social distinction?" I said.

"Precisely," he said.

"So do all shamans, at one time or another, experience such a psychotic incident?"

"Not necessarily," he said. "They know the doorways and can learn how to open them. And to step through them, sure-footed."

"I suppose the myth of the exodus from the garden has had a profound effect on Western thought," I said.

"It is a given!" He exclaimed. "Look at the great Western philosophers of the twentieth century: Nietzsche, Sartre, Camus, Beckett, these existentialists! Brilliant *reasoners.*" He tapped the side of his head. "Virtuosos of logic. But they *begin* with the premise that man is alone, a fugitive from Nature. They never question this, but go on logically to describe a philosophy based on the uniqueness and isolation of the individual in a universe indifferent or even hostile to man!" He turned away and washed his hands in the stream and splashed the spring water on his face.

"The ultimate realization is despair," I said. "The ultimate solution is often self-destruction."

"Yes," he said, and pulled a bandanna from his pocket and wiped his face. "But we were never banished from the Garden, you see. The ground was never cursed on our account, as your Bible claims. Nature is not hostile to us. We are her caretakers."

We passed a village that first day. I saw it at the base of a little terraced hill to the north.

"Should we go there?" I asked.

"No, I don't think so," he said, and we headed away from it to follow a dry riverbed around a small hill, and it was late afternoon before we came upon another.

We had been hiking a steep embankment and found ourselves on top of a ridge, perhaps five hundred feet high. The slope below was terraced Inca-style. The terraces were at least two hundred yards long, six to eight feet high, and faced with smooth, interlocking granite blocks. We skirted the edge of the terraces along a pathway paved with large flagstones and descended to the village at the base of the hill.

The distinction between poor and primitive is important here. The people live in ancient thatched-roof stone huts and more modern adobe ones. They farm the fields and terraces, grow corn and potatoes, raise pigs and chickens and llamas on the same land that their ancestors cultivated three thousand years ago. The men farm, the women help in the harvest and weave.

There was a *tienda* sporting a bent and pitted Coca-Cola sign, selling stuff from the city, such as soda and beer and some canned and packaged foods, soap, cigarettes, a few hardware items, bridles, belts, burlap and nylon bags. There was a little market area on one of the two streets. There were seeds, grains, coca tea, a few fruits, baskets, some clothing. Primitive, yes. But poverty is subjective.

Some miles to the south, the *altiplano* fell away to low jungle valleys, and the fruits we purchased were tropical: mangoes, a papaya, a couple of streaked orange bananas.

The fruit stand was tended by an Indian girl of ten or twelve: dark complexion, Asian eyes, high cheekbones, and a long, curved nose. Her shining black hair was pulled back in a long braid that fell from beneath a narrow-brimmed hat. She wore a long black skirt, a red-and-green patterned blouse, and a burlap shawl. She was shy with strangers and as we selected our purchase, a hard-faced older woman appeared in the stone doorway of the *casita* behind her. She eyed us suspiciously, but when Morales greeted her in Quechua, her face softened toward him, although she couldn't keep her eyes from my clothes and the bandanna that covered the mark on my forehead.

He interpreted his conversation for me afterward.

"We are looking for a healer," he said after the pleasantries.

"Your companion is sick?"

"Well, yes. He has a very bad stomach ailment."

"He should take *manzanilla* tea."

"Do you have some for sale?"

"Oh yes!" she said, and disappeared into the house. We completed our transaction with the girl, and then the mother returned with a little cloth bundle.

"Thank you, señora," he said, and asked the price.

"No, no. Please take it for your sick friend."

He bowed and said thank you. "I am sure this will help, although if the cause of his sickness is not physical, he will need to see a good healer."

"There is one," she said, "and he is very powerful. A sorcerer who came to Zunita last summer." She pointed over our shoulders, toward the hill in the direction of the village that we had passed by. "He is a magician."

"Do you know this *laika's* name?"

"He is called don Jicaram."

We thanked the woman and headed west.

"So shouldn't we go to that village?" I asked when he had recounted the conversation.

He looked to the western horizon. "No," he said. "It is in the other direction, and there is only an hour or so of daylight. There are other villages and this sorcerer she spoke of sounds like the traveling variety. He won't be there now."

"But perhaps they know where he is from," I said. "He must have a village of his own."

"Not necessarily. I have heard of some who keep moving from village to village."

Morales set off with determination, and I reminded myself that I was his guest. I tried to guess his agenda. He had never mentioned the purpose of his little walking tour, and I had assumed that he was going to visit relatives, perhaps the village of his birth. Fine. But my time was limited and I was getting anxious.

As the sun set and the high-altitude chill set in, we stopped by the edge of a pine grove, where a tumble of smooth granite boulders marked the site of some unidentifiable Inca structure. Morales built a neat little fire: a grid of twigs, dried moss in its center, and I lit it with a disposable lighter. We ate fruit and dried beef and potatoes wrapped in corn husks and baked in the coals. I removed the bandanna from my head, and he gazed at the mark, now a faint reddish circle that looked as though I'd pressed the rim of a glass into my forehead.

"Tell me about this," he said. I described the carving of my third eye in graphic detail. He was delighted.

"So what do you make of it?" he asked.

"I don't know," I said. "I think I was the victim of an elaborate ritual designed to induce massive hallucinations."

"Do you really?" He cocked his head. "That leaves much that is unexplained, does it not?"

"Plenty. I know that Maximo cut me, and it felt as though permanent damage was done, but that was three days ago and look at it!"

"I can see."

"When I saw that horse and told Anita, she was pleased, but what if I'd seen a . . . a salamander! She could have agreed to anything."

"But you did not see a salamander, because it was a horse."

"You think it was real?"

"These so-called power animals are energies of Nature, elemental spirits that we personify as animals. I like to think of them as a merging of you and a force in Nature. A manifestation of an archetypal energy in time and space. Primitive consciousness personifies them as animals, and they assume that form when we connect with them. That is a good theory at least."

"Like any theory in this realm," I said. "Untestable."

"Well, what do you expect? In a dream we may witness some very real event that we experienced when we were awake being interpreted into symbols. In the same way you may define one of these Nature energies as an animal, but that interpretation does not take place in our rational, reasoning mind—that neocortex that you spoke of to my class. Theory and the testing of theories are part of our rational processes. They are intellectual and academic. Those conventions cannot apply to these phenomena."

"That's a fine argument," I said. "But *if* Anita has 'connected' with this energy form and sees it as a horse, and *if* I see it as a horse, and all this takes place on, say, a symbolic level, then that implies a common consciousness."

"A common ground," he said, and nodded emphatically. "That is why the symbols are universal. You find them in every culture in the world. What do you suppose it is that makes people respond in the same way to a particular painting, story, or song? Is it not appealing to that common ground, expressing something that is commonly felt deep within humanity's consciousness?" He placed another chunk of wood on the fire. It popped and sizzled and a cluster of sparks arced to the ground and died.

"The shaman," he said, "knows that there is a sea of consciousness that is universal even though we each perceive it from our own shores, an awareness and a world that we all share, that can be experienced by every living being, yet is seldom seen by any. And the shaman is the master of this other world. He lives with one foot in this world"—he placed his hand on the ground,—"and one foot in the world of spirit."

"The conscious and the unconscious?" I asked.

"If you must," he said. He paused. I remember staring across our fire, watching the firelight play with his soft, hawklike features.

We fell silent and stared at the fire. The fresh log was burning now, charring, cracking, and the flames grew from the contours of its sides.

"Buckminster Fuller—the architect?" I looked up to see if he recognized the name.

"Yes?"

"He once said that fire is the release of the energy of the Sun from the wood of the tree."

He rocked back and grinned. "That is wonderful," he said. "Another common ground. The energy of the Sun, the source of everything there is."

"Maybe that is why many aboriginal people refer to even rocks as 'thou.' Ultimately, animal, vegetable, mineral, we all come from the same source. The Sun. And we are just temporal forms of that energy."

"Of course," he said. "And the power animals are another form, at least to our people. And the light, the aura that you are so unwilling to admit that you saw around Anita, is to her what the flame is to this log: a body of energy, formless, radiating her energy."

"Do you believe that?" I asked. I felt like a kid, telling ghost stories by a campfire.

"I believe that man has become accustomed to this state of consciousness, this waking awareness, and it is presumptuous to believe that it is the only state in which our perceptions are real."

He poked at the fire with a stick, and the chunk of wood split in half and collapsed in a shower of sparks.

"It is pure folly," he said. "And such a belief places severe limitations on the very objectivity that you value so dearly. Experience is always subjective and to deny the *reality* of any experience is to deny a part of oneself."

March 15

Writing by the lingering light of the fire. Morales has blanketed himself in his poncho. I've rolled out my sleeping bag.

So many stars. In the darkness of this night and at this altitude you feel closer to them.

He is a wonderful companion. Somehow, arguing over such issues as the nature of awareness, subjectivity, comparative mythology, etc. is more persuasive when one's classroom is in Nature and not a lecture hall. The issues seem more tangible, more poetic, and less discursive.

The concept of the shaman as an individual holding dual citizenship in the conscious and the unconscious mind has fired my imagination. A primitive explorer in realms of consciousness which he or she regards with as much respect and reverence as we assign to the "un-altered" waking state in which we are accustomed to living. Western science is only now approaching the subjective nature of reality. Quantum physics, the outcome of an event is influenced by our observation of it, all that good stuff.

Yet the shaman begins with this assumption—no, with this belief— a belief acquired in the course of his own experience, not as the result of a preexisting philosophy, religion, paradigm. Shamanism worships no Christ, no Buddha, no Muhammed or Krishna.

So where will we find a *hatun laika?*

The separation of Man from Nature provokes the hell out of me.

Note: Look up passage in Genesis re God creating the birds, the trees, and all of the Earth to serve man. Shamans believe in the contrary, that we were created stewards, caretakers of the Earth.

That the rift between man and Nature happened is not in question. It's appealing to think that it happened along with the advent of the neocortex, self-reflexive thought, awareness of self, when he was first able to distinguish between himself and others, himself and his environment, good and bad.

Isn't the Exodus from the Garden merely an allegory of this Cartesian revolution? This "I am," this conscious separation of Man from Nature? Six, eight thousand years ago, with the self-assertion of the neocortex?

"Of course it is an allegory," said Morales when I put the question to him over a breakfast of tea and fruit.

"There is nothing wrong with the tale," he said. "The problem is the way it has been told, the way it has been taken to heart and taught by the priests. Instead of an elegant description of an historical event or evolutionary step, it is seen as a literal statement of fact, as humanity's condition. It is always dangerous when the metaphor of myth becomes a religious dogma enforced by priests."

"Our shamans."

"What?"

"The priests."

"No."

"Hasn't the priest taken the place of the shaman in the Western culture?"

"No," he said. "The priest is a functionary. Men enter the priesthood and come to a preexisting dogma. They come to understand it and maintain it and teach it. Their experience of religion is an experience of faith, but not of direct communion. Their communion is with a tradition, rarely with an experience. They accept the faith and its conventions and its faults. They are the caretakers of myth, not the makers. The shaman is a mythmaker, and the source of his faith is his own experience of the Divine in Nature."

March 16

Have never walked so much in my life. Have no idea how many miles we've covered.

We've visited two more villages, much the same as the first, and bypassed another. We live on a diet of ground corn, fruits and vegetables purchased in villages, an occasional piece of meat, tea made with fresh spring water, and snacks of Morales's yucca and corn paste. I've become accustomed to its blandness and it is quite fortifying.

We continue our discussions. Wandering across this vast plateau, the snow-capped Andes in the distance, the jungle lowlands and the Amazon to the south, I have begun to feel less of a visitor to this place and more of an inhabitant. The vista is a constant reminder of the true nature of my home. I don't need all this stuff—frame backpack, waterproof parka, thermal socks. I look at Morales and he is at home here. He moves through the forests and across the meadows with a lighthearted assurance, an elegant simplicity that I can't help but admire. He takes nothing for granted.

His contentment is the same contentment that I've seen on the faces of the people of the little hamlets that we find at the base of a hill or a gently sloped terrace or near the bank of a stream.

The values of the rural Indians are dictated by the land they live on, not assigned by the community. I remind myself that most of the world, geographically, is inhabited by such people, ruled by such standards.

No great revelation there, it's just a firsthand perspective.

He hardly needs to point out that Nature informs the primitive philosophies of the world directly. Nature exits the Judeo-Christian scene after condemnation in Genesis and only appears in cameo here and there—usually in moments of epiphany and revelation: Moses climbing a mountain to receive the commandments, Jesus going into the wilderness for forty days and returning with his message. . . .

We continue to talk about such things. And others. We pass a half-buried Inca structure, tumbled down, reclaimed by meadow grass, and we talk about his ancestors. He inevitably brings the conversation around to the shaman, the individual whose "testament is Nature itself, whose hymns are the music of the rivers and the winds." I would like to believe that such people exist like I once wanted to believe in Santa Claus.

As for this don Jicarum, we continue to hear of him. Hearsay. No one knows where he is from, but his reputation has spread on the wings of rumor.

They say he can change the weather.

In the morning we head west southwest, where there is a healer named Jesus.

8

The unknown always passes for the marvelous.

—*Tacitus*

Had it not been for his reputation as a sorcerer and master healer of *susto*—the "evil eye"—Jesus Zavala probably would have been the village idiot. Twenty years ago a stroke had paralyzed much of his left side, including his face. The corner of his mouth curved down in a permanent pout, and he had a habit of wiping it with the first knuckle of his right hand, so the lip was chapped and flaky. His left eyelid was nothing but a flap of dead skin drooping over most of his eye, but the good eye, the right one, reminded me of doña Rosa's. It glistened.

He lived in a time- and weather-worn adobe hut on the edge of the village. The adobe blocks were bare, inside and out, gray-brown dried mud with bits of rock and straw showing, and the roof was half tile, half straw.

Jesus sat on a woven rug in the middle of the swept dirt floor. There was a clay stove, a bed made of pine needles, and a little altar to the Virgin Mary. Morales told me that villagers brought food to Jesus twice a day.

I sat cross-legged before him, and Morales squatted, resting comfortably on his haunches, and Jesus grunted and drew three coca leaves from a little woven bag. He blew on them, dropped them on the mat, and we all stared down at them. Without moving his head he raised his eye to look at me, then his eye moved past my face and roved the room, the walls, the ceiling.

"The *rastreo de coca*," whispered Morales. "A simple form of divination."

Jesus slapped the mat with the palm of his hand, drew three more leaves from the bag, blew on them, and tossed them to the mat. They fell to form a V with a line under it. Jesus raised his head and touched the lower lid of his bad eye with his forefinger, then leveled the finger at my face.

"Black magic," said Morales, and then asked him a question in Quechua. For a reply the old man lifted his hand above his head, palm flat, and moved the thumb and little finger up and down.

Morales grinned. "A bird," he said. He fired off a string of questions, and Jesus variously nodded and shook his head.

"He says that a powerful sorcerer has sent a large bird after you. Have you offended any sorcerers recently?"

Naturally the incident in Ramón's hut suggested itself, but I said I didn't think so and asked what Jesus recommended I do about this bird. The old man's answer, gleaned from another series of rapid-fire yes/no questions, was that this bird would stalk me until I knew what I had done, that I would need to confront it, and, eventually, confront the sorcerer. He told me to beware. I agreed to do this.

"Do you have any questions for señor Zavala?"

"Tell him we are looking for a *hatun laika*," I said. "A powerful sorcerer known as don Jicaram. Has he heard of him and does he know where we will find him?"

Morales nodded and put the question to the old cripple. I could not understand the Quechua, but I caught the words *hatun laika* and the name we had heard twice now in the past four days: don Jicaram.

I watched Jesus' withered face, watched his eye widen as though with surprise. He grunted. It was like a laugh. He eyed Morales with suspicion, then me. Confusion? He raised his hand, palm up, gestured toward Morales and then toward me. Then he brought his palm to his chest with a dull slap. I didn't understand. I looked at Morales, frowned, and shook my head. And Jesus spoke, a short series of forced grunts, for the stroke had left him unable to articulate.

"What did he say?"

Morales's face was not altogether expressionless; I think one eyebrow might have been raised a quarter of an inch. "That he is with us now," he said.

I turned my head and smiled back at the disabled Indian who thought himself a master shaman.

"*Ayee me*," I said. Thank you, in Quechua. Morales got up and placed a coin among the pine needles at the base of the altar to the Virgin Mary.

Jesus led us to the door. He place his hand on my arm and I looked down at him. He was smiling. He dropped his hand, reached behind him, and drew his fingers up the seat of his pants as though wiping himself. The healthy side of his mouth curved up in a grin, and the skin around his good eye crinkled in good humor, and he wagged his finger at me and shook his head.

We left the village and walked in silence for at least half a mile, heading west. At length we stopped and Morales turned and looked back in the direction of the village, but it had disappeared behind the crest of a hill.

"Why did he stop you at the door? Wipe himself? Did that mean something to you?"

"In the jungle," I said. "That night with Ramón. *Ayahuasca* is a purgative. . . ." We were in the forest again, or it could have been a eucalyptus grove. We never knew until we came out the other side.

"What happened?" he asked, grinning.

"First I threw up, vomited my guts out—that's when I saw the snake."

"Yes?"

"Then I ran into the bushes and shit everything in my bowels. It was incredible. Violent. Cathartic."

"I shouldn't wonder."

"I wiped my ass with a couple of leaves . . ." He started to laugh. ". . . and they must've been poison ivy or a jungle relative." He was holding his stomach now, leaning against a tree. "I got a rash you wouldn't believe." I turned, faced the direction from which we'd come, and screamed, in English, "How the hell did *you* know!" And my companion slid down the tree that was supporting him and sat, laughing, on the ground. I fell to my knees and joined in. The fact was that I'd purchased ointment at the *farmacia* where I bought Anita's lipstick and I'd run out of it just the day before. The rash was gone, but the thought of it lingered.

"You civilized folk," said Morales, wiping the tears from his eyes. "When you're not pissing in a creek, you're wiping your ass with poison leaves!"

"Well, what about it?" I asked when we'd picked ourselves up and were on our way. "How do you explain his knowing?"

"How do you explain his knowing," repeated Morales thoughtfully.

I shook my head, waved my hand in vague sort of way. "No, no, let's not get off on semantics and philosophical flights of fancy."

"It is just that your question reminded me of the old problem of defining the ultimate truth: that which can be known but not told." He pulled a stick of cinnamon bark from his pocket and chewed on it. "There is knowledge that cannot be explained."

"I know that," I said. "You know . . . that I know . . . that you know . . . that I know that."

"I am not so sure," he said. "So do not be impatient. Jesus Zavala would fall into the category of a soothsayer. He is more technician than shaman."

"Technician?"

"The *rastreo de coca* is his art. A form of augury not unlike the I *Ching* or the tarot. In his case it is combined with rather well-developed visionary capabilities."

"Anita mentioned that there was an eagle following me," I said.

"Did she? Perhaps it has something to do with your time in the jungle."

We stopped by a cluster of rocks and a narrow *arroyo* cut into the forest floor. A spring. Water gurgled from between the granite stones. Morales soaked and filled a goatskin *bota* that he had purchased in Jesus's village.

"Divination is a curious art," he said. "It has survived so many thousands of years."

"At least 2000 B.C.," I said. "Mesopotamia. There are cuneiform texts that describe the practice for consulting destiny by pouring oil on water, studying the shapes made by smoke rising from burning incense. A thousand years later the Chinese were using the I *Ching*."

"And what has your research told you about its meaning?" he asked.

"I think that it's related to the development of the neocortex," I said. I shrugged off my pack and sat on the edge of the little *arroyo*. "The frontal lobes gave man foresight, the ability to look—or at least plan—ahead. He was curious and perhaps threatened by, the uncertainty of the future. By seeing destiny as a series of chance events and creating a way to consult it, he began to bring order to the future, narrowing down all the possibilities into one or two. You could guess that those whose frontal lobes were better developed became the prophets and soothsayers of their community, divining love, fortune, war, illness. . . ."

I got up, impatient with myself. "But what difference does it make? It's all speculation. Oil on water, smoke, sticks, leaves, tarot cards: ways of approaching the randomness of the future in a random way. Chance patterns."

"Patterns *interpreted* by the mind," said Morales. He slung the water-swollen *bota* over his shoulder. "It is intriguing that modern man is fascinated by the possibility of such things, yet discards them as meaningless, superstitious games. But don't psychologists use ink blot patterns on paper to tap into the minds of patients?"

"The Rorschach test," I said.

"Precisely. The theory is that these random patterns will suggest certain things. Your thinking brain may tell you that it is a meaningless blob of ink, but you respond *instinctively* with 'butterfly,' or 'tree,' or whatever else 'comes to your mind.' Where do these things come *from*? The unconscious?"

"So you think the *rastreo de coca* is a way of tapping into the unconscious mind of the soothsayer who uses it?"

"Perhaps," he smiled. "It's a thought."

"But if the interpretation is right, then the information was already *in* the unconscious."

"As you said, it's all speculation."

"In any case, Jesus said nothing about the future. He came up with this bird issue and knew about something that happened to me a month ago."

"A memory."

"Well, yes."

"There are shamans who will tell you that memory is not kept in the brain—neither is consciousness, for that matter—but in the body and in the fields of energy that surround the physical body. They are able not only to see these fields, but to reach out with their own and see the other's history, their present, their possible destinies, even. Señor Zavala's coca leaves are childish compared with such a thing."

"So where do we find such a shaman?" I asked. Tradition and folklore was fine, but I was growing impatient with all the theory.

Morales just smiled and shrugged his shoulders.

We made camp early that day. It turned out that the little rock spring where we stopped was met by another underground source fifty yards away, and we followed the widening *arroyo* all afternoon. It became a creek, then a ten-foot-wide stream, and we stripped and bathed in its sparkling cold water. Morales cooked beans that night over our fire.

I did not write in my journal that evening. I fell asleep almost immediately after dinner. And I dreamed a funny sort of dream. In it, Morales and I were playing hide and seek with a seed pod. A mimosa seed pod six inches long and two inches wide. He'd hide it in the forest while my eyes were closed and then tell me to find it. Without looking for it.

The next morning I figured it had something to do with finding the *hatun laika* named Jicaram.

And when I awoke I knew that we never would. That we'd never find this master shaman, this sorcerer, this "man who had already died."

And then we did.

9

Neither the sun nor death can be looked at steadily.

—La Rochefoucauld

It was midafternoon when we emerged from the floor of the valley we had been following since late morning. We were near the edge of the *altiplano,* where it began to fall five thousand feet to mountainous jungle, green like moss, mist-filled valleys. We stood, entranced by the tropical vista below us, and then someone coughed.

There were three of them. Three men. Two were in their thirties, dressed in patched, threadbare jeans. One wore a faded baseball cap and something like a hunting vest with zippers and pockets, the other, a soft felt hat with a floppy brim and striped shawl crisscrossing his chest and tucked into his pants. He wore a pair of old lace-up boots with cracked leather and broken soles. The third man was older. He could have been sixty or seventy; at this altitude and in this climate it was hard to judge. He was thin and wrinkled; his clothes were baggy, and a poncho hung from bony shoulders. His hat was broad-brimmed, tightly woven straw, a domelike crown with two thin braids.

As we turned the old man stepped forward and removed his hat. He half-glanced over his shoulder at the other two and they followed suit. Then he faced forward and dropped his eyes to the grass.

"*Tutacama, taytay,*" said Morales.

"*Tutacama,*" said the old man.

Morales gave me a look. "Stay here," he said. "They are Quechua. I will speak to them."

I took off my pack, set it on the ground, and leaned on it while Morales approached the trio and engaged the old man in conversation. They spoke for about three minutes. Clearly the old man wanted something, and he seemed self-conscious, almost embarrassed. The two younger men said nothing, merely exchanged glances and stared at my backpack. The old man also glanced up over Morales's shoulder and gave me a deferential look. He turned and pointed past his companions, back into the hills. Morales nodded, said something, and looked at me. The old man smiled in my direction and then they all nodded. The professor placed a hand on the old man's shoulder, then turned and walked back.

"They are from a village back in the hills. We passed it this morning."

"I didn't see a village," I said.

"There is an old woman. A white woman, and she is dying. They saw us passing and have asked for our help."

"So let's go," I said.

The village was tucked into a hillside a mile or so away. It was built around and incorporated a substantial Inca ruin. There were sections of wall built of granite blocks so expertly cut and fitted together that friction alone had held them in place for centuries. Plants grew from square niches meant to hold the ends of wooden support beams. In many places sections of walls had been repaired by the villagers with adobe and uncut stones. Grass-thatched wood and adobe huts had been built against the Inca walls and around a stone-flagged central courtyard where two large stone mortars had been carved into the rock floor. We had passed within three hundred yards of the place.

The Incas had built a hamlet here, near the edge of the *altiplano,* an outpost of their civilization. Now, a thousand years later, their descendants were living in its ruins, farming the terraces that sloped down the hill from the village, repairing their masonry with mud and rock, for the artistry had been lost, the skills long forgotten. Their heritage, like their village, lay in ruins.

There were chickens, pigs, a llama in the courtyard. An Indian woman was grinding maize in one of the mortars. She stopped when we entered, nodded her head, and disappeared.

The old man led us to one of the huts. In the courtyard the shadows were growing long, and it took a moment for my eyes to adjust to the darkness of the room. A woman, her head covered by a black shawl, stood holding a candle and murmuring at the head of a bed, a pallet supported by two wooden crates in the center of the room. She looked up at our entrance and moved to leave, but Morales held up his hand, and she just stepped back against the wall. He said something to her in Quechua and she handed him the candle. Its flame cast our shadows wavering against the adobe walls.

There was a woman lying there, stretched out on the pallet, an Indian blanket pulled up to her chin, her arms resting outside of it and by her sides. It was impossible to judge her age, she was so emaciated. Her skin was yellow with jaundice and stretched taut over the bones of her face; the tendons in her neck were sharp ridges. Her hair was short and gray; her eyes stared blankly at the ceiling from hollowed-out sockets. Her mouth was open, her lips cracked and colorless, drawn back slightly from dried, calcium-spotted teeth, and her breath came in raspy whispers in and out.

Her hands were large but the skin was yellow and withered. There was a simple gold band on the fourth finger of her left hand, loose, leaning forward against a swollen joint.

She made no movement, no telltale sign of awareness, nothing to show us that she knew we were there.

Morales turned and looked at me, held up the candle, and I stepped forward and took it. He passed his hand over her face and her eyes remained fixed on the ceiling. With the forefinger and thumb of each hand he took the edge of the blanket and folded it back down from her chin to expose the top of a simple cotton dress buttoned up the front. A silver crucifix at the end of a string of rosary beads lay on her chest and around her neck.

"A missionary," he whispered.

Morales turned his head and rested his ear on her chest, listened for a moment, and then straightened. He turned and asked the old man a question. I leaned over and passed the candle back and forth across her expressionless face.

Her pupils were fixed and dilated. I watched the candle flame move back and forth, reflected on the glassy surface of her eyes. I listened, as Morales had, to her heart, so slow, so very faint that I could barely hear it for the whispered conversation taking place in the corner.

I looked down at the tarnished silver crucifix and wondered how she had come to this place.

Then Morales touched my sleeve, and we walked out into the sunset-lit courtyard.

"She was brought here two days ago by Indians from below." He gestured toward the hillside and, beyond it, the jungle.

"Her liver has failed," I said. "I think she's in a coma."

"Yes." He looked up at the sky, clouds tinged with pink and orange. "We have been invited to stay," he said. "We will spend the night here."

"Of course," I said. Behind him, there were women moving in and out of the hut. "What can we do?"

"Nothing. She will die tonight. We can only help to free her spirit."

I didn't know what to make of it.

Twenty or thirty candles had transformed the mud-and-straw hut into a sort of chapel. I sat on a sack of corn husks by the door and watched my companion, seated across the room from me, eyes closed, head resting back against the stone Inca wall. Motionless.

The Old Man was with us. I had learned that his name was Diego. An old woman, who I supposed was Diego's wife, gently applied a moist cloth to the dying woman's face.

I had thought of fetching my journal and writing of the experience, but abandoned the idea as inappropriate, too clinical. Besides, what would I have written? My thoughts in the presence of death? Would I have wondered about her life, the things she had seen, the inspiration she had felt to leave her native land and bring her faith to the jungles of Peru? Would I have compared her to Jennifer's dissected cadaver, by now incinerated in a furnace at the University of California? Probably.

Would I have related the experience to Early Man witnessing the death of one of his tribe, and the dawning awareness of his own mortality? Maybe.

But I didn't write any of these things. I didn't really even think them at the time. I felt nothing but the solemnity of a moment that had lasted nearly two hours.

A room had been prepared for us. Someone of the village had been displaced, a room swept clean, and I had left my backpack there. Morales had left his hat, *bota,* and little food pouch, and we had returned to stand vigil.

Suddenly there was a long, loud, rasping breath, and then it stopped. Was that it? Diego's wife stepped back from the head of the bed. Morales opened his eyes. Nothing had changed on the dying woman's face.

Then she exhaled and the rhythmic breathing began again. She was still alive.

Morales stood, looked at Diego's wife and inclined his head toward his place against the wall and she went there and sat.

The room was warm from so many candles, insulated from the cool of the evening by its thick adobe walls. Nevertheless, I was surprised when Morales took the top of the blanket and pulled it down to expose the missionary's body. Her dress reached to below her knees and she wore sandals, and her feet, bony and yellow with jaundice, had shrunk within them. He folded the blanket, lifted her feet, and placed the blanket, like a pillow, under them, then removed her sandals and handed them to Diego. Then he closed his eyes and massaged her feet for half an hour.

When he was through he moved to the head of the bed, and, ever so gently, lifted her head and removed the rosary beads from around her neck. Nothing changed in her breathing or her expression as he eased her head back into place. He placed the beads in the palm of her left hand and closed her fingers around them.

He looked at Diego and nodded, and the old man got up and motioned to his wife. She rose and so did I. Eyes to the floor, she moved around the foot of the bed, bowed slightly to my companion, and went out. Diego bent over and placed the sandals just outside the door. He straightened, looked at my friend, bowed his head, and whispered: *"Ayee me, don Jicaram."*

And he left us alone.

What?

I looked at my friend, now standing at the head of the bed, his hand on the dying woman's forehead. He raised his eyes and we stared at each other for a moment. He said: "Blow out the candles. One by one."

I just stood there, staring at him. Was this possible?

"The candles. Please."

I moved to the little ledge that ran like a shelf around the room. My mind was racing, but out of gear. I leaned over and blew out a candle. I couldn't think clearly. I must have misunderstood Diego. Then I heard Morales chant, a low, murmured Quechua song. I looked back over my shoulder, and his eyes were closed, his hand still on her forehead, and his lips moved almost imperceptibly. Slowly he opened his eyes, those Rasputin eyes, and they held my gaze for a moment, told me to get on with it, and

I did. I blew out the candles until his chanting stopped and he said: "That will do."

There were three candles left, and the smoke from those snuffed hung in the air. He was at her side now, and he placed his hands just above her right leg and swept them down toward her feet as though brushing something away. Again, from her thigh, down her leg, over her foot, and his hands stopped in the air just beyond her foot, and he flicked his fingers, flicked them like flicking water, away toward the wall. Three times he brushed his hands down her leg and flicked his fingers. Then he moved to her left leg and repeated the procedure.

I moved to her head and listened for her breathing. It was the same, a shallow, labored respiration. Morales lifted her right arm by the wrist and "brushed" this too with a decisive movement. Then the left, but he was careful to keep her fingers curled over the rosary; the little crucifix dangled in the air. There was something eerily methodical and workmanlike about him as he replaced her arm by her side and began to unbutton her dress from the neck down.

When he had finished, there was nothing exposed but a three-inch-wide midline of yellowed skin, sharp outlines of ribs and sternum, a shrunken stomach, and thick cotton underpants too big for her now.

He started at a spot a inch or so above her groin. His hand, first and second fingers extended, began to make a circle in the space between her legs, a counterclockwise circular motion, and he drew his hand away, still spiraling, away and up into the smokey air. First chakra. He did this three times, then started on the second chakra, beginning at a spot half an inch from the surface of her underpants, a perfect circle, three-inch diameter, slow, faster, spinning, up and away.

Her stomach, her heart, the deep hollow at the base of her throat, her forehead—I stepped to one side—and then the top of her head.

When he was through he stood near her head, and I saw his eyes lose their focus, an almost imperceptible shift in the direction of his pupils, and then a blank, almost glassy . . .

"Look."

I took my eyes from his face and looked down at the body, the ever so slight rise and fall of her chest.

And Morales hit me in the head.

It was lightning fast. His elbow came up and struck my forehead a hard, sharp blow. My head swam for an instant. My hand flew to the spot reflexively.

"What the hell . . ."

"Look!" he said.

It was an instant, nothing more. There was something on the surface of her body. Something milky and translucent an inch or so above the contours of her body. Then it was gone.

"Stand here."

He took my arm with a firm hand and brought me around to the head of the bed.

"Look now. Soften your focus."

I let my vision go blurry, and he tapped a delicate circle on my forehead with his fingers and then struck it with his knuckle.

And there it was. Out of focus, but clearly there, an ever so subtle glow now three to four inches from her skin as if a luminous mold of her body were emerging from the flesh. I had to concentrate not to focus. I felt an involuntary chill up my back.

"Keep breathing now," he said.

I exhaled, inhaled as evenly as I could that nothing would disturb the quality of my vision.

"Am I really seeing this?" I whispered.

"Oh, you are seeing it, my friend. A view that we have forgotten, that has been clouded by time and reason."

"What is it?"

"It is she," he said. "It is her essence, her luminous body. She would call it spirit. She wants to let go. Soon now. We will help her."

I turned to look at him and there was . . . something, but it was gone. Something around his head, on his shoulders, but I blinked and saw nothing but the sharp outlines of his face, softened only by the orange candlelight.

Morales worked on her for another hour. He repeated the procedure that I had witnessed before, repeated it with the same patient intensity, never hesitating, dedicated to the work at hand.

I stepped outside. For a moment. I breathed in the cool night air and tried to clear my head, but . . . Don Jicaram? *Truly?*

Outside the sky was clear. There would be a full moon in another week. The stars were brilliant, and in the courtyard fifteen or twenty villagers were gathered around a large fire. Someone was singing a lilting tune, in Spanish, which surprised me. There was activity and the air carried the smell of rich food. All was as it should be. Normal.

And behind me, in the candlelight, a man I had come to think of as a friend, this idiosyncratic, strangely poetic professor of philosophy was disengaging a dying woman's "luminous body" from her physical body, helping her to die. And Diego had said, "Thank you, don Jicaram."

I rubbed the spot on my forehead. It was tender. I turned back into the room.

The contrast between my view of the outside—the courtyard, the activity, the moon and the stars—and that which greeted me when I turned will always give me a thrill.

Morales was bent over by her head, his lips less than an inch from her ear, whispering. Suddenly her chest heaved and she gasped as the air rushed through her mouth and into her lungs. It stayed there.

"Exhale!"

And there was a long wheeze, like a labored sigh, as her last breath seeped from her chest, out through her open mouth. And then I saw, suddenly, as though out of the corner of my eye, the milky luminescence, which I had not noticed since I had turned back into the room, lift and coalesce into something amorphous, without specific shape; something translucent and milky like an opal hovered there over her chest, twelve to eighteen inches over her chest. Then Morales clapped his hands sharply over her sternum, and then it was over her throat, her head, and then it just wasn't there.

"My God," I said. Morales looked up.

"Did you see it?"

I approached the bed and looked down at the face. Strange how you can see the death. She had been in a coma, expressionless, yet death still managed to show itself in the softening of her face and rigidity of absolute stillness. The face of death is unmistakable. No blood moves beneath its surface, no veins pulse imperceptibly. No living thing can be so inert. Life, like death, is a visible thing, and death *is* a mask, a mask of final stillness.

"What was it?" My voice was a whisper.

"What the Quechua call the *viracocha*." He drew down her eyelids with his fingertips. He buttoned her dress and pulled the blanket up to cover her completely. "I am glad that you saw it," he said. Then he blew out the remaining candles.

The village had cooked a pig in don Jicaram's honor. They had dug a pit and slain a hog and roasted it on a spit. And there was *chicha,* a beer made from corn.

Melchor (the one with the baseball cap) spoke Spanish. He told me that Diego had met don Jicaram many years ago. The *hatun laika* had been passing through and had stopped at the village and cured Diego's father of something that he couldn't translate, but I think was emphysema. The old man had since died but, said Melchor, he could breathe his last breath freely thanks to don Jicaram. Two days ago, when the Indians had appeared, carrying the old missionary woman on a litter, the villagers had not known what to do. Diego had gone into the *campo* and left there an ancient carved stone that the shaman had given to his father. It was a blessing that we had come.

Digesting the meal took all my remaining energy. The *chicha* beer had gone to my head, already spinning with the events of the past few hours. I excused myself and found my way to our room, where fresh straw had been laid down. I was too confused, too stupid with sleepiness to write in my journal. I unrolled my sleeping bag, unlaced and pried off my boots, and slid in.

I dreamed.

On my back, belly up on the sand. Looking at the sun, whiteness of sunlight, no need to squint. It's okay, I'll just lie here and look at it. But that's bad for the eyes.

Close them. Eyelids orange now. Breathing sweet desert air rushing into my lungs. Warm peacefulness, sunny comfort. Can stay here forever. . . .

Movement. A jagged shadow lurches across the field of light glowing through my closed lids. My stomach flutters danger and my eyes open on fear. A sudden threatening shadow from nowhere . . . far off . . . coming *fast*. . . . It swoops and screams and I roll sideways in the sand with the impact of the bird's talons tearing across my stomach. Roll, again on my back, sweating fear. I prop up on elbows in the sand, crane my neck to look down at the sandy, bloody gash in my taut belly, red with blood, yellow fat, then the black eagle, the monster is back, filling the sky, battering my body with its wings, pinning my arms under its blows, the dull ache of dream pain in my thighs, its bone-white talons embedded there. Pinching, clamping my guts, my intestines, in a surgical beak, wriggling its feathery neck, tugging wildly, out of control frenzy of hunger, working my organs out through the tear in my stomach.

Take it! Tear it out and be done for Christ's sake! It stretches its wings, blots out the sky, and jerks at my entrails, and feathers bristle and I scream as it spreads its wings and flexes its feathers, bristling . . .

"Wake up!"

I gasped for breath and sat up, half out of the sleeping bag, fingers dug into the straw. Morales was leaning on his elbow, his poncho a blanket.

"You should not have made love with Ramón's daughter," he said.

March 20

Don Jicaram. How? Does he lead a double life? One minute the mild-mannered Professor Morales of the city, then into a nearby Inca temple and it's . . . don Jicaram! Shaman! *Shazam!*

Well, why not? Still, it's stunning to think that all this time my companion was the very man we were seeking. What a charade. And to what purpose?

He was biding his time, watching me, testing me. My intent. My trip into the jungle, my time with Maximo and Anita—have those been trials too? When we first met, that day in the cafeteria, he told me that there was a custom that a shaman would share his knowledge with any who asked as long as they presented themselves with impeccable intent. Purity of purpose.

Have I done this? Or has his identity come out by accident, by our happening upon this village and this old woman? The revelation came with such simplicity, such dramatic elegance. . . .

All this time that I have been seeking a *hatun laika*, a subject to study, *he* has been studying *me*. Teaching me. What next?

And what has happened to my vision? Did I see her energy body disengage?

Mornings always seem to bring into question the events of the night before.

When we left the village, we did not retrace our steps back to the edge of the clearing, but rather headed north across the tundra. An hour passed before I asked him about the dream.

"The eagle is from Ramón," he said. "It has been following you ever since your return from the jungle. It showed itself to you in your dream."

"But you have seen it," I said. "Jesus Zavala divined it. Anita and Maximo talked about it."

"Yes?"

"Well?"

He stopped and cocked his head. "Do you hear that stream?"

I listened. A distant pattering of water over rock. "Yes."

"It is somewhere over that little hill."

"Right."

"Let us say that I am familiar with this particular spring and its rocky shore. I sit here and build a fire while you wander off in the direction of the spring. You come back an hour later, completely wet. Your hair, your shirt, your pants, your boots. I say to you, 'You have been swimming.' You would not be surprised."

"Of course not."

"Of course not! You are wet. The water shows. Then I mention that you should have taken your clothes off before swimming."

"But what if I had tripped and fallen into the stream?" I asked, thinking the example childish and the reasoning flawed.

"But remember, I know the stream and the sharp rocks that make its shore and bottom, and I see that your clothes, although wet, are not torn or damaged in any way."

"All right," I said. "That's just deductive logic, based on what you know and what you observe."

"Yes, like Sherlock Holmes," he said.

"Anyone would have come to the same conclusion."

"Undoubtedly, because we are all accustomed to reasoning based on what we are used to seeing: the evidence of our conscious, waking awareness. But that awareness is only a fraction of our total awareness. It is as easy for me to see that you are all wet as it is to see this power that Ramón has sent after you. It clings to you like the wet clothes. Sight is a skill. So is vision. You have had glimpses of such things. You should begin to understand."

"My training, my conditioning, prevents me from understanding."

"Yes. Your conventions tell you one thing, your experience, another. It is characteristic of Westerners to need to understand something before acknowledging its worth or even accepting its existence."

"Well," I said, "I *haven't* seen this eagle."

He shook his head. "You did last night."

"In a dream."

"So although you are not conscious of this power, you are *unconscious* of it. Close your eyes and dream, my friend. Master dreaming and you master the unconscious. The truest experience of life is when we dream awake."

"So you are suggesting that a shaman can see the unconscious of another?"

He shook his head. "Why must you reduce everything to a simple sentence? You will never grasp the essence of these concepts with simple word formulas. You must think like a poet. Think in terms of metaphor and imagery.

"Take, for example, the lagoon that you have described behind Ramón's hut. Here is a poetic expression of the psyche. The surface that we are accustomed to seeing is dependent upon what lies below. The unseen depths support the surface, yes?"

"Yes. I thought of that analogy."

"Good. Then perhaps you will understand."

We were off again, walking down a grassy hill.

"We are used to standing on the shore and seeing the surface of the lagoon. We can deduce very little of what lies below the surface. Anyone can fall into the lagoon, but they would have no idea of what dangers the depths might contain. It could be very deep, there could be plants waiting to entangle, dangerous currents. There could be *pirañas*."

"Fear could keep you from diving in," I said.

"Indeed, it could. But if you change your perspective on the water, see where the Sun shines on its surface and look at it from that point of view, from above, where the eagle flies, then you can see into its depths, see what supports the surface, see what lies below."

"The unconscious," I said.

"If you must." He sighed. "Once you acquire the vision, you can know the lagoon and swim where you will."

"I understand," I said. And I did, completely. Then he took the metaphor one or two steps further.

"That perspective allows you to see not only the present condition of the lagoon, but much of its history, everything that has touched its surface and sunk to the bottom. You can even see the effect that whatever has penetrated the surface has had on the life of the lagoon: a sunken log that plants have grown on and fish must swim around. Everything that has ever fallen into the lagoon has somehow altered its character. Some things are deeply embedded and are no longer distinguishable, but all of them are visible."

"Its past is visible."

"Yes, and the effect that the past has had."

"It's a good metaphor," I said. "But if you compare the mind to a pond, you imply the geography, the banks that hold the water there. The vessel that contains the liquid. A specific place within which the mind resides. That's an argument for the localization of consciousness within the brain, that the mind is inside the skull."

"I did not compare the mind to a pond, I compared it to that lagoon that frightened you. A lagoon is part of a stream. It is a place where the shore widens and the center deepens and the water slows, but the water is, nevertheless, constantly flowing through it." He grinned. "I can even travel upstream, nearer the source, and affect the lagoon in any number of ways by affecting its source. I can place an object in the stream that, eventually, if nothing interferes along the way, will reach the lagoon, and, if it stays there long enough, it might sink in." He glanced up at me out of the corner of his eye. "I can place my hand in the water and cause a ripple in the stream that will eventually reach the lagoon and reverberate through it. It might even upend the canoe you are sitting in, or save you by washing you ashore."

I laughed. "So what do I do about this eagle?"

He stuck a stick of cinnamon bark in the corner of his mouth. "Learn to see it. Learn what it has to teach you and then return to the jungle. You will need to return. To complete your work of the West."

And so began my apprenticeship with Antonio Morales Baca. Don Jicaram. He had told me that were I to meet a master shaman I would need to approach him as a student, not as a psychologist. But although I use the word *apprenticeship,* it was friendship that formed our bond.

At the end of a day's journey from Diego's village we came to a little hill in the middle of a meadow. At the crest of the hill was an Inca ruin, tumbled down, its foundation half-buried in soil and brushed by grass. It looked as though it had grown out of the hill. It was dusk as we ascended and turned to gaze back down at the sparsely grown forest on one side and, on the other, the slope of a valley that descended more than a mile from the *altiplano* down to the deep green Urubamba valley.

"An observation post," said Antonio. He slapped the side of the granite wall with his palm. "One of hundreds that linked the Inca Empire."

He led me through a gap in the wall into a little enclosure of fallen granite blocks, and grass. One of these blocks, a near-perfect specimen of Inca stone carving, lay by the base of one wall. He motioned for me to grab one corner, and we turned it onto its side to expose a rock-lined hole eight inches deep, a foot wide, two feet long, probably part of an ancient irrigation canal. There was a long bundle there, wrapped in an old brown-and-red woven Inca cloth.

"What's this?"

"My *mesa,*" he said. "We need a fire."

I trotted down the hill and gathered some firewood, and returned to find that he had built a four-sided framework of twigs, a tiny pyre, with a pile of dried grass in its center. He lit this with a match, and we built our fire around it.

"We won't eat tonight," he said, and untied a bit of twine around the parcel and spread the cloth on the grass. Inside there were two short staffs and a soft leather pouch.

"The *mesa,*" he said, "is a collection of power objects through which one engages the forces of Nature. It is the center of ritual."

"And this is your *mesa?*"

He nodded. "It is very simple and very old. You will find others to be quite complex, with power objects for every occasion." He winked at me. "Every phenomena. But a *mesa* can be as simple as a bed of pine needles and a few stones."

He planted the staffs in the soil at the upper corners of the cloth. The staff on the left was of a dark hardwood carved like a lefthanded spiral. The one on the right was of polished bone or ivory, and was crowned by a handle in the form of a hooked beak.

"They represent polarity," he said. "Darkness and light." Then he proceeded to place objects from the pouch onto the cloth.

There were not many and he did not explain their individual significance to me at the time. There was a piece of carved obsidian, half jaguar, half bird: earth and sky, the winged realms. There was a wooden fish or dolphin for access to the underworld, water, the psyche; a tiny gold owl, no more than two inches high, that represented night vision and the wisdom of the darkness. Many years later I would learn that such an object was dreaded by some shamans, for it held the power of lost and ancient knowledge and had little to do with simple healing. There was an eagle, carved from some dark gray stone and inlaid with diamond abalone shell slivers. "Each one of us has a universe within," he would later tell me, and this object was used to fly into it. And there were other things, stones and shells, a shard of crystal, a small wooden bowl. All were worn smooth from centuries of use, like fetishes in an anthropological museum.

Finally he withdrew an antique glass-and-silver flask from the pouch. It was half filled with a greenish brown liquid like Chinese tea.

"Tonight we will engage with ritual," he said. "You have made important steps in acquiring vision, but you still move through Nature like an outcast, awkwardly. You should move through the forest or across a meadow as you should move through life: with confidence, respect, and grace."

The sun had disappeared over the horizon, and our fire crackled, sent sparks rising into the graying sky.

"Tonight you will take San Pedro for the first time," he said. "San Pedro, Saint Peter, the keeper of the gates of heaven. It is also called *huachuma*, 'flesh of the Gods.' "

"Communion," I said.

"Yes. Imagine the San Pedro cactus, standing alone, its arms raised to heaven and its roots growing deep into the Earth. It is the medicine of choice of the shaman, helping the shaman to enter the body of the Earth, to meet the Mother Goddess, to come face to face with the power of Nature. It grows in all of the temperate zones of Peru: the coast, the *sierras*, the desert, and the jungle. Its preparation is a closely guarded secret. When simply boiled it produces a mild euphoria, but when the essence of the plant is distilled and married with the flavors of cleansing herbs, it becomes a visionary medicine of great spirit and power. It must not be abused.

"It is the plant of ritual, of vision. In the South it helps you to see your past in its most brazen form; in the West it gives you the strength to face death; in the North it shows you the way to mastery; and in the East it helps you to call upon your power animals, to acquire their skills as you need them to acquit yourself effectively in the world, to cast no shadow, to leave no tracks." He paused and nodded. "Yes, and it conditions you to be able to access these . . . higher capabilities of your own accord. These higher states."

He unscrewed the silver cap of the flask and poured a small quantity—about half a jigger's worth—into the bowl.

"Its use is specific and sacred. You have used drugs in the past, but without motive, purity of purpose, and a connection to the Earth, any 'mystical' experience is psychological drool. The irresponsible use of any drug only mimics and forestalls the real union with Nature and the Great Spirit. It is like entering a spiritual whorehouse and debasing your highest self in the most dangerous way, by burning up your life force. The shaman's task is to strengthen this life force, expand the envelope of energy that surrounds the human body, and vitalize it, by accumulating personal power." He stopped and blew a puff of air to one side as though to dismiss the subject, like blowing out a candle. "What you are about to receive is a natural plant substance that will cleanse and bring balance to your body and the energy fields that surround you. Only when the body, mind, and spirit are in balance can the shaman make a real act of power."

He handed me the bowl. "Stand and salute the four directions."

I took the bowl, stood beside the fire, turned my back on Antonio and faced south. I didn't really know what to do. Then his voice came softly, in gentle Spanish tones, from behind me.

"We call upon the Satchamama, the great serpent of Lake Yarinacocha, the spirit of the South, to come to us. Wrap yourself around us, ancient Mother, fold us in your coils of light."

I raised the bowl to the southern sky. I felt self-conscious, toasting the air.

"Hey!" he said, and it sounded like an *amen,* and I said: "Hey!"

I turned to the horizon, looked at the distant peak where the sun had left us.

"We call upon the spirit of the West, Mother-Sister Jaguar, golden jaguar that eats the dying Sun. Come to us, you who have seen the birth and death of galaxies. Let us look into your eyes. Teach us with your grace."

What was it that Ramón had said about the jaguar?

"Hey!"

"Hey!"

I told myself to concentrate on the ritual and faced north.

"We summon the wisdom of the North, the place of the ancient masters, grandmothers, grandfathers. I bring you one who is not of my people, but of our people. Receive him, welcome him. Bless us in our work that we may one day enter your crystal palace with but a single thought and sit in council among you. Hey!"

I raised the bowl to the north and turned to the east.

"Hey!"

"And we call upon the spirit of the East. Come to us from your mountaintop, great eagle. Teach us to see with your eyes, that our vision may penetrate the Earth and the heavens. Fly with us now and watch over us. Teach us to fly wing-to-wing with the Great Spirit. Hey!"

"Hey!"

I turned and Antonio motioned for me to bring the bowl down to the Earth. "To the Pachamama, great Mother Earth . . ." The intonation of a prayer. "You who feed us and nurture us at your breast, teach us to walk on your belly with beauty and with grace. Hey!"

"Hey!"

He raised his hand and I lifted the bowl to the sky.

"Great Spirit Viracocha, mother and father, we salute you, that all we do is in your honor. Hey, hey!"

"Hey!"

He nodded for me to sit across from him. He nodded again and I drank the San Pedro. It tasted faintly of anise.

Antonio closed his eyes and began to breathe deeply, exhaling through pursed lips. I followed his example and soon the rhythmic rustle of a rattle marked the tempo of my breathing in three-three time. His chant was Quechua. I wondered where the rattle had come from. I thought about what he had said, about San Pedro, a plant I had heard of, about his discourse on the use of substances without motive, purity of purpose, connection to the Earth. Experience and experience served. Then I gave myself over to the hypnotic rhythms of rattle and chant. I became aware of my body. There was a tightness in my neck and shoulders, a soreness from the straps of my backpack. Eyes closed, I dropped my shoulders, moved my head from side to side, sinuously stretching the muscles. It felt wondrous. I lifted my shoulders and rotated them back, and never before had I experienced such musculature, such an immediate relief and relaxation, and I realized that my motions were unusually fluid, sensitive to each sore muscle, stretching, unclenching. Eager to explore this new facility, I twisted my upper body, placed my right hand on my left knee and pulled myself, torqued my body to the left and felt three vertebrae crack. Then to the right and three more popped and the relief was tremendous. I wanted to move, to stretch and exercise, and the light of the fire was beating against my eyelids—a light show of pinpoint colors, as though single pastel photons were passing in between the cells of my lids, penetrating to the pupil and registering at the visual cortex at the back of my brain.

I had no idea how much time had passed, but then I opened my eyes and, for an instant, there was something so hawklike about Antonio's face that I blinked it away. He was smiling at me over the *mesa*. He sipped from a tiny bottle that I had not noticed before, then reached down and lifted the gold owl from the cloth and held it between his palms as though in prayer. Then he took the little object in one hand and held it before him and blew a fine spray of sweet oil on it. The smell of the oil penetrated my nostrils and hummed in my head. The gold owl caught the light from the fire and seemed to glow. Then he made a fist around it, extended his arm toward me, and opened the fist.

"Take it. With your left hand," he said.

I took it.

"Hold it, and close your eyes, and see it with your inner vision. A power object is a focal point, like a tuning fork."

I closed my eyes and imagined my forehead opening . . . glowing . . . the light was violet.

"That is the way. Excellent, my friend."

And I saw a woman, a dream image woman with owl wings folded around her, a feathered shoulder lifted, head turning to look at me over the shoulder, eyes opening, feathers . . . opening . . . with eyes. Eyes in the feathers. I caught my breath. I opened my eyes and looked down at the object on my palm, then up into his eyes.

"How do you feel?"

"I feel wonderful."

"Get up and walk," he said. "Go down the hill and into the forest."

I leaned over to replace the object. His hand touched mine.

"No, no. Take this with you. Never leave a *mesa* or medicine circle without protection."

I nodded for some reason and stood. My legs were aching to move and

I did. I moved out of the light of the fire and down the hill and into the forest.

A pine tree grove that resonated. The trees were defined each by their own light, glowing pastel outlines that moved with the branches swaying ever so slightly, pine needles vibrating in the northerly breeze. Living things with flesh and nutrient fluids coursing through them, drawing upon the Sun's light, which seemed to linger in each of them, rising from the soil. . . . How was it that I had never noticed that before? Their gentle presence was tangible, known to me for the first time, and I had walked among them only hours before, not seeing, unaware of their spirit, their gently pulsating life. Their consciousness. Our kinship was profound and I felt the breeze at my back and I began to run. Did my feet touch the ground? Yes, so perfectly, swiftly across the pine needles.

I had never run like that, running from nothing, toward nothing, moving so swiftly for the sake of the movement itself, the exhilaration of grace, slaloming though the forest on no path, the cushion of cool soil and pine needles, faster. I ran with my whole body, feeling every muscle loose and tuned in perfect harmony, the air parting, swirling around my back. . . .

"Close your eyes. . . ."

The light shed by the trees reassured me that they were still there, and I moved, ran, liberated from sight, through the forest, like the air.

I knew that something was moving me, something inside of me that I had never felt before.

10

March 22

Still reeling from the events of the past few days. The death of the missionary, my first experience with San Pedro. The revelation of Antonio's identity sits undigested in my stomach.

I saw a magician once, a slick trickster. He, or rather, his sequined assistant, rolled a footlocker to center stage. With her help he stepped into a mailbag secured at the top by a chain and padlock, and the bagged magician lay down in the locker. The lid was closed and locked at four points. His assistant stood atop the chest, lifted a curtain from the floor to surround herself, and . . . dropped it. Or did she? For it was the magician who stood smiling from atop the case, and when the padlocks were removed, his assistant emerged from the mailbag. In the blink of an eye.

I was eight. I remember the moment, how it forced me to think, to replay all that I had seen.

Let me see it one more time.

Just one more time to discover the secret of the wonder of the thing.

Antonio lifted a palmful of pine forest earth and gazed upon the pine needles with the earnestness of a tea leaf reader. The coarse brown dirt fell to the ground through the spaces between his fingers.

"There are two kinds of people in this world, my friend. There are those who are dreamers and those who are being dreamed." His eyes glanced at me sideways.

"There comes a time in every man's life when he must encounter his past. For those who are dreamed, who have no more than a passing acquaintance with power, this moment is usually played out from their death-beds as they try to bargain with fate for a few more moments of life time." He moved his hand from side to side, sifting, then dropped his gaze to the stuff on his palm.

"But for the dreamer, the person of power, this moment takes place alone, before a fire, when he calls upon the specters of his personal past to stand before him like witnesses before the court. This is the work of the South, where the Medicine Wheel begins.

"You see, we assemble our present with the bits and pieces of our past, seeking to avoid those circumstances that caused us pain, seeking to recreate those that brought us pleasure. We are helpless captives."

I cleared my throat. " 'Those who do not remember the past are con-demned to relive it,' " I said.

"Or to avoid it," he stressed. "And I am not speaking of *remembering* the past. Anyone can *remember* the past and, in remembering, we reframe it to serve and justify our present. Remembering is a conscious act and there-fore subject to embellishment. Remembering is easy."

He blew the remaining pine needles from his palm to reveal a charred wood chip, an acorn-sized cinder, a relic from a *campesino* campfire.

"The person of power sits in the prisoner's dock alone before the fire. He *confronts* his past. He hears the testimony of these . . . specters. And he dismisses them one by one. He acquits himself of his past. Do you com-prehend this?" He lifted his eyes from the cinder and fixed them upon mine. "The man of power has no past, no history that can claim him. He has cast aside his shadow and learned to walk in the snow without leaving tracks."

He looked down at his palm and raised an eyebrow, as though seeing the tiny cinder for the first time. He grinned, let the cinder roll down his palm to his fingertips, and held it before him. "How appropriate. Isn't it lucky I found it here."

Our work has begun in earnest. By Antonio's reckoning we will reach Quillabamba by noon tomorrow and catch the train back to Cuzco, from there to Aguascalientes and on to the ruins of Machu Picchu, where I will perform my "work of the South."

Have spent the last two days exercising my vision and trying my patience, the last two nights discussing the theory of things past.

Antonio has refused to discuss my San Pedro experience, how I ran in the forest at night with my eyes closed. He became impatient when I blamed it on the psychoactive effects of the San Pedro. It was the ritual, the summoning of power through ceremony—why must I always dismiss an experience with the handiest explanation? What happened, he said, was that my mind had spread its wings and taken flight.

Why, he asked, must I wake up the next morning and think myself again an outcast from Paradise when I had run in Nature free, unfettered?

I have been touched by power, he said.

I call it a wild and magical run through the woods, lucky that I didn't fall and rip my face open.

It rained the night before last. Torrential. We found half-shelter under a granite outcrop in the forest. Yesterday, while our things dried in the sun, Antonio instructed me to sit on a boulder that stuck out above a rain-swollen pond.

For three hours I sat there, contemplating the reflection of my face and the clouds in the sky above and behind.

Fascinating thing and so simple: Both the clouds, thousands of feet above, and my face, three feet from the surface of the pond, are reflected on the flat plane. Antonio told me to focus on the reflected clouds and, when I did, my image split into two out-of-focus blurs. The trick, he said, was to work the muscles of my eyes to bring the two faces into focus while maintaining my concentration on the clouds.

This is not easy. Just when I thought I had it, I'd realize that I'd stopped focusing on the clouds. . . . start again. But the trance state that it produces is profound. There were moments when I lost myself altogether. He told me also to concentrate on the space *between* my two faces and there were moments, flashes, when I thought I saw things. Other faces. My father's, my grandmother's. I don't know. These occurred later, when I was in such a meditative state that I know I'd lost track of time and situation. My awareness of the moment was abnormal, deep trance, and Antonio had to shake me out of it. Later he reminded me of the myth of Narcissus, spurned by Echo, so captivated by his own image in a forest pond that he was transformed into a flower growing on its bank.

The exercise is designed to retrain the eyes to look at the spaces in between things. Like Anita, who he said could look at a spot half an inch from my face while keeping my face in focus and there see my aura. My chakras spinning. My energy body.

"You are trained to focus on objects, on things," he said. "The world of the shaman happens in the spaces in between things."

Games with consciousness. Awareness games. A curious meditative state can also be created by watching myself watching myself. Aware of awareness. Aware of myself breathing myself breathing. Hard to describe. I sit looking at our evening fire. I start a dialogue with myself:

"I'm sitting here, looking at the fire."

Sitting, looking at the fire.

"I'm sitting, looking at the fire."

Sitting, looking at the fire.

"I *really am* sitting here, looking at the fire!"

Yes. Still sitting, looking at the fire.

On and on, over and over, like a mantra. The I who a nanosecond ago was preceiving myself looking at the fire through my eyes, really is looking at the fire. It is a strange duality, watching my own mindstream. The duality of the self that is engaged in the act and the self who is aware of the first self's reality and can describe it as it happens. It is almost a way of stopping thought. Antonio calls it stopping time.

Tomorrow I will begin a fast to prepare for my work of the South, to shed my past like the serpent sheds its skin.

The past. As individuals we are at the mercy of our past. The traumas of our past prey on our fear in our present. The joyous events feed on our present, limiting our future as we seek to recreate the circumstances of past joys.

Does this hold true for a family? A tribe? A nation? A race? A culture? The species?

Antonio's answer would be that it does until the individuals gain control over their destiny. Free themselves from their pasts. And he proposes that in this shamanic model one can confront one's past.

Literally.

We boarded the train at Quillabamba station and got to Cuzco by noon. My dream of a fresh melon and papaya juice downtown was waved off by my companion, as were the taxi drivers who offered to take us there. From the station we headed on foot for Tambo Machay.

"It is called the Bath of the Incas by most," said Antonio. We climbed to the top of the hill. "Imagine." He squatted down, resting on his haunches, elbows on knees, hands clasped before him. "The United States is overrun by another race of people, who do not believe in your ways. The population is killed or beaten into submission, the cities are laid waste, the Library of Congress is destroyed utterly, so that no records remain. A thousand years later an archaeologist picks his way through the rubble and uncovers the reflecting pond that now stands before the Washington Monument. In a few years the guidebooks refer to it as the Bath of the Americans."

"And what *is* Tambo Machay?" I asked.

"The source of Cuzqueña, the finest beer in Peru." He laughed, pushed himself up, and shoved his hands deep into the pockets of his trousers. "The Temple of the Waters. A place of cleansing and purification. Its source is the convergence of four underground rivers from the four directions. The four niches in the wall of the upper level once housed figures representing the four *apus*, the four great snow-capped peaks that surround Cuzco, the four cardinal points of the Medicine Wheel. The Inca trail to

Machu Picchu begins there." He pointed to a ridge ten kilometers to the East. "It is eighty kilometers to Machu Picchu, and it was here that the traveler filled a *bota* and cleansed the chakras before the trek to the citadel."

"We walk to Machu Picchu?"

"We take the train. At," he consulted his watch, "1:10. The Indian train," he said. "There is time for you to fill your canteen. There is a ritual."

March 24

Ritual. Ceremony. Are they the mechanisms with which early man accessed the limbic brain of imagery and the reptilian brain of body function? Turned on the visionary faculties of the neocortex? If one approaches ritual with pure intent and the firm conviction that it will transform them somehow, alter consciousness, heal, then is it not a placebo of sorts? We behold a feather. Our neocortex allows us to reason that it came from a bird (we may even know what kind of bird), that feathers are used by man as ornaments and for dusting. . . . But we are told that this feather has special power, that when held in the left hand and passed under the nose while chanting "do wop do wop, sha na na," it will cure hiccoughs or even a serious disease.

For those who truly believe this to be so, the feather has become a magical symbol with healing properties. It has been transformed into an *image* that the limbic brain can believe. The neocortex understands, the limbic brain believes, the reptilian brain effects the change by relaxing the muscle spasm when the feather is passed under the nose.

Those who cannot free themselves from the logic of the neocortex, who see just a feather, will sneeze when it tickles their nose. Their hiccoughs remain; their condition is unchanged.

Hospital studies have shown that a placebo is as effective as morphine in 80 percent of the patients that are told that what they're getting is a revolutionary new painkiller.

The placebo effect is based on tricking the brain into believing in a powerful cure. Is it possible that instead of tricking the brain as one would a child, that we can ally its healing resources?

If our primitive brain, our unconscious mind, expresses itself through symbols during our dreams, can we not use our neocortex to string together symbols (as we do words) to communicate with *it*?

If we can consciously communicate with our primitive brains, the brains of body functions and the four F's, can we not reprogram them?

I stripped to the waist and followed Antonio's instructions, beginning at the uppermost spout, working my way down and across the second tier, where the water branches into two streams, to the bottom, where they meet again as one, drinking the ice cold water, cleansing my seven chakras by "unwinding" them counterclockwise. Then I "charged" them, spun them clockwise. It felt, as it had before, vaguely ridiculous, numbingly cold in the thin Andean air.

Antonio met me at the base of the temple.

"Fill your canteen." He handed it to me and I placed it in the stream of sparkling water. "Some will claim that the purpose of the ritual is to cleanse the psychic debris attached energetically to your chakras, loosening the energy coordinates of who you have been so that you may reorganize them to serve who you are becoming or, at least, who you will be today."

He folded his arms across his chest and regarded the temple. "Water is a universal ritual cleansing agent. John the Baptist was its greatest advocate in the West." He smiled broadly and turned to look at me. "But self-conscious ritual is no ritual at all. Attend fully to the steps we take. You must give yourself to the process, as you did when you ran in the *altiplano*. Try not to let your focus blur or your attention stray. You must honor these exercises and honor yourself as you perform them."

March 25

Despite our friendship, Antonio thinks I am conceited. A twenty-four-year-old hotshot psychologist brimming with information, data, academic and paperback philosophy, lugging a backpack full of thermal underwear and toilet paper.

I can see it now and then in his eyes and in his smile, and on his lips when he refers to my "*study* of shamanism."

Just when I thought I'd passed his tests, earned his respect, impressed him with my earnestness, I catch this smile.

Machu Picchu, grandfather peak. Huayna Picchu, lover peak. Their mossy granite slopes rise dizzily from the protective serpent coil of the white waters of the Urubamba. We left the dingy train station at Aguascalientes and made our way to the edge of the river.

"You may cross the river here," Antonio said. He squatted and produced his bag of yucca and cornmeal. "You should follow Bingham's course up the side of the mountain, retrace the steps of the first white man who entered Machu Picchu. There is a cave, there." He aimed his forefinger at a spot two-thirds of the way up the mountain, to a dimple in a sheer bald spot of white granite. "Take your thermal blanket, the water in your canteen. It is comfortable, though cold at night. Tonight, tomorrow, tomorrow night, and the day after, stay there and fast. Before the Sun sets on the third day, make your way to the top, to the ruins. As you go, collect wood for your fire. Choose it carefully, but do not enter the ruins. I will meet you there."

"And then?"

"We will lay out the *mesa* and summon the frayed ends of your past, and you will do your work of the South." His tone was matter of fact.

He sighed and squinted up at the late afternoon sun. Before us the Urubamba tumbled and roared through the valley. Near us, near its shore, little eddies swirled bits and pieces of flotsam into spirals.

"This is what you must do, my friend. You are young, but have left much debris behind you. You are a bundle of loose ends. The past keeps you bound to your image of yourself. You must put yourself into a fire that will consume your past, but will not burn you. Erase your personal history." His fingers, kneading together yucca and cornmeal, moved quickly. "Shed your past as a serpent sheds its skin. This is what you will do in Machu Picchu, but first you must prepare yourself as best you know how. You must spend this time remembering, calling upon your memories of the past, thinking about who you have been and what you have become. Apply *your* psychology to yourself. See where it takes you. You will find it difficult, yet this is what you must do . . . as a student. What you do in the ruins you will do for yourself as a man." He leaned forward and handed me a portion of yucca and cornmeal paste.

"Knowledge can be had only when one can exercise power over destiny, and your destiny is a daily victim of your past. Spirit cannot grow with the dead flesh of the past clinging to it. You must bring no history to your study of shamanism." He looked down at the food in his hand and laughed.

I smiled at his good humor. "What's funny?"

"I sound like a real mystic, eh?"

I took the course prescribed by Antonio, following, as he had remarked, the footsteps of Hiram Bingham, the "discoverer" of the sacred city of the Incas, in 1911.

Later

Western conceit. Hiram Bingham, intrepid gentleman explorer in the golden age of adventure, when rugged individuals were knighted for their rugged individualism. Wide-brimmed felt hats, leather boots laced to the knee, or leggings, travel-worn notebooks with rough pencil sketchings of the masonry of a bygone race perched atop a beetling crag or masked by creeping vines and dripping orchids.

Romance, adventure, and the satisfaction of revealing to the world the treasures of ancient cultures in faraway lands.

Perhaps that is how Bingham saw himself. But when a "civilized" man is shown a place where third-world natives have lived for centuries, he is called its discoverer. As if the natives were keeping a secret from the rest of the world.

I think there's some truth in this, although my tone is cynical. If Bingham hadn't "discovered" the lost city at the top of this pinnacle, I wouldn't have had to climb it on an empty stomach.

The cave that Antonio had pointed out from the far bank of the Urubamba was little more than a hollow, a cleft in a bold granite wall. A lip of mossy soil led across the face to the entrance, and along this I groped. The sun was setting in deep orange, and I moved hand in hand with my shadow across the smooth rock face two thousand feet above the river. There was room to turn at its entrance, and I did so, to gaze back down into the Urubamba Valley.

Later

Tucked away in my little hole I feel abandoned, embarrassed. A little scared, and I know how hungry I can get. But I've transcended all of that before. I've pushed myself before, denied myself comfort in the name of adventure or to acquire some experiential trophy.

The sun has set and the last rays of March 25 are brushing the underbellies of the clouds with salmon pink and orange. I can sit back eight feet, back against the stone wall, and see this through the irregular opening of my tiny cavern, framed by the lips of the mouth of this cave. I feel like Jonah.

And day sighs into night.

I've made my nest—unpacked my backpack—all the shit I've been carrying. Survival kit, including needle and thread, fishing hooks, salt tablets, waterproof matches, band-aids, snake-bite thingamajig, thermal blanket. A Hershey bar.

With almonds.

I'd forgotten about that. I've placed it on a little granite shelf.

Later

This is not easy. My mind is so filled with recent events, and I am hyperconscious of my situation and the purposefulness of this effort.

Perhaps that's it. I am trying to make this preparatory time into a significant self-revelatory experience. I am trying too hard, and I know better.

Frustrated though. So much information. Need time to digest and distill and instead I am preparing myself to engage with my past and this fourfold path of knowledge.

Random thought: Seems that those who seek spiritual adventure inevitably end up social castaways. As if they lose themselves somewhere along the way, redefining their identity in terms of their "quest." Silly sycophants. Sycophanatics. Disciples, promoters of a mystical convention or spiritual tradition. Astrology, numerology, Judaism, Catholicism and all its et ceteras, Hinduism, and all the other isms. Belief systems, paradigms. Reductionism? The scientific method? The crowning glory of Western thought? How many professors have I seen genuflecting before the altar of hypothesis and clinical validation?

And then there are the figures of worship: Jehovah, Christ, Guatama Buddha, Mohammed, Krishna.

But Antonio, professor of philosophy, amiable companion, shaman. Awfully well adjusted for a "person of knowledge." He seems to take it all in stride. A pragmatic mystic.

I miss the *altiplano*.

Tired. I'll try to sleep now. Face my situation in the morning.

I dreamed that night, but the memory scattered, helter-skelter, displaced by the panicky disorientation of waking in a strange place. I gargled with the water from Tambo Machay, rolled up my sleeping bag, and ventured out onto the ledge.

The morning was Andean, and a few deep breaths of chilled thin air restored me. A mist had settled into the green Urubamba Valley, obscuring the river nearly half a mile below my little hermitage.

I sat cross-legged on the ledge, closed my eyes to the splendor of the vista, and willed myself into as blissful a state as I could manage.

In his preface to *Freud: The Mind of the Moralist,* Philip Reiff writes, "Man is tied to the weight of his own past, and even by a great therapeutic labor little more can be accomplished than a shifting of the burden." The Western tradition of psychotherapy certainly substantiates this observation. Western people excavate their past with the tool of memory, an unreliable instrument at best. And we are ill used to exhuming our past fully and alone. We are more accustomed to summoning our pasts to represent ourselves to others with the stories we choose to tell, the incidents we select to embellish our personalities. We are iconographies of carefully framed impressionistic and abstract paintings. During my brief time on an Indian reservation in the U.S. Southwest, I heard of the tradition of telling your life story to a stone: a distinctly humbling experience if taken seriously. It is easier to address to an object, be it a pebble, a rock, or a passive therapist, than it is to address yourself. Perhaps the act of telling lends order to an otherwise shapeless quantum of memory.

I cannot recreate the structurelessness of my experience in the side of that mountain; but I can touch on the highlights, for they form the conscious foundation for much of what happened on the evening of the third day and the early morning of the fourth.

My paternal grandfather. Large, liver-spotted hands too rough for a surgeon's, but he was an old man. Wispy gray-white hair, and a softly creased aquiline face. I think he smiled at my father. He was graduated from Columbia School of Medicine in 1905 and became chief of surgery at a New York City Hospital. In the 1920s he returned to his native Cuba and built a small clinic in the city of Havana, only to find that the municipal public works could not provide his facility with adequate electricity. He built a hydroelectric plant to light his hospital. He was an eclectic Catholic and a devout capitalist.

My father was an attorney and businessman with a healthy practice and a vigorous bank account. A handsome man with wavy hair and a pencil mustache, dashingly aristocratic. He lunched with Batista. Stubborn, opinionated, self-absorbed. In the 1940s he successfully sued the Vatican for a divorce from his first wife, maintained custody of his son, and married my mother a few years later.

My birth was incidental to my parents' preparations for a European vacation. When they returned from "the Continent" my mother is said to have been surprised to find a new addition to the household. She was a beautiful lady with liquid brown eyes lifted in adoration of my father.

I was raised by my nanny, and I like to think that I was saved from many of the more mundane parent-related neuroses that are a psychotherapist's bread and butter. Tati was an Afro-American, third-generation Cuban, the descendant of salves. As I remembered her, she must have been in her mid twenties. We bathed together, showered together, played together, but she was a servant, like our chauffeur. This was before the revolution. I loved her dearly, treated her shamefully.

March 26

The impotence of my feelings of regret for past behavior is exaggerated by my isolation here. It's a lot easier to fast when you know

that food is at least available. I listen to my stomach and force myself to meditate on its noise. This may be an appropriate visualization as I reach into my gut to bring up memories. And the longer
I apply myself to the task, the emptier my stomach becomes.

Tati was a spiritist. She used to flush medicines down the toilet. I remembered sneaking down from my room to peer through the bushes at old
Rodolfo, Tati, others of the household staff, and friends of theirs who were
strangers to me, singing, dancing, spinning in the moon and candlelit night
in the yard by the sea wall when my parents were away. Dark adventures,
armed with a pocketknife and Boy Scout flashlight, climbing down from my
window, crawling over the sea wall to hunt for hermit crabs.

When I was ten years old I heard gunfire and felt our home rocked by
nearby explosions. Time was meaningless to these early recollections, and it
may have been weeks or months that we lived with these sounds. People
walked in different ways on the streets of Havana in 1959. A woman—a
neighbor whom I do not remember knowing—hosed blood from her sidewalk. I stopped going to school and my father's face was lighted by the
yellow glow of burning papers in the fireplace. That was in the house of a
family friend, close to the airport.

My fingers were smaller than his, and I shoved tight rolls of hundred-
dollar bills into cigar tubes; he removed the light switch plates and dropped
the tubes down between the walls. I remembered that he had not been there
when we left Havana. The airport confused me.

Miami was surf fishing for lunch with my older half-brother, my sister
playing in the sand, and my father meeting with people, a house full of
white-collar refugees and leaders of the counterrevolution.

I thought we were a family again in Puerto Rico, but hindsight had
touched up the faded snapshots of my memory. Father was reestablished in
business, the construction business, and I felt like a freak at the Jesuit High
School of San Juan. Summers at the Caribe Hilton. I was on the swim team
and thrilled to win medals, which I still keep in my sock drawer at home.
And I helped the surveyors at construction sites. After all, I was the son of
the owner.

Teaching SCUBA to tourists. One couple had a daughter with wavy
blond hair, and we made love awkwardly in a coral forest twenty feet down.

Today should be easier. I can leave here before the sun sets. The end is in sight.

Have thought a lot about Victoria. First love, first commitment. Driving across country, her purple VW. I loved her as much as I was capable of loving. Perhaps I have never loved, just labeled my feelings with the word. The definition changes over the years.

She taught me to play bridge. Determined to impress her and her friends with my intellectual prowess, I struggled manfully through the night. Performance anxiety. The intensity of my concentration was trancelike. I stumbled into bed countless hours later, only to fall into a waking sleep, dreaming vividly hand after hand, spades, hearts, diamonds, clubs, bidding, tricks, slams and grand slams. I woke up exhausted.

Like this morning. I cannot remember falling asleep, merely waking to memories of my memories of the night before.

All the loose ends, all the polluted relationships, all the sorrows and joys.

The second full day was humbling. I found that I could no longer meditate on the condition of my stomach. I focused instead on the Hershey bar. Exercise was out of the question; after three push-ups I felt that I was burning precious fuel.

My memory of that day is with me still. I can call upon it now and relive its ruthlessness. We all experience moments of mortality, pangs of insignificance in relation to the Earth, the cosmos. You may be walking along a beach. The dog has bounded off after a piece of driftwood or a Frisbee. You gaze thoughtfully after her, down the long sweep of shoreline. The sound of the surf wafts through your subconscious, a whimsical *leitmotiv* reminding you of the omnipresent rhythm of Nature. You turn to the horizon and the setting sun; your personal concerns become meaningless and you sigh at your smallness, the immortality of a grain of sand, the infinitely abiding universe. The dog is back, errand accomplished, wet and frisky. She drops the Frisbee at your feet. You smile at her, pick it up, and get on with the game. My experience in that hillside cave was somewhat less sentimental, saved from cliché by the heartlessness of hunger and the intensity of my loneliness.

I dwelled upon my choices, the identity that I had created for myself, the people I had touched and how I had touched them. The people I had used and how I had used them. How I had been used.

Later

Today I feel abandoned, *desterrado,* like that time with the peyote only more so.

If I were to die tomorrow, what would I leave behind? Is there anything of value? Anyone I've helped? Or are my acts handouts, like that *propina* at the train station? How authentic is the work I do? Am I handing out therapy like Band-Aids? Maybe it's even worse. Maybe doing therapy is a handout to myself. Am I merely acquiring stature?

Trying to nap. Unable to sleep. Waiting for the sun to drop. I close my eyes, exhausted from the effort of remembering, and I think I can feel the walls of my stomach rubbing against each other. Water from my canteen coats my insides. I can feel it go down. I close my eyes, but I've started something I cannot finish.

Renting the house in the woods with Victoria. Holding forth on the subject of my bachelor's thesis, playing the world-wise rebel. A romantic rogue with the soul of a poet. She saw right through me.

You con artist.

I open my eyes. The sun has intruded upon my hole. Half of my face is sunburned. I'm sweating. My neck is cramped. I drink.

I am hungry and stupid enough to think that I know hunger. But even the salt of my tears refreshes me. I am spoiled and continue to spoil myself.

Hunger is the greatest teacher. No wonder the psychology of the west is oral and anal. We are overstuffed.

Sometime in that late afternoon I realized that measured by my peers I was a success, a twenty-four-year-old *wunderkind* psychologist, a wild-ass protegé; yet measured by the Earth, whose granite walls enveloped me, I was a parasite. My purpose was, as yet, ill defined; I was living for myself.

And then I left. I packed my gear, then sat for a time watching the Earth rotate away from the Sun. There was still another hundred feet to climb, and I had no idea of what waited for me at the summit. Would Antonio be there? Would I confront the ghosts of my past?

I wondered also if I would encounter the memory of the past two and a half days, and, if I did, what it would look like.

The ruins of Machu Picchu have been assigned many functions since their discovery in 1911. They have been called the last refuge of the Incas, the last Inca capital, the Lost City of the Incas, a secret hideaway for the Chosen Women, the Virgins of the Sun. Salcamayhua, the seventeenth-century Peruvian historian, recorded that the first Inca, Manco the Great, ordered works to be executed at the place of his birth, consisting, in part, of a masonry wall with three windows. The presence of such a structure indicated to Bingham that rather than being the last capital of the Incas, Machu Picchu may have been the birthplace of the first. Later it would occur to him that it might have been both, that he had, in fact, discovered Vilcapampa, the principal city of Manco and his sons, the Incas' final refuge from the Spaniards.

Half an hour of climbing brought me to a rounded granite promontory, and, around this, a flight of a dozen stone-faced terraces, each the height of a man. With less than half an hour before the sun set behind the distant range to the right of Huayna Picchu, I made my way along one of the widest terraces. Here and there I saw walls of ruined houses, glimpses of the exquisite granite joinery of the Sacred City. A huge overhanging ledge; below it a cave lined with perfectly fitted stone, above it and behind, the Temple of the Sun following the natural curvature of the rock, keyed to it by master stonecutters. I proceeded along the side of the mountain, knowing that I was edging along the perimeter of the city, below the ruins. The altitude and my anticipation conspired to make my breathing short and labored. Ahead of me and to the right, a grassy knoll sloped up and away from me. The glow of the setting sun touched its summit: a small thatched structure, an irregular object, and the figure of Antonio waited for me in the dusk. I realized that I had neglected to collect my wood, had forgotten his instructions. A long flight of stone steps led to the base of the hill and hugged the side of a moss-grown broken wall. I made my way up, pausing to pick up a twig here, a small branch of mesquite there.

I passed the Gateway of the Sun without turning to look in, and, turning my back on it, panted resolutely up the hill. Halfway up I stopped to lift a sliver of wood from a tangle of weeds. I turned and caught my breath at the spectacle before me. Overgrown and semiexcavated shells of buildings, granite ashlars, temples, walls of mortarless stone, plazas and courtyards, all in shades of flecked white-and-gray granite, green moss, and pastel lichen. A hundred terraces. Beyond the ruins, towering above them to the north, the pinnacle of Huayna Picchu. Below me, to the west, the Temple of the Sun and a sheer cliff falling away to the Urubamba. To the east a small ruined temple with three great windows facing the direction of the rising sun. Fog was rising from the valley below and to the west, the direction from which I had come. It rose vertically and bent slightly to the east, swirling over itself as though to cover the city or like a hand groping for a handhold.

Before a thatched-roof hut at the top of the hill the Death Stone sat like an abandoned canoe, a miniature ark high and dry on the summit of Ararat.

Antonio's smile of welcome was expansive. My ordeal must have left its mark.

"You look terrible," he said.

"*Gracias, profesor.*"

"And you will need more wood."

I sloughed off my pack and wandered away to complete the errand. Where had Antonio been for the past three days? Twice I caught myself staring in wonder at the setting of my adventure, a fossilized citadel, an aerie of pre-Columbian culture shrouded in mist like the ruins in an Arthurian legend. I remembered Antonio's instructions to choose the bits and pieces rather than to collect them like kindling, so it took more than half an hour to produce two armfuls. At the top of the knoll Antonio handed me a length of twine, and I secured my bundle and set it aside.

"When can we enter the ruins?"

"You cannot."

"I cannot?"

"You can enter the *ruins* as a tourist whenever you wish, although that is a profanity born of ignorance." He turned his back on the Death Stone and gazed at the ruins below. "But you may not enter the *city* until you have completed your work of the South and the West, until you have learned to live the life of a spiritual warrior, until you have freed yourself from your past and faced death, until you have disengaged yourself from your physical body, as we do when we die."

"Then why are we here?"

"For you to begin your work of the South, but you will do this outside of the city limits. There is a cave below the Temple of the Condor." He gestured to the right, toward the edge of the ruins.

"To fully address your work of the South, you must release yourself from fear. Fear is in the realm of the West, where you confront death. But you cannot exorcise death until you have completed your work of the South. It is something of a vicious circle, a Mobius strip . . ."

"A catch-22."

"Your work of the West will come later. Tonight we can only put death on the agenda, do what we can to prepare you for your ritual. The Death Stone is in the shape of a canoe, with its bow facing west. It is here that an initiate's spirit leaves the body and travels West to the regions of silence and death. The legends say that it returns from the East, where the Sun rises and new life is born."

"The legends?"

"Yes. Lie on the stone, with your head facing the bow. Take a few minutes to calm yourself."

I stretched out on the cool granite slab and tried to will my heart rate to a meditative rhythm. He left me alone and I closed my eyes on the twilight. The temperature had dropped to a comfortable cool, and I had forgotten the hollowness of my stomach. The stillness of the approaching night was complete, its silence enhanced by the stirring of the dry grass. What was Antonio doing? As my breathing became regular I heard his whistle, faint and almost breathless. I sensed him beside me and heard his chant, a polysyllabic rhythm reverberating like the hum of a tuning fork. The temperature was dropping and a faint stirring of air at my forehead sent a shiver down my spine. It would be another cold Andean night. I looked up through my eyelashes as he passed his hands from my forehead to my throat, on to my sternum. Disengaging my chakras; spinning them counterclockwise; charging them; spinning them clockwise; chanting into them. I took stock of my sensations and felt nothing but relative tranquility, a slight easing of my anxiety and anticipation, concern over the lack of specific sensation.

I felt nothing.

The chant ended with a decisive *¡hoy!* He whistled again, softly, and it faded with the breeze.

"You can get up now."

I opened my eyes and though scarcely five minutes had passed, the night was upon us. Sparkling stars above low cirrus clouds, and the ruins were luminous in the moonlight. Antonio was squatting by his *mesa,* a few feet away.

"Sit there."

I sat cross-legged, facing him over the Indian cloth.

He handed me the wooden bowl. There was more San Pedro in it this time. "Your work is with the serpent tonight. Call upon the spirit of the South, summon it here, and salute the four directions. You know what to do."

I stood and raised the cup to the south and tried to remember the formula. "I call upon the spirit of the South, the serpent, Satchamama. Come to me, help me to shed my past." It had sounded better when he said it. "Hey."

"Hey!" he shouted. "Power, my friend. Purpose. You needn't address yourself to the wind. You do not need to say anything. Think it. Summon the power and salute the Four Winds as you would form a prayer."

That was easier. I did my best, said a silent prayer to each of the cardinal points, visualized the animals that represented them, the jaguar, the dragon, the eagle. Then I saluted the Mother Earth and the Great Spirit, drank half the contents of the bowl, took my place, and offered it back to him.

"All of it," he said. Just like Ramón.

I leaned my head back and drained the cup and set it on the cloth. Then I closed my eyes and breathed slowly, rhythmically, trying to orient myself to some center.

I opened my eyes and he was looking not at me, but at something between us; the focus of his eyes was not on my face, although he seemed to be looking directly upon me. The spaces in between things.

What was he seeing?

His focus shifted and he fixed my eyes with a searching look.

"You have been avoiding power all these years," he said. "Not acclaim or recognition—you barter for them regularly—but power in the face of Nature. Before you connect with your power you must shed your past. And the past must be recaptured before it is freely released." He handed me the little bottle of sweet oil and then drew the carved bone staff from the soil.

"The sword of fire, of light," he said, and handed it to me. "Charge it. Hold it in your hands and summon its power. From the East, the place of vision and the rising Sun. Blow sweet oil on it."

I took the liquid into my mouth. It was strong, pungent on my taste buds, but I held it in my mouth and raised the staff and blew a mist of the stuff into the air, onto my hands and the staff they held.

"Take this with you. Hold it in your left hand. If you sense danger hold it firmly in your right. It is to sever your connections with your past."

He lifted my bundle of wood from the ground, took my arm, and led me away from the *mesa* and down the hill. My heart pounded with anticipation. I felt nothing from the San Pedro.

"Can I enter the ruins when I am finished?" I asked.

"You are not going to be finished," he said.

"Where are you going?"

"I have my own work to do."

The entrance to the cave was hidden in a fold of granite on the side of the hill beneath the Temple of the Condor. On the ground before the entrance was a small stack of wood and dry grass.

"The cave is shaped like an L," he said. "Go to the turning point, and use this wood to build your fire. Not a white man's fire; do not burn all your wood at once. Build it four by four. Place your memories in the fire one by one. Do not put a stick or branch in the flames unless it has a memory."

"All right."

"Face the wall. Concentrate on the fire," he said. "Do not allow it to die. Do not take your eyes from it. You can lose yourself if your attention strays. Call upon the vision of the eagle. The song of the East, *hoy, hoy, charaguay, charaguay, hoy*." He placed a hand on my shoulder. "I will see you in the morning."

I found the apex of the cave by the sulfur flare of six or seven matches. There must have been two entrances, for the place was ventilated by a gentle cross-breeze. I planted the staff in the dirt floor of the cave and built my fire as he had: four-sided, four groups of four sticks, dried grass in its center. I had almost exhausted my match supply by the time I lit the little pyre. The grass crackled, the kindling held its flame, and the granite walls were illuminated by its light. I remember asking myself if the flames were not slightly more defined than most, or had the quality of my vision changed? Was this an effect of the San Pedro? I could not recall ever seeing anything with such clarity.

I fed the fire with bits from Antonio's pile until I felt confident of its flames. I sat back and even as I looked, the flames changed, my perception of them changed. My focus was shifting and what had been sharply defined became luminous, glowing, as though seen through a gauze. I lifted the staff from the dirt and checked my vision against its edges. Though I could see every detail, every crack and imperfection in its ivory surface, the fire still shimmered opaquely.

I closed my eyes and breathed deeply, mimicking Antonio's style. The light of the fire beat against my eyelids and the sensation was dizzying. Then the light began to flicker and play its game behind my eyelids as it had on the *altiplano,* but there was a sound, a rushing sound associated with the tiny particles of light. The colors were luminous, pastels, glowing like embers.

I opened my eyes. The fire was radiant and I felt comfort in its glow. I looked at the pile of wood I had collected. Which to choose? A worn piece of mesquite caught my eye. It was smooth like driftwood, like a small bird with wings pressed close to its side, streamlined for a dive. I set aside the staff of the light, lifted the object from the pile, and placed it squarely in the center of my fire. It settled into the flames; its weight pressed down on a charred branch and its edges browned. My eyes shifted, searching for an image, not knowing what to expect. There was something, movement in my peripheral vision. I turned slightly to look for it and felt a surge of adrenaline. But the light from the fire played against the walls of the cave, tricking me. I exhaled, realized that I had been holding my breath. My body was tense, my back and shoulders rigid with expectation. I was trying too hard.

Breathe.

Again I closed my eyes to assess my condition and wonder at the effects of the San Pedro. The lights were there still, but larger, more luminous, and they rushed past me with a sound like wind through the trees and the regularity of ocean surf. One luminescent orb lingers before me. Another. I raise my hand and brush aside the mosquito netting of my little bed and wriggle on the cool sheets to make room for this presence. It moves, hovers next to me, and I feel that it is smiling.

I cannot remember opening my eyes. All I know is that one instant I was a very little boy, snug in bed, and in the next I was back, in the cave, below Machu Picchu, before the fire. I looked at my watch. 8:04? The bird-shaped hunk of mesquite was charred, black and gray, glowing. Had I fallen asleep? A dream image, a memory of a dream. Experience of a memory of a dream. A child's secret. Suddenly I thought of Tati. A picture of her intruded itself into my thoughts, and I reached for another offering, a curved mesquite branch still bearing a few leaves at the end of a twig. I leaned forward over crossed legs and placed it on the fire.

I shivered, shuddered convulsively, and my stomach sickened with adrenaline. There was fear on the back of my neck, and my eyes shifted away, reflexively probing the darkness beyond the dancing shadows and the firelight. The staff of the light! Which hand to hold it in? A bolus of something rose in my throat. *What!* I haven't eaten for three . . . I retched, coughing spasmodically, and a draft of cool air lifted ash and spark from the fire. Smoke, a pungent haze of incense, beeswax votive candles, cheap Cuban cigar. Tati is stripped to the waist, and her skin glows with sweat in the candlelight as she rocks rhythmically back and forth over a bowl of smoldering leaves. She is doing something with her mouth, but her back is to me.

"Come here, boy!" Her voice is low, guttural, like Rodolfo the gardener's.

"Tati?"

She turns and I catch my breath. Her face is twisted, grimacing; her eyes upturned and heavy-lidded. A cigar hangs pendant from her pouting lower lip.

"Come here." The cigar wags at me. "Stand here."

I am four. She is my nanny. I do as I am told, and stand before the bowl of burning stuff. She takes the cigar from her mouth, turns it around, and molds her lips around the wrong end, the burning end, and inhales, smoking backward, filling her lungs with smoke and blowing it back into my face, purifying me with smoke. "You are a good boy, a good young boy, and strong. I will visit you in your dreams."

"Tati?"

"No."

I reach out and touch her wet mahogony skin.

"I want some milk, Tati. Get it for me. Now."

The mesquite leaf sizzled, hissed, and blistered above the embers. I felt my face, touched it with my hand, seeking reassurance. Wet. My face was wet. Three days' growth of beard. A tear caught in the corner of my mouth, and I tasted it with the tip of my tongue. A sob convulsed my chest and I realized that I was weeping. This is not a dream. Not a dream. Distinctly visual. Straight to the perception centers . . . limbic. Hallucination. No. None of the whimsy, the eccentricity, of hallucinogenic states. Stay with it.

The branch collapsed, its center crumbled into the live coals.

Focus.

The next branch was heavier than it should have been. Or was I getting weaker? Nonsense. But it was just a little branch. I placed it in the fire's center. Rounded bluish flames hovered above and around dying embers. Was there enough flame to ignite this wood? How could I have let it burn so low? And . . . what is on the palm of my hand? I turn it palm up and stare with wonder at the brown-and-white-striped conical shell that fills the center of my childish little hand. Grains of moist sand cling to my skin, in the delicate creases of my palm. The shell tickles and moves. A pointed, furry leg like a tiny finger ventures out from beneath the shell. I grasp my wrist to steady the hand. Musn't scare it. The shell shifts and the miniature crab appears. Hermit crab. Tiny legs and delicate claws. It moves, scurrying sideways across my open hand, tumbling from it onto the sand at the water's edge.

I looked down at my hands. The right was clenched, the left covering it, holding it close to my stomach. I pried open the fingers and held it close to my face. It was moist with sweat. No sand, my palm, familiar, adult.

I looked up. The walls of the cave seemed to have reformed themselves, closed in on all sides. I was in the center of a granite eggshell. Fear spread from my belly up, into my chest, my heart, my throat, and the light from the fire seemed to throb as its color changed from yellow to orange, and blackness threatened to snuff it out. I could not let it die, yet the only fuel left was that which I had gathered. No choice, but a pile of choices.

Without taking my eyes from the embers I reached blindly for wood, placing a mesquite stem and a tiny bough of heather into the coals before recalling Antonio's admonition. One at a time.

My father. His despair at the loss of his fortune, his land, his place, his world. He holds his head in his hands and weeps as I reach for him across the flames. He is a victim of a persona that has lost everything, everything taken from him, but he clings to it, a stranglehold on his identity. There, across from me, separated from me only by a fire that is consuming me.

I hold myself, hugging the ivory staff to my chest, rocking back and forth, keening with the weight of his pride and my own desperate desire to please him, to play his game, to adapt to the world of *his* values, *his* standards, his conceit. I see that he will never be free from his pride, and that I will release myself from the competition. I wipe a tear from under my chin. I will free myself from his example and distance myself from his disdain, but my *abuelita,* my grandmother, shakes her head. "Take care of him, Bombi." My baby name. "Do not abandon him."

From that instant I could not stop. I fed the fire with the cuttings of my past, and the vapors rose from the fire, swirling, spiraling, cavorting, in a babble of moments and emotions.

Of all of my experiences in the realms of healing and consciousness, the twelve hours I endured beneath the Temple of the Condor were perhaps the most poignant. I have carried its memory in my heart ever since.

Someday I shall shed it too. I shall encounter those twelve hours and release them into the flames of another fire. But for now, I can see myself still, cross-legged before the steadily burning cinders, crying, laughing, deep in the throes of self-induced catharsis. Cell by cell, hair by hair, finger by finger, limb by limb, placing myself into the fire. Friends and relations, patients, the faces of Huichol Indians staring with wonder at a map of the world drawn in the sand. There were instants when I thought it was over, when the fire would burn down, and I would invoke Antonio's chant, summoning the vision of the eagle and blowing on the embers, raising smoke and sparks before consigning another twig or branch or bough to the flames. A draft of air would clear the room of smoke, but images would linger, their presences surrounding me, penetrating me.

And there were unidentified emotions, a woman I did not know, a face familiar but unknown to me, images that were not mine, that bore no relation to who I had been, and, with them, the urge to dump my remaining wood into the fire.

Sometime that morning the fire died. The ordeal ended and the walls of the cave were once again the walls of the cave.

I walked out, carrying the ivory staff by my side. Antonio sat on a rock, silhouetted by the bright morning sun. I remember that he placed his hand on my shoulder.

"Did you have enough wood?" he asked.

"Yes. There was some left over."

"There always will be," he said.

Together we climbed up to the Temple of the Condor, the edge of the ruins. A busload of tourists had arrived, and we watched them make their way down the hill from the Death Stone and enter the Lost City of the Incas. Then Antonio led me down a path, away from the ruins.

"You will return here many times," he said. "The next time you will enter the city, and the stones carved by the hands of the ancestors will speak to you."

I was too tired to wonder about the meaning of his words.

March 28

Perhaps there are two kinds of memory. All those we carry with us, available to conscious recall, like those I remembered during my fast. Subjective memories. Sounds, images, feelings, trivial details that are made all the more vivid as we assign significance to them with the benefit of hindsight. They are the memories of retrospect.

Under hypnosis an adult can remember the color of his crib. Objective memory. Like those I engaged and wrestled with. They had a life of their own. Like a dream, not subject to conscious control, they ran wild. Independent of me. Not retrospect, but retrospectacle.

But I am in no condition to write about this. We are in a small hostel in Aguascalientes. There are hot springs here at the base of Machu Picchu.

I remember that Albert Einstein once defined science as the attempt to make the chaotic diversity of our sense experience correspond to a logically uniform system of thought.

So how do I approach what has happened to me in a scientific fashion? I leave for California in two days.

My pen is getting heavy and my writing sloppy, but it occurs to me that as the nature of our sensory experience changes, so must our science, our definition of our system of thought, the way in which we think.

I'll think about it in the morning.

Serpent fire:

- collect wood as past issues to shed
- burn only one at a time
- open sacred space
- issues can be events, people, habits...

West

11

Canst thou not minister to a mind diseased,
Pluck from the memory a rooted sorrow,
Raze out the written troubles of the brain,
And with some sweet oblivious antidote
Cleanse the stuffed blossom of that perilous stuff
Which weighs upon the heart?

— *William Shakespeare*

The airport in Cuzco was socked in. The sky had fallen, the clouds settled over the city. Visibility at the airport was measured in feet; the last departure had been more than two hours ago, and flights were backing up into the following morning when, I was assured with a Latin grin and a definitive nod, the fog was "scheduled" to lift.

I had returned to Cuzco to find a message waiting for me at the hotel. Though I was no longer registered there, a handful of *soles* at the reception desk had bought me an address and phone number in case of emergency. There was even a letter from Brian. The phone message was from my father. My paternal grandmother had suffered a stroke. Perhaps, he suggested, I should return to California via Miami.

I had booked a flight, Antonio and I had dined together, and, the next day, he had accompanied me to the airport.

I shook my head, hefted my backpack over one shoulder. "You can't *schedule* fog," I said.

He looked at his watch. He was as I had seen him that first day, Professor Antonio Morales Baca. A baggy suit, frayed white shirt, dark tie, hair combed back, pockets bulging. Impeccable sloppiness. His skin was a few shades darker from the sun of the *altiplano,* and there was a healthy lightness to his manner, a rejuvenation that showed at the corners of his eyes and on his mouth when he smiled.

"It will clear," he said. "Half an hour."

I looked down into his eyes and smiled. "You think so."

"Of course."

"How do you know?"

He grinned. "Because I am an Indian."

I laughed. "I almost forgot. Indians know everything."

"Everything but how to live in a godless world of physical objects and right angles." He placed his hand on my shoulder. "I must go. I have a class at one o'clock."

"Thank you," I said.

"Thank *you,* my friend. We are good traveling companions."

I opened my mouth, but there were no words.

"You have tasted knowledge," he said. "Soon you will have an experience of power. But do not wait for it."

"Goodbye," I said.

I offered him my hand, and he just looked down at it and shook his head. "It is said that shamans say goodbye only once."

I kept my hand before him. "Who says such things?" I asked.

"We do," he replied. "You and I do. For us it will always be *hasta pronto.*" Until we meet again.

And he took my hand.

Half an hour later the fog cleared. The sky opened up over the airport, and a young woman in an Aero Peru uniform announced the boarding of the flight from Cuzco to Lima.

I spent a day in Miami. My father looked me up and down. His eyes were tired and he frowned at my hair, uncut since California, my mustache, and rumpled clothes. "You should see your grandmother," he said.

"That's what I came for, Papi," I said.

I shaved, and Soledad, my parent's maid of forty years, gave me one of my father's pressed and starched shirts. I took my grandmother to lunch.

The stroke had been minor, a cerebrovascular accident. Her frailty was nothing more than old age. She took my arm and I led her into a brightly lighted restaurant near the water.

We talked of this and that. She was excited for me, or sensitive to my excitement. I looked well, she said, and she liked my long hair. She was squinting a lot and I asked was there anything wrong.

"It is so dim. They should turn up the lights."

I reached across and removed the thick glasses from her face and wiped them with a linen napkin and slid the bows back through her gray hair and over her ears.

"That is much better," she said, and laughed without embarrassment. We had always laughed like that together. Her hand sought mine across the tablecloth and we sat there, at a table for two, holding hands like lovers. This woman who had mothered me, who had appeared to me in a fire in Machu Picchu, whose spirit was so strong, but whose body was wearing away with the friction of time. We would never sit like that again. I knew it then, and I smile at the memory now.

I returned to California. It had been winter when I left, and it was the first day of spring when I returned. I started compiling my notes for my thesis, resumed my work at the mental health clinic, obtained a grant from the Office of Child Development to develop mental health programs for the Head Start school system, opened a small private practice, and fell in love with Stephanie.

Brian's infatuation had gotten him nowhere. Mine was a one-way ticket, a package tour to a place I had been before and would return to again and again. Yes, the human experience depends on pairs of opposites, yin and yang, and darkness and light cling to one another; the darkness enhances the light and the light defines the darkness, and the centers of pleasure and pain lie next to one another in the human brain, and you rarely experience one without stimulating the other. I loved Stephanie and we shared the anguish and ecstasy of being together and being apart.

As I had suspected, she was a handful: a stubborn romantic, a sensitive feminist. She was still recovering from a traumatic separation, a two-year relationship with a dental student named Edward, when we fell in love. We feasted off of one another that spring. We agreed on monogamy that summer.

My work at that time was unique in its diversity. I began to incorporate my thesis notes into a book, *Realms of Healing*, that I would write with Stanley Krippner. At the clinic I was exposed to examples of extreme psychosis: multiple personality disorders, schizophrenia (an ill-defined condition), sociopathic breakdowns, and attempted suicides. In my private practice I guided patients through depression, sexual insecurity, substance abuse, and trauma. And at the Head Start school I witnessed firsthand the standards for achievement and the criteria for normality that is imposed on the young. I watched underprivileged and minority students, children of half a dozen cultures, conform to our culture, become assimilated to an educational system. Children customized to fit in, to serve the program so that the program could serve them. It should have been the other way around. A question-and-answer–oriented system of evaluation and teaching that failed to play to the personal and cultural strengths of the individual child was, in my radical eyes, producing systematically mentally retarded kids.

It didn't take long for me to develop a reputation as flamboyant and eccentric in my work at the clinic, as hotheaded and arrogant with regard to education.

Strangely enough, although I was acutely aware of the effects of my work with Antonio, I didn't talk about it much. I thought about him a great deal in those first few months, even made a point of finding a spot in the Sonoma hills, a nature retreat, a waterfall an hour's hike into the hills, where I would go on weekends to meditate and exercise my vision. But for the most part, my work of the South was confined to my consciousness and the pages of my journal.

June 1, 1974

Back from the clinic. Glass of wine and . . . thought I'd crack you open and fill a page. It's been too long. Gloria was readmitted to-night. Ascension Thursday. First it was Ash Wednesday, then Good Friday. They saved her again and tomorrow morning it'll be my turn. Back to the drawing board.

Still feeling centered, potent. The effects of my work in Machu Picchu? Gut-wrenching, soul-searing ritual—an evening's worth in a state of consciousness in which the elements of my personal history were dealt with directly, visually, cathartically. Not analytically, in-tellectually . . . neocortically? There I go, trying to localize the stuff that dreams are made of. Assign it to the limbic brain. That's the problem. There are no straight lines, no convenient theories, no pigeonholes. So how do I integrate my experience? I know that the work of twelve to twenty-four month's worth of intensive therapy was accomplished in a night. If I accessed my unconscious, do I need to explain the process? If I want anybody here to understand it, I do. If credibility is important to me . . . who am I kidding? Science has determined the nature of our reality ever since the age of reason, and you can't apply scientific method to consciousness, be objective about that which is the very essence of the subjective experience. I must content myself with having experiences, *serving* experiences, collecting "data."

Sounding sour and cynical. Why?

Stephanie hasn't called.

Gloria is back.

Gloria Pierce was almost a nun, a novitiate on leave from a convent near Napa. She was twenty-three years old, a contemporary Mary Magdalene: sensuality touched by piety. She had made her novitiate vows on the first of the year after twenty-three years of preparation. Christ had appeared to her mother during three days of labor, and Gloria's devotion to God was pre-ordained, prenatal.

A nun's vows are her wedding vows, her ritual marriage to Christ. Here was a young woman who had been engaged to Him since birth. An arranged marriage. Her devotion was genuine and passionate, and passion was her demon. Gloria's emerging sexuality had taken her by surprise, had proved too much for her. Lust was the object of her despair. She was, in her mind, a virgin living in sin. So she had cut her wrists crosswise on Ash Wednesday.

She had been stitched up at the county hospital and hustled over to the mental health clinic for evaluation and counseling by one of my colleagues. Then she did it again, on Good Friday. I was on call.

I took a lot of flak regarding my "approach." We used the hospital as our therapy environment: the emergency room, the intensive care unit, the maternity ward. Trauma, death, birth. We snuck out for long walks in the Sonoma woods, and she began to open up, share the anguish of her feelings of lust and her love of Christ, the agony of her self-inflicted orgasms.

Soon her history began to assert itself, and we got past the emergency and started scraping away at her past. Her scars were healing; one the color of oyster flesh (Ash Wednesday), one delicate and rosy. Daily sessions became weekly. Then she missed one, then another. She had failed to return my call the day before. She couldn't. She'd drunk from a can of Drano.

Now the scars were forming inside. Throat, stomach, Drano-scorched mucous membranes.

I'll never forget walking into her room. She did not look up, just stared at the wall, clutched a pillow like a child or a lover. The fear in her eyes was infectious, and something snapped inside of me. I told her that if she wanted to die she could use my Swiss army knife, but she'd have to cut *down*, not across. She'd have to make the sign of the cross with the slashes on her wrists.

I dug into my pocket and pulled out the knife. Nickels and quarters scattered across the sheets and rattled on the floor.

"Here," I said, and tossed the little red knife onto the bed sheet. "Do it right."

She threw it at me.

I sat on the bed and held her until her tears turned to laughter, and I realized that I had a lot to learn. Nothing anyone had ever said to her had made the critical difference. The decisive moment had evolved spontaneously out of fear, through drama.

She was discharged the following week. She quit the order soon afterward. I was summoned to the chief psychiatrist's office and thoroughly chewed out for my unprofessional conduct. I argued that our profession had become a palliative. We were psychoparamedics, patching up people's psyches until the next crisis. I saw Gloria months later, when she called to introduce me to her fiancé.

One Friday in June, I realized that I had a free weekend. Stephanie was visiting her parents in Santa Barbara; I'd seen my last patient at the clinic, my last client at my office, and, although I could have spent a couple of days working on my thesis, I opted instead to prepare some San Pedro. The cactus itself was fairly common, readily available, and, although I knew little of its preparation, I sliced one up, boiled it for a few hours in a liter of water, funneled it into a canteen, and headed off for my spot in the woods, an hour's hike from a dirt road above the far end of a private vineyard.

It had rained late into the spring that year, and there was still water flowing over the thirty-foot rock face and into a shallow pond at its base and along a rocky creek bed into the woods. I sat on a tiny sand bank in the middle of the stream: coarse sand and smooth stones and leaves and twigs from the overhanging oak trees. Sat there and meditated on the sound of the water trickling over the stones; robins arguing over piracantha berries; the smell of oak, oats, wine country earth; the sun on my upturned face.

And I felt as though I had returned to be in the company of my natural environment. I felt closer to the life of my little nature retreat than ever before. It was as though I had learned how to feel at ease with Nature in Peru and had brought the lesson back home with me. The life of the *altiplano* had been Antonio's, and this was mine.

Sometime in the midafternoon I drank a cupful of San Pedro. I paid my respects to the four directions, called upon the archetypal spirits of the Four Winds to come and sit with me, and drank. I had gone without breakfast and lunch, nevertheless, after another hour I felt nothing. My blissful state was altered only by my expectation of the effects of my con-coction. I started to think about Antonio's references to the distillation of the plant and the use of "cleansing herbs." Then I realized that, deep down, I was recalling his last words, his reference to an experience of power.

Years later I would learn that only certain San Pedro cactus, grown, tended to, and prayed over by shamans in "power places" in the mountains, had any effect. The American garden variety that I had prepared produced nothing but a toxic stomach upset.

It was a hot day. Sunlight reflected off the surface of the water that rippled gently on either side of my sand bank. I took off my shirt and stood. Testing my sensations. Is anything happening? Do I feel anything? Forget it. I'm becoming preoccupied with the substance, and that's getting in my way. I feel fine. I feel good. Relax and feel the strength of a body at ease. I'll walk over there to the waterfall. Through the water. My boots are wet now, and besides, they're awkward. I'm not hiking, I'm standing in a stream. Take them off, throw them back onto my sand bank, my *mesa*. The water falls so carefully over the rock, steep, it slips and slides down the slick algae-slime face from . . . thirty feet? I can climb that. There would be a good spot there beside the stream. Easy. I can climb it quickly, elegantly, hands and feet.

Swiftly. Like a cat.

And there I sat, in near bliss, where the little brook fell over the rock cliff, level with the tops of the oak trees, my sand bank and my hiking boots looking very small.

There was nothing particularly mystical. There were no great epiphanies, merely a mildly euphoric sense of accomplishment, a sense of coming home and being there fully.

I don't know how much later it was when I realized my situation, realized that I didn't remember climbing up the rock face. It was growing dark when my reasoning brain kicked in, and I peered down the face of the cliff and was astonished to see that there were no handholds, there was no conceivable way of getting down. To the right, where the water ran, it was slick with organic film. To the left and directly below, it was a vertical drop of thirty feet. My boots were down there. My little daypack, canteen, car keys. I knew that I had to go down, had no idea how I'd come up, and, as the sun set and darkness fell, I felt fear in my stomach. There was movement in the trees below. Lights and shadows. My fear was palpable, intensified by the coming night. I debated how to proceed, resolved to recapture the power and strength I had felt hours before. I visualized my cat.

My cat. For some reason the thought of this alleged power animal presented itself to me. Here, I reasoned, was an opportunity to test it, to call upon it. I closed my eyes and imagined it emerging from the jungle—no, woods, these woods, moving steadily, purposefully, head low to the ground, legs moving in perfect cadence, paws flopping forward, perfect placement, infallible, one after the other, hands on rock, left, right, loose and fluid movement, knowing without thought, forward, inexorably, inch by inch.

And then there was a moment of such exhilaration, such intoxicating power, that can be known, but only poorly described. It was an instant, a breath in time, it was the sensation of a cat realizing that he is a cat.

I caught my breath and slipped into a rational state, and there I was, ten feet from the bottom of the cliff, facing down, a 45 degree angle, one palm resting against a slight bulge on the rock, the other on a tiny ledge hidden under the falling water, and I fell, head first, broke the fall with my left hand, spraining my wrist, and rolled over into the shallow pond. I jumped to my feet and shook the water off. The pain was nothing compared to the exhilaration. For an instant, an unmeasurable moment, I had become the cat.

The next day, Sunday, I got a phone call from Miami. My grandmother had had a heart attack. I tried to reach Stephanie in Santa Barbara, but she was out. I left a message with her mother and left for Miami.

June 14

Hospitals belong to the night. The dead of night. What curious places they are. Whitely sterile, disinfected, fluorescent. The place we "visit" until we come here to die.

A waiting place. We wait in it and it waits for us. Here we wait to feel well again, wait to die, wait to be free from disability. Patients cultivate patience and patience is the art of hoping.

Maria Luisa is dying. My father found her, gave her some kind of CPR, brought her back from the brink, and now she's being kept there artificially.

Four IVs. A central line in her neck to push drugs and fluids, one in each arm for good measure, an arterial line in her left arm to draw blood and for hooking up to a transducer for constant blood pressure readings. There's a nasogastric tube running through her nose and into her stomach. It's hooked up to a suction machine on the floor to drain her stomach constantly so that she won't aspirate, regurgitate into her trachea. And there's an endotracheal tube down her throat, a ventilator because she can't comfortably breath by herself. She doesn't have the energy. And she's on a steady diet of intravenous morphine, nitroglycerin and Valium. Sedated because anxiety increases the heart rate and uses more oxygen and everybody's trying to save that heart muscle. Anxiety? It occurs to me that the only thing she has to be anxious about is all the crap they're shoving into her, all the discomfort they're causing her. There she lies, plugged in at six places to a life support system in a whitely sterile, disinfected, fluorescent cubicle.

And she'd been at home.

She told me so. She saw me. I bent over her face and her lids, heavy with drugs, slid up and she looked into my eyes and said: "I was at home."

And then I took her hand and she squeezed it with a strength that surprised me and then let go and her forefinger began tapping—a nervous tic—on my palm, and I began to sob. Her hand tightened on mine again, comforting me in her pain.

Then I had to step out because they were inserting the endotracheal tube, and it's usually a bit of a struggle to get it down the trachea when they're conscious.

My God! We fear death so much that we take eighty-year-old women ready to die and pick them up off the floor of their homes and plug them into the technology we've created to keep that precious life alive because anything, *anything* is better than death.

It's barbaric. Where's the humanity in this? And all these interns and residents, all these smart, smart young men and women, all these health care professionals nodded when their college philosophy professors talked about life and death, the great circle, the noble uroborus, the nature of things, the natural cycle. They understood, didn't they? Or did they write it down in their notebooks and choose the correct multiple choice question on their final exam and leave it at that?

Do they, does anyone here know what it is to face death honorably?

Do I?

Know what it is to exhale that last breath freely rather than holding it, holding it in, holding onto life so hard that we crush it, strangle it.

Death is not a tragedy. The tragedy is how we face it. It's pathological.

Oh, Maria Luisa, can't I help you to die?

I could not. I stayed there long after my father had left. We had had an argument. It was he who had initiated this treatment. He had called the ambulance and told the paramedics to do whatever they could and they had done just that. Standard operating procedure.

"She's ready to die," I had said.

"How do you know? I saved her life."

I had made the mistake of taking issue with him and he had reminded me that she was his mother and stormed out.

I went into her room and listened to the whir and hum of the suction machine draining her stomach, the wheeze of the ventilator. She was drugged senseless. I held her hand and thought of that night on the edge of the *altiplano,* the face of the missionary, the elegance of her death. The contrast was unbearable, and then a nurse pushed open the door and asked what was I doing there? I told her I was Maria Luisa's grandson, that I was a doctor, that I'd come from California to be with her. But visiting hours were over. She was willing to argue, so I led her out of the room and we stood in the hall and I demanded to see the on-call resident and went back into the room.

He showed up half an hour later. Again, we stood in the hall. He was a mess, four hours to go of a thirty-six-hour shift. Red-eyed and weary, he didn't have time for me. He quoted policy, tried patiently to make me understand, told me that she would be fine through the night; there was a chance she'd hang on for days.

"I don't think she's fine."

"I'm sorry, but I don't think you're qualified . . ."

"Yeah, I know," I said. "I'm just a pain in the ass."

He gave me a half-laugh. "She's in stable condition. If you have an issue with her treatment, you'll need to talk to the immediate family. Now I've got to get to the E.R." He sort of patted me on the arm, and then turned and took a few steps. He stopped. "I'm sorry," he said, then his shoes squeaked off down the hall, and his white coat billowed out behind him.

I turned and walked back into the room. I told her that I loved her and kissed her forehead and kissed her hand. There were two nurses waiting for me at the door, deciding whether to call security. I told them goodnight and walked out into the hot Miami night.

Up the drive and to my right, an ambulance idled by open emergency room doors. A couple of paramedics moving with professional urgency slid a stainless steel stretcher from within, and the intern met them at the door and placed a hand on the chest of the admission whose emergency this was.

Maria Luisa died two days later, in spite of all of the attempts to keep her on the brink.

My return from Florida was marked by a peculiar incident that would serve as a preface of things to come. Stephanie had extended her stay in Santa Barbara and returned a few nights after my arrival. I was feeling particularly sentimental. As the months had passed, my dependency on her had grown. I longed for her when we were apart, and her ambivalence regarding her separation from Edward gnawed at me.

We dined at my place.

I lit candles, a dozen in the living room, and we made love in their light. For more than an hour we toyed with each other, teased each other's bodies, indulged in each other's sensations, caressed the possibilities . . . here? or . . . here. What about . . . this? Anything is possible when you abandon your detachment, yield to the flesh, perceive with your body, focus with your touch, and I ran my finger from her forehead to the tip of her nose, over parted lips and down her throat and between her breasts, and shuddered and I saw a man.

Saw him, felt him, sensed him completely in an instant.

"Don't stop. . . ."

I caught my breath, and held it as long as I could.

"Not now. . . ."

I was aware of the room, the candlelight, the sweat cooling on my body.

"What is it? What's wrong?"

Adrenaline, that breathless, heart-thudding sensation of danger, the body's protective device, strength when you need it most. When you are threatened. For it wasn't merely the sensation of him, but the knowledge of her loving another. Fresh. Recent. I knew it like a hound knows where a fugitive has run.

"Who did you see?" I asked, not a whisper, and the sound of my voice broke the erotic state, cracked the shell.

"What?"

"You slept with someone."

Her eyes widened and her brow and ears moved back in an involuntary spasm.

She drew away from me, scooted up against the pillows, stopped with her back against the sofa. "What did you say?"

"You heard me."

"What *is* this!" Anger. "What are you doing?"

"What am *I* doing?"

I stood and slid into my pants and walked away. I drew a glass of water and leaned against the tile kitchen countertop. Then I put a hand to my chest and felt the palpitations there. The tips of my fingers were tingling, and I realized that I was almost hyperventilating. My whole body was reacting. Systemically. The demon jealously rising from my stomach, through my chest, my throat. . . . A minute later she was behind me, a towel wrapped around her, held in place over her breasts.

"What's happening here!" I demanded. How could you . . ."

"*What!* How could I *what?*"

She shook her head, looked at the floor as though searching for something. "You have me *followed?* Then you wait? You wait to accuse me when we're making love?"

A nervous laugh caught in my throat and I shook my head. "Don't do this. Don't turn this around." I drained my water glass. "I didn't have you followed."

"Turn it around? Turn *what* around! I can't believe this!"

We got over it, but she was right. She wouldn't believe it. Wouldn't believe that I could describe the man, that I knew how he had touched her. It spooked her and, ironically enough, I don't believe she ever really trusted me after that night. It happened again, a month later, but I kept it to myself, and, although we agreed to attempt a committed relationship, and although it lasted for most of the year, every so often I would catch her looking at me, evaluating me out of the corner of her eye. Some part of her would always suspect that I was a little nuts.

January 2, 1975

A dream.

I am sitting at a white-painted wrought iron table in a Spanish-style courtyard with Stephanie. Talking nonsense like *Alice in Won-*

derland. I tell her that she can choose either to sleep with (or marry?) me or to sleep with others (there's an obscure figure in gray overalls). Next I am entering a room where Stephanie is lying in bed. I climb in from the roof, like a spider, down the wall of the narrow little room. I know that she still has a sexual debt to pay. A sexual debt?

In bed we are having sex. She is on top of me but facing toward my feet, squatting, then she turns and looks over her shoulder and says, "Now we can have the baby you want to have."

But I think to myself, No, we must be making love face to face— we must be face to face before we can have a child.

In Machu Picchu, on the hillock beside the Death Stone, Antonio and I had "put death on the agenda," and, curiously enough, death became my companion that year. Peculiar how the transient themes, the subtextual patterns, of your life are illuminated by hindsight.

I thought often of the Medicine Wheel, the journey of the Four Winds. The mythic South, where you exorcise the past that haunts you, binds you, restricts you. The West, where you lose fear by facing death, free yourself from an unknown future. And, although I had no sense of when I would return to Peru, if I would resume my work, return to Ramón and engage with the work of the West, death made its presence felt.

I found myself continually confronted by the specter of death, and with each confrontation there was a lesson. It had begun with the death of the missionary, and I had learned by witnessing, learned something of my vision and the *viracocha*. Gloria's flirtation with death had taught me something of the drama of psychological healing. And then there was Maria Luisa, an astonishing, painful demonstration of death in the Western world.

August 22

There is a hospital bed waiting for me too.

Maria Luisa was eighty–two. The resident who had ministered to her was probably thirty. So. Twenty-five years from now, when I am in my early fifties, a child will be born who will grow to become the doctor who will pull the plug on me.

How will I die? What will I die from? Playing with the concept of future life progressions. . . . I see myself dying of a heart condition at an early age. Oh, maybe that child has already been born. I see myself lying in a hospital bed, surrounded by family members not telling me the truth.

Denial.

Denial.

Denial.

Why?

Death is fearful. We cower so from it, and deny it when it comes.

But we incubate it within us, like a germ within us.

Why a heart condition? What is the condition of my heart? Have I ever really opened it up to anyone? Have I ever allowed anyone to come very close? Perhaps I'm setting myself up to die of a heart/ love condition. That's it.

Must change that.

Have had a measure of success leading Holly and her family to hold her imminent death in a life-positive way. Easier for Holly than her parents. Her mind is too young to have been permanently imprinted with tradition and taboo. She is eager, willing to explore death, to approach it as a life experience. Her parents are so over-whelmed with her loss that they could well miss the gift she is giv-ing them, the lesson she is willing to teach them. But her pain is in the way. I've tried everything. Balancing her energy, visualization techniques—closing pain valves, discharging her pain into the Earth. Today, in a light meditative state, she saw a banana.

Holly was seventeen years old and dying of ovarian cancer. She had been referred to me by a friend at the University of California Medical School, and we had worked together for six weeks. Her cancer had metastasized in spite of drug and radiation therapy. All that was left was the pain and her death.

After four weeks she had asked if she could work with me alone, without her family, and in my desperation I took that as a sign of progress. Her request was not a rejection of her parents, but a declaration of her need to work with her pain and face death alone. Her attitude toward herself and her disease was healthy. We discussed the importance of examining her past, her illness, her pain, and freeing herself from her obligations, from the ties that kept her bound to this life, from her parent's desperate desire that she live. I asked for their permission to take her to my home one evening, and there, in my backyard near the edge of the woods, we built a little fire and she consigned to the flames the bits and pieces of her past that haunted her still. She characterized each one of them with words or simple drawings on square bits of fine Chinese paper, folded them or twisted them into shapes, and we sat before the fire for three hours. We laughed together, cried together.

But the pain was getting in her way. Then, at the end of a session in which we had continued to work on a self-induced trance state, she had seen a banana. The next week she saw a whole bunch. She started to dream of a banana tree, and, in a light meditative state, could summon the image. It was the only thing we had to work with, so I encouraged the image, began to guide her imagery, and eventually there was a whole banana tree. Neither of us had any idea of its significance, and I discouraged her from analyzing it, although we were equally curious.

August 31

Breakthrough with Holly.

My clinical supervisor keeps insisting that the banana is a phallic symbol, repressed sexuality. Jesus! Let's put her in a pigeonhole in a conventional Freudian rolltop desk!

Then today, the banana tree acquired roots. I told her to focus on those roots, see how they grow, their delicate, translucent tips, pushing slowly deeper, deeper through the soil, deep into the Earth.

"An underground stream," I said. Her eyes were closed. Her head, covered by a bright blue scarf, was bowed slightly forward. Her breathing was perfect, from the stomach, her hands hanging loose and relaxed from her wrists. She was good at this. "An underground stream of cool, mineral-rich water, spring water running through a vein in the Earth, a channel in the rock and soil, quartz crystal walls shining, glowing with phosphorous, and the water trickles steadily. And look up. Look where the roots of the tree have broken through the soil above. Little bits of soil fall and are carried away by the steadily trickling stream. Your roots, the roots of your tree, thirsty, seeking that water, seeking to tap into the clear, cool, nourishing vein of the Earth, reaching down. . . . Feel them. New cells forming, roots growing, tenderly reaching . . . almost . . . there. . . ."

There were tears in her eyes and she drew a long, deep breath, opened her eyes, and smiled.

Six months later she died, consciously. In those six months she achieved a 50 percent to 60 percent reduction in pain. The roots from her banana tree had grown, reached deeply into the Earth, nurtured her with the cool spring water we found there, and she was able to release much of her pain through those same roots, back into the Earth. Her father had taken her into the hills of Napa to run in a field of poppies, and her ashes were scattered there later.

I went to Brazil later that year, and the results of my work and experiences were documented in *Realms of Healing*. During that trip, and during the course of my later research in Brazilian spiritism, I experienced a lifetime's worth of paranormal phenomena. I met Dr. Hernani Andrade, a physicist and the director of the Brazilian Institute for Psycho-Biological Research, and we became lifelong friends. With Andrade as my guide I began to investigate the spirit religions of the Candomble, the Umbanda, and the outlawed Quimbanda, techniques of mediumship and astonishing healing skills, yet all the while I was aware of a fundamental difference between the spiritism of Brazil and the shamanic creed. The practices of spiritism maintain a strong subject/object relationship with the supernatural and the "spirit world." Healing and insight are achieved through a medium, a person who channels a spirit and becomes the spirit's instrument. The healing states and ecstatic states of shamanism are specific to the individual, and the elements of "spirit" are instruments of the shaman's consciousness. A spirit medium will yield his or her body and voice to be used by a spirit, but the shaman never loses control. The shaman is a spiritual warrior and engages directly and masterfully with the domains that he or she visits in the "spirit flight."

Dreamed of Antonio again. Walking in the *altiplano*. He has a mimosa seed pod. Hide and seek. I remember having a similar dream
when I was there. This time he hides it, and I am to find it by asking the trees to help me. The wind is whispering through the
pines, and they are shimmering with their own light. I address a
tree. "Where is the seed pod?" Antonio laughs and tells me that I
look very stupid standing there talking to a tree. I become angry
and stomp off, and later I ask without asking, I think my question
and a bush begins to glow just ten feet away. I go there and find
the pod.

Tonight Andrade has invited me to attend a seance.

Called Stephanie. She sounded tense.

It's 2 A.M. Exhausted but must write this down before sleep. The
seance. All M.D.s and psychologists interested in channeling. They
meet every Thursday night, like a poker game. Andrade explained
that the purpose of the sessions was to heal certain people who had
died but whose spirits were still tied to their biological experiences.
People who had died unconsciously and were "caught between this
world and the next," still experiencing their pain, the symptoms of
the diseases that had caused their deaths. Andrade frequently func-
tioned as a sort of spirit therapist. There was a medium, a beautiful
middled-aged Brazilian woman named Regina. We all held hands
and she went into a deep trance and "incorporated" a variety of
"spirits," and Andrade engaged them in a sort of classical psychotherapy dialogue. Three cases, two men and a woman, and Regina's
voice changed remarkably with each. The session was conducted in
Portuguese.

Close of session, Regina seems tired, confused. The Lord's Prayer is
recited and the lights are turned on and suddenly Regina starts
speaking Spanish. A gentle, tremulous voice. "Where am I, God
help me . . ." Andrade begins to speak to her. She is in great dis-

comfort and she is scared, her lips are so dry, such a hollowness in her chest. Andrade explains that she is now beyond death, no longer in her former body.

"That is confusing me. . . ."

"Look!" he says. "Look down. Feel your body." Regina's hands move over her dress.

"Are those your hands, your breasts?"

"No. . . . They are young."

Andrade tells her that she is occupying the body of a medium. Her spirit has regained consciousness and awakened from the nightmare she was caught in, not fully alive, not quite dead.

Then Regina looks at me and gasps.

"Bombi! Is that you, my little one?" I stand up, knock over my chair, and Regina throws herself into my arms. "Help me! Help me, please."

I go blank. Andrade and another pull her away from me and Andrade counsels her. I listen in a daze. Only my grandmother called me by that name. As I listen, Andrade encourages her, tells her to look about her and see that there were others there to help, that it is safe to reach out and be guided into the next world, and she starts to see things, identify her mother, her father, her husband—my grandfather—by name.

Her pain and discomfort diminish, she feels younger, stronger, and Andrade tells her that she is leaving the physical world, the nightmarish realm between the worlds.

She turns to me again and says:

"Thank you for being here. I will always love you and be with you. Take care of your father."

No one here knows about Maria Luisa.

Perhaps Regina was a sensitive. Perhaps she sensed my loss and obtained all the relevant names and information telepathically. I know no more now than I knew then, for I did not feel compelled to analyze the experience. Andrade was sympathetic, yet matter of fact about the whole thing. I was moved, deeply, and admittedly consoled by the thought that my grand-mother had been released from her suffering and allowed to die.

But I had had enough of death.

October 13

Could I have done more for her? Eased her suffering and helped her to die in Miami?

I'm returning to Peru. Tired of being stalked by death, cats, eagles. Booked a flight: São Paulo–Lima–Cuzco.

I suspect my "work of the West" started back on the *altiplano*. I'm going back to finish it.

12

Should this my firm persuasion of the soul's immortality prove to be a mere delusion, it is at least a pleasing delusion, and I will cherish it to my latest breath.

—Cicero

The news of Professor Morales's illness struck me as wholly unreasonable. There are some people that you never conceive of as unwell.

An intense-looking young man with wire rim glasses had taken over his classes, although the university was once again on strike. I introduced myself to him, and he told me that the professor had been away for more than a week with pneumonia.

"Can you tell me where he lives?"

He drew his head back and squinted at me. "You are a friend?"

"Yes," I said. "A very good friend."

"Pardon me, but you do not know his house?"

"No. We have spent most of our time together traveling."

His eyes widened behind his glasses. "Ah, I know you." He nodded. "You are the psychologist from California."

We shook hands and he directed me to a house ten or twelve blocks from the university. It was an old house of whitewashed adobe, and the walls were at least three feet thick. Small windows, tiled walkway, red-tiled roof. I knocked on the door and it was opened immediately by a fat, middle-aged man with a pencil mustache. His head was half-turned back into the room, and he was fiddling with the catch on an old black leather bag.

"*Penicillium notatum!* Mold, my friend! It grows on rotten fruit and ripe old cheese, and if you don't take the medicine, it'll probably grow on you! Just because it comes in a little white pill doesn't mean it isn't good for you!" The yellow rubber tube of a stethoscope was caught between the handles of the bag, and the man shoved it inside.

There was a cough inside and Antonio's voice: "Don't patronize me."

"Then stop being such a sanctimonious old fool! You have a visitor." The man turned to me and said excuse me, and he walked out, down the path and up the street. I pushed on the door and it swung open. The room was stocked with simple wooden furniture: chairs, a dining table. The ceiling was beamed and the walls covered with bookcases crammed with old volumes and artifacts. There was a window with a view of Salcantay and the ruins of the Inca fortress of Sacsayhuaman. Antonio stood by the window. He was wearing his traveling pants and *manta* shirt and tying a small bundle of something or other with a piece of string. He looked thin and pale, shadows around his eyes, but his face brightened as he turned to see me. He crossed the room in three steps and gave me an *abrazo*. He had certainly lost weight.

He pushed himself away and regarded me at arm's length. "So! Are you ready to travel?"

"Travel? But you're ill."

"No, no. I am convalescing."

"Who was that man?"

"Dr. Barrera. He is an old friend. We live to argue with one another." He lifted his poncho from the back of a small sofa. "Like George Bernard Shaw, I enjoy convalescence. It makes the illness worthwhile."

"Are you taking penicillin?"

"Of course. That and my own herbal preparations. I tell Barrera that I am not taking it. It irritates him so much." He chuckled. "I have been away from the countryside too long. My lungs congest when they are not refreshed."

"Where are we going?"

He lifted a long hardwood staff from its place in a corner near the door.

"To visit a man who has died," he said.

October 17

Second leg of the trip. Second bus. In spite of his good humor, Antonio is tired, and he is asleep in the seat across the aisle of this rattletrap. Have ridden buses through most of Latin America, but this is an experience. Pen jumping all over the page, but I've nothing better to do, just thankful I have a seat. First bus, gave my seat to an old Indian woman with gas and stood in agony for two hours while she relieved herself and Antonio slept.

We travel to see Antonio's teacher in some rural hamlet north of Cuzco. Word came (how I don't know) that this old man is dying and Antonio is traveling to be with him. I gather the man we will meet (if we are in time) was his mentor. He referred to him as "the man I learned from."

Death. Again.

Traveling light this time. Just a daypack. Exhilarated.

We've stopped on the road. Barren *altiplano*. There is no sign, not a building or ploughed field in sight, but three women and a young boy with a pig and two chickens. I count only two seats. Here we go again.

We got off at a similar stop two and a half hours later. Although we were still on the *altiplano*, the character of the land was less wooded and reminded me of the Mexican chaparral: dense scrub, few trees, outcroppings of granite. We followed a dried-up riverbed until the sun set, and then made camp in the little gorge.

We built a fire and its light bounced off the walls of the *arroyo*.

"There are acts of power," said Antonio, "acts of confrontation with spirit, with Nature, with the unconscious mind, with life. Your decision to abandon traditional practice and venture into a realm unknown to you was such an act. Your confrontation with your past in Machu Picchu was such an act."

"And my work with Ramón?"

"No," he smiled. "That was more an act of boldness, of imprudence, although it was instructive. Curious, is it not, how the quest for an exhilarated state leads one to test themselves against death."

"The centers of pain and pleasure lie next to each other in the limbic brain," I said. "Although fear can paralyze us, it can also stimulate. Look at the warriors, the heroes of old."

"Fear is a volatile emotion." He drew a grenada fruit, green with brown speckles, from his bag. "Nothing so robs the mind of its powers as fear, and, as Seneca said, such is the blindness of mankind that some men are driven to death by the fear of it." He pried the fruit in half and handed me a portion. "But you cannot face death by creating experiences that bring you near death. Death is the greatest act of power to the shaman. The spirit flight, the ecstatic state of the shaman, is a journey beyond death. To learn how to die is to learn how to live, for you are claimed by life and can never be claimed by death. In a sense the person of power spends a whole life learning how to die."

"The person who has already died," I said.

"The shaman is a spiritual warrior with no enemies in this life or the next, free from desire and fear: desire formed by our experiences of the past, and the fear of death that haunts our future. They are the twice-born, once of woman and once of Earth."

"The work of the South and the West."

"Yes. By making the journey West and facing the jaguar in life, the spiritual warrior not only frees himself to live in his present fully, but when death finally comes it will know him and he will know the way." The West is where the body and spirit, the *viracocha,* part." He wiped his hands on a red bandanna. "This is dying consciously, with your eyes open. The way to leave this world alive."

"Immortality?"

He shrugged. "The body is a vessel of consciousness, of life . . ."

"Of energy."

"Yes." He reached toward the fire and slowly passed his cupped hand through the flames, then made a fist and held it before me. "When one dies consciously, one leaves behind the vessel and identifies oneself with that which the vessel holds."

He opened his hand and, for the life of me, I thought I saw the light. "And that is . . . ?"

"And that is God." He shrugged his shoulders. "The life force, energy, call it what you will. The stuff that dreams and the cosmos are made of."

Later

We travel not only to be with this old man, this teacher of Antonio's, but to share in his rite of passage, to partake in the final act of power of a shaman.

Sitting by the fire in a dried-up riverbed. Antonio has excused himself and wandered off to exorcise his mourning, so that he may be fully present to celebrate the death.

We are a half day's journey from the old man's home. We got off the bus because, as usual, the way we get to where we are going is as important as what we do when we get there.

I hoped out loud that we wouldn't be too late, and Antonio said no, we would be in good time, and I asked him how he knew.

"He will wait for me," he said.

Thinking of Maria Luisa.

Thinking of my father.

Thinking about mortality.

Dying to your flesh, born into your spirit. The body is a vessel of spirit, of energy, of consciousness. Remember comparing the psyche to a lagoon. Lagoon a place where the river widens, deepens, but the river flows through it. I sit in the bed of a river, but where is the stuff that this riverbed held? Where is the water that ran between these walls? Something stopped the water from flowing and that which was here continued on. To the ocean? And its particles will rise with evaporation and fall to Earth elsewhere to flow again in another riverbed, or to cut a new one in some far corner of the world. To nourish a plant, to flow through the veins of a blade of grass.

Stream, streams of consciousness.

Sitting in the corpse of a river.

Now, off in the distance, I can hear Antonio singing. What is it? Beautiful, faint, a melancholy tune.

Bone tired. I'll sleep.

We set off the next morning, and there was a lightness, a peaceful resolution to Antonio's manner that I had not seen before. I sensed that we were climbing most of the morning, and trees began to appear. The land was looking more familiar.

At midday we stopped by a solitary eucalyptus tree and ate yucca and cornmeal and fruit, and Antonio cleared a small space at the base of the tree and dug a hole. From his bag he withdrew the little bundle that I had seen him tie together at his house.

"What is that?" I asked.

"Fishmeal." He opened the packet and held it under my nose and laughed at the face I made. He placed the paper-wrapped bundle in the hole and covered it over with soil and poured water over it from his *bota*.

"What's the idea?"

"The idea!" He sat back on his haunches and his face broke into a smile. The weariness was gone. It was as though his face was regaining its life, its health, its character. He leaned forward and slapped my knee with his palm. He was pleased that we were together again.

"The idea, my friend, is that you give something in return."

"In return for . . . ?"

"You know, or at least begin to suspect, that the plants as well as the animals have spirits. When you use a plant for sacred purposes, you connect with its spirit. That connection becomes unique to you. Last night I engaged with the spirit of the San Pedro to help me to summon my power so that I could attend to my old friend. I offer this fishmeal as a gift in return. One should always leave something: hide a crystal in Nature, plant a plant, bury a coin at a crossroads, even, to honor the gift, to give something in return for what you have been given. Fishmeal is a precious fertilizer from the coast."

"You used San Pedro last night?"

"Very little, nothing more than a homeopathic dose." He stood and filled his chest with the air of the high plateau. "My lungs are clearing. Let's go."

I had assumed that we were destined for a village, but, sometime before dusk, we crested a hill and there was a fringe of pine trees and, just before them, a *casita* with a low stone wall forming an enclosure for chickens and goats. There were a couple of burros wandering behind the house, and a young Indian boy was removing a simple saddle from the back of an old horse by the break in the wall.

Antonio told me to wait and he headed down the hill and I watched him disappear into the house. I started to feel self-conscious. Was it appropriate for me to be here? I saw one or two people move out into the enclosure and back inside. How many were there? Who were they?

They were friends. They were students, healers, shamans. They were *El*

Viejo's only living family, and there was a roomful of them, sitting in chairs and on stools arranged around a rocking chair in the center of the room. His only blood relation was a granddaughter in her fifties, who served little sesame cakes to those gathered.

Most of them were Antonio's age, early sixties, Indians. I counted six women and four men. El Viejo, the old shaman, sat in the rocking chair. He was a small man, shrunken with age, covered with a brightly woven Indian blanket. His hands were unusually large and liver spotted, the nails were long. His nose was arched and thin and seemed to start high on his forehead, also high and sloping, accentuated by baldness on top. The fringe of long gray-white hair that surrounded his pate was pulled back and tied in a ponytail, and his eyes, under sparse brows, were soft and gray. His skin was delicately wrinkled, like tissue paper, thin and pale, almost translucent; the only color was high on his cheekbones, a blotchy pinkness, wine-stained tissue paper. He was a remarkable-looking man.

Two of the visitors, a man with a white shirt buttoned up to his neck, and a young woman with a purple shawl, had left their seats for us, had moved to sit on burlap sacks against the wall. I felt like an interloper. I protested to Antonio.

"It is a place of honor," he whispered. "Accept it graciously."

He sat in a chair beside the old man, and I took the stool behind him. Next to me sat an old woman, a Peruvian crone with peppery gray hair parted in the center and braided on one side, the braid tied off with a strip of woven ribbon.

El Viejo squinted over at my companion and nodded his welcome, a corner of his mouth lifted in a grin, and Antonio placed his hand on his teacher's and spoke to him in Quechua. He mentioned my name and the soft gray eyes shifted in my direction, but did not seem to look at me. Like the eyes of a blind man, they had no focus. I smiled at him and he whispered something to Antonio and Antonio nodded. I felt the blood rushing to my face, felt lightheaded and embarrassed. Then Antonio placed his other hand on my knee, and I smelled something acrid, heard a crackling sound. The old woman was lighting a pipe, a long hardwood bowl carved into the face of a fanciful owl with a stem and bit of bone like an antler. She puffed the tobacco without inhaling and the smoke wafted across my face, and she touched Antonio's shoulder and he took it from her and handed it to the old man, who raised it ever so slowly to his lips and drew on it, inhaling the smoke of the glowing tobacco.

He exhaled through his nostrils, like a dragon, two narrow streams of white smoke, then blew it out his mouth and this stream caught those from his nose and carried them into the center of the room, and I noticed the bed there. The floor was wooden planks. There was an adobe fireplace or stove in one corner, and each of the four walls had a large latched wood-framed window.

The old man handed the pipe to Antonio and he drew the tobacco deep into his lungs and I thought about his recent pneumonia. Then he handed it back to the crone, and this time she inhaled before passing it to the man on her left. El Viejo closed his eyes while the pipe was passed to each of the guests, and the room filled with its pungent fumes, stronger than any cigar, stronger even than Ramón's jungle tobacco, but the windows stayed closed. Not a word was spoken. No one save Antonio and the old man had breathed a sound since our entrance, and when the pipe had made the circuit and come back to the crone, she touched my arm and offered it to me. She smiled, a crack in her face, and I took it and looked at the old shaman and he opened his eyes and inclined his head and I drew on the bone bit, inhaled, and thought that my lungs would explode.

I coughed out the smoke and doubled over in an uncontrollable paroxysm of coughing. The crone turned to her neighbor and made a wisecrack about *"el jovencito,"* the young one, and the room laughed. The ice was broken and she patted me on the shoulder and took the pipe from me.

"What *is* this?" I whispered, not out of respect, but because I was still fighting for breath.

"The most powerful *huaman* tobacco," said Antonio. "Its spirit is the falcon, and it is visionary although it is nothing but tobacco. You are an honored guest."

"Thanks." I looked around the room and they were smiling. The old man's granddaughter was at my side. She offered me a sesame cake and I thanked her. She moved to her grandfather's side and whispered in his ear, and he nodded and lifted his hand as though to acknowledge her words. There was a murmuring of Quechua behind me, and I half-turned to see a middle-aged couple holding hands, heads together, staring at me in a distracted way. I smiled and gave them a nod, and they looked almost embarrassed, smiling back at me. Then Antonio touched my shoulder. He cleared his throat and leaned close.

"We need to perform a healing," he said.

"Uh huh?"

"The room has been cleansed with sage and tobacco and all present have prepared themselves, cleansed themselves, for El Viejo's death. When he makes his final journey to the West, he will go alone, the moment is his."

"Yes?"

"A number of the guests have noted the presence of another, uninvited."

"I'll leave," I said, anxious not to interfere.

"No, no. You have been invited. You are an honored guest. It is not you, it is a spirit that you have brought with you."

"What?"

"I do not know how I missed it. Perhaps my illness. It is very clear now."

"What is?"

"A woman who has died. Her spirit is still attached to your heart chakra." He touched my chest. Beside me, the crone was loading the pipe from a cloth pouch.

"They can see this?"

He nodded. "A dim bubble of light, connected to you by a cord, like an umbilical cord of light. El Viejo has asked that we perform a simple healing and release this soul. They have agreed."

I turned and looked at the people seated behind me. It was one of the eeriest sensations I have ever felt. They were looking not at me, but at something before me, something near my chest. Maria Luisa? The old witch had the pipe going now, and she drew the smoke deep into her lungs, eyes closed, then opened them and blew the smoke at a spot eighteen inches or so from my neck. There was a tapping sound and I looked to see the old man, the dying shaman, tapping the arm of his chair with the fingernail of his middle finger. Tap . . . tap . . . every two seconds.

"Turn around," said Antonio, and I shifted on my stool to face the gathering. The crone had started to hum, a low, resonant sound with no melody, and it was met by a similar sound at a higher octave by the second person to blow smoke at my chest, pass the pipe, close her eyes. Others were lighting their own pipes, filling them from the crone's cloth pouch, inhaling the acrid fumes, and soon I was enveloped in a cloud of dense *huaman* smoke, and the room was vibrating to the haunting sound of the shamans' song.

"Close your eyes," said Antonio. "Concentrate on this spirit. Exercise your vision."

I closed my eyes, watery with tears from the smoke, and felt Antonio's fingers tapping a circle on my forehead. I thought of Maria Luisa, the seance in São Paulo. . . . There was talk in the room, someone giving an opinion and another agreeing.

"What is happening?" I asked Antonio, without opening my eyes.

"They are directing energy toward her. She is glowing with their love. They are charging her spirit so that it can free itself from you."

There was a general murmur now.

"What are they saying?"

"She is angry with you, this woman. You have taken something from her." I felt the warm bowl of the pipe placed in my hands. "Take the smoke and give it to her. She died in a hospital, and you have taken her dignity."

I placed the stem between my lips and drew the smoke into my mouth and exhaled. El Viejo coughed.

"*Hurgó los huesos.* . . ." He picked at the bones. . . .

Antonio said, "You have picked at the bones of one who has not yet died. She is not free."

I opened my eyes and the smoke was there, suspended before me, egg shaped, the size of a watermelon.

"You have taken something from her. . . ."

My hand flew to my chest. My medicine pouch, a leather pouch, a gift from Stephanie.

". . . her head. . . ."

I grabbed the leather thong at my neck and pulled the pouch out from under my shirt, opened the flap, and withdrew the slide, a microscope slide dipped in plastic, a slide containing a microthin slice of Jennifer's brain. The crone drew in her breath through her teeth, a gentle hiss. There was an astonished silence.

The man with the white shirt stood up.

"What is that?" Antonio.

"It is a slide, for a microscope. A human brain."

He raised an eyebrow. "Why do you carry it with you?"

"I . . . a friend gave it to me."

"You carry it like an object of power," he said.

"It is," I said. "For me. I . . . learned more from this brain . . . from holding this brain in my hands . . ."

"Do you see her spirit? Do see how she is attached to this?"

"No. I thought I saw . . ."

"You must make peace with her. Free her spirit. She is ready now. She has stayed with you because through you she can find her final rest. It is not your fault. Spirits are drawn to light, like fireflies to a burning candle. Go. Go outside into the woods and offer this to her, return it to her and release her. She can go now, you will perform her final healing."

I looked at him pleadingly.

"I will explain it to them," he said. "Come back when you are through."

I stood and the room rocked, shifted dizzily, and I steadied myself, a hand on Antonio's shoulder.

October 18

We must find our own ritual. We must find our own ceremony, our own access to the realms of consciousness that exist within and without.

Writing has become an ingredient of my ritual, and I faithfully execute it here, within the tree line of the little wood beside El Viejo's *rancho*. Waiting in the dark.

Jennifer, a woman I never knew, could never come to know because I can't find the essence of life or self by picking at the bones of the dead. I don't know how you died, but I can guess that your moment came in a hospital bed while the healthy and the living did everything they could to keep you in their world.

You may have been well schooled in living, but surely, death was unfamiliar to you and came early and you fought it and if you have been somehow attached to your physical body, the vessel that held you, I am sorry. Sorry that it was not honored, that you were not helped to be free from it before it was defiled. It is our tradition.

Now, I am sure that your body has been burned and the Sun has been released from the flesh and all that is left is this morsel of tissue that is yours.

But all that was you has not ceased to be, and isn't it a wonder that your spirit should follow the last remnant of flesh and find freedom here, so far from home, in the company of such remarkable men and women.

I have broken the slide and removed what it held and buried it here, near the base of a pine tree.

I feel your presence.

Will this place be a reference for you?

Thank you for what you taught me. I will cherish the knowledge in my head and your spirit in my heart. Forever.

I begin to understand what is sacred.

I spent more than an hour there in the woods with Jennifer. The moon had passed between the Earth and the Sun. A new moon, a crescent sliver, and the night was unusually dark. When I returned to the house the room had been filled with candles. The windows were open now, but no wind disturbed the fifty or so tapers of light. The old shaman was lying on the bed in the center of the room, and the crone was singing a faint melody. I took my place on the stool, behind Antonio, beside the crone, four feet from the old man's body. His head turned toward me as I sat, and he stared at me, stared into my eyes and my mind went blank, blank like the gray of his eyes. Then he coughed a shallow cough and turned his head away, eyes toward the ceiling, and he closed them.

The *shush-shush* of a rattle started up somewhere behind me, and someone whistled, like you whistle when you call to a bird, and a song started, a murmured chant, and it was as though this simple song was a vehicle that carried with it the peace that settled on the room. I leaned forward slightly and saw that Antonio's eyes were closed. Before us the old shaman's chest was rising . . . and falling, and a sort of tremor shivered through him. I wanted to take his pulse. Instead I closed my eyes and allowed my body to measure itself to the rhythms of the rattle and song. . . . Found myself transported effortlessly to a state of serenity, perfect harmony with the song. . . .

It was much later when I opened my eyes, and the recent past had the feeling of a dream. I woke to the dream of the room, the faces, the dying man before me. The rhythm of the rattle, constant. The old man's breathing, slow and regular, and the rattle shook thirteen times for each breath. There was time to count the breaths, time to feel the texture of the air, the charge of it, the sweet intensity of it. The candles had burned low since I had closed my eyes.

There was rapture in the air, on the faces of these men and women, these students of El Viejo, and it was bewitching, as tangible as the smell of spring in April.

Then Antonio half-turned to look at me, and I realized that I had been staring at the old man, the rise and fall of his chest, counting the thirteen shakes of the rattle, breathing with him. Antonio reached out and touched my left temple with his middle finger, then tapped, drummed his fingertips, in a circle on my forehead.

"Look," he whispered. "Look carefully."

I let my focus go, and my eyes shifted to a spot six inches above the old man's chest, and there it was, that intangible form, a hazy violet hue there . . . and gone . . . there again, disappearing with each long breath, rising with every exhalation.

The crone squeezed my left hand. I turned and looked at her, then down at her brown, callused hand, dry and cool. I covered her hand with my right hand and nodded, and her eyes wrinkled with a smile. She raised the pipe to her lips and inhaled and blew the smoke at me, dipped her head and neck and blew it from my lap up, up my chest to my face, and there was something wondrous about her face and the dip of her head and neck, something tender, caressing. Something almost erotic.

She put the pipe into my hands, clammy, palms sweaty. The rattle stopped and the room hummed with silence.

When I turned my head, I could hear the cartilage crackle in my neck.

I couldn't see the energy body; the glow was gone. I saw the old man's body convulse once, twice, and sigh in the silence.

And I raised my eyes to an orb, a luminous ball of opalescent light, cords of light spiraling from his forehead, wrapping around it, blending into it, a radiant egg supported by a helix of spiraling light, and if I looked at it, it was gone, so I focused on empty space, for it could be perceived, but not seen.

Then Antonio took the pipe from my hands. I had forgotten that I was holding it. He puffed on it and the last ember glowed and caught the dry tobacco. He rose and blew the smoke across the dead man's forehead, and, as though out of the top of my vision, I saw the *viracocha* pulsate and scatter into a thousand points of light, like the light you see when you close your eyes and press on the lids. They scattered through the room, leaving trails, tracers of light, and seemed to touch the heads of the old man's students and the rattle went *shush* and when I looked again, the orb was back, hovering in the center of the room, and Antonio was standing with the granddaughter beside the shaman's body, dipping his fingers in a bowl of herbs and touching the shaman's chakras, his kneecaps, the soles of his feet, his elbows and hands.

And there were hands on mine. The old woman to my left, the man with the white shirt to my right. Antonio and the granddaughter were joined by others, and we stood, hands joined in a circle, and the old woman beside me sang a plaintive song. Her voice sounded like a flute, and I recognized the weird melody. I had heard it the night before, heard Antonio singing it in the night. It was the song of the woods, the high plateau, the song to summon the spirits of the grass and the pines, for, as Antonio later explained, the elementals, the forces of Nature that were El Viejo's power animals, had been set free. And I saw the energy body, the light of this old soul swirl and dissipate like a drop of dye in a glass of swirling water, and Antonio led me to the window, rubbed my forehead, stimulated my vision, and said: "Breathe. Breathe deeply and look quickly!"

For that instant the woods were alive with a light like I had seen in the jungle, radiant halos outlining the trees with pinpricks of light like fireflies scattering, flashing, playing in the spaces between the trees, and the tops of the pines swayed ever so slightly and the scent of the pines swept on a breeze through the room.

The candles wavered, and the smoke cleared. And the song ended.

13

Every parting gives a foretaste of death.

—Schopenhauer

The morning after the death of the old shaman, the party feasted on fried yucca, fruits, breads, and cornmeal. The mood was festive and there was much talk, mostly about local diseases and afflictions. Antonio explained that these people had traveled great distances to be present for the old man's birth into the spirit world, that they were shamans, healers, all touched by the teachings of El Viejo. He smiled at the mood of the group. Their joy, he said, was from the knowledge that the spirit of their teacher was with them fully now that he was free from the confines of this world.

The old man's *mesa* was laid out, and each of his students went to it and took an object: a staff, a crystal, a stone, ancient objects of power; and there was no argument, no hesitation or indecision. Antonio told me that specific objects had been given to them during the old man's death. They had been told what was theirs by the spirit of the shaman.

October 19

We left the house near the woods at about 11 A.M. We talked about immortality.

The knowledge that we are made of somatic and spiritual matter is fundamental to the shamanic experience. If one learns during their lifetime to separate themselves from the physical body, to experience themselves as "beings of light," to learn the spirit flight, one may die consciously, die to the flesh and be born into the spirit—a spirit that one has already met and claimed. If one does not die consciously, one's energy body returns to the "Great Pool of Consciousness."

When I pressed Antonio to explain this Great Pool, he shook his head. I hate it when he does that.

"It is a metaphor of the myth," he said, "a poetic expression of a concept. Leave it at that. If you are not satisfied with the image, then form your own, my friend, but do not base it on the experience of others."

"All right," I conceded. "But this . . . *individuation* of the spirit: is it believed that by dying consciously you maintain your individuality after death?"

"Individuality?" he asked. "Now there is a muddy concept. If you must insist on reducing everything to theoretical formulas, you would do better to be more precise."

"Damn it!" I stopped, shrugged off my daypack, and dropped it on the ground. "I'm trying to understand with the means that I'm accustomed to!"

"Yes," he said, "you are in a delicate position. You are on the path of experience. A path that will lead you to understanding. Caught between two worlds, between a waking state and a dream state. You have experienced power, yet you are still confused by the difference between your experience and your beliefs. But your beliefs are based on the theories of others."

"Theory is important," I said. "For God's sake! Theory is what allows us to exercise foresight! It's what has led the human race into the future: think ahead, propose a possibility, test it, prove it, move forward. Neocortical thinking, logic is a fact, a forum of Western thought. It cannot be discounted just because other cultures approach the mystery of the cosmos from the opposite direction! Besides, even Western science is ending up in the mystical realm. Look at quantum physics. . . ."

"What will I see?" he said.

"What you already know. That consciousness is a determining factor of reality. That the outcome of an event is influenced by the observation of the event. That a photon, subatomic light, is not a wave and not a particle. It is neither and it is both. It's astonishing! The whole process of the Western scientific method is based on reduction. . . ." I started ticking off points on my fingers. "We're trying to explain brain function by studying the molecular biology of the central nervous system. Molecular biology is studied in terms of atomic physics, and atomic physics is the realm of quantum mechanics, the uncertainty principle: the observation of an event influences its outcome, the mind of the observer is integral to determining the nature of reality."

"So," he said. "Scientific reductionism has reduced itself to consciousness. Physicists are becoming poets."

"Yes. The study of the human mind inevitably turns to the consciousness of the one who studies."

"And the new shamans will come from the West."

"What?"

"It is a vision I once had," he said.

He lifted my pack from the ground and handed it to me. "Now," he said. "For the sake of theory, let us say that one may maintain not *individuality,* but integrity of consciousness after death."

I slipped the pack over my shoulders. "All right," I nodded, and we continued on.

"What does that suggest to you?"

"Immortality," I said.

"And?"

"I'm not sure. It's like infinity. How do you resolve such a concept in a practical way?"

"How do you apply quantum mechanics to everyday life?" he challenged. "Does quantum theory teach you how to walk on the Earth? How to change the weather? How to identify yourself with the creative principle, with Nature, with the Divine? Does it teach you how to live every moment of your life as an act of power? No. Theory. Logic. Conceptualizations. Games to amuse ourselves with something that transcends all human research and conscious thought." Now it was his turn to stop and face me.

"It is through the experience of life through death that one becomes a spiritual warrior and identifies oneself with the life force." He held his hand in a fist before me, reminding me of the fire of two nights ago. "My old teacher has died to his flesh and yet maintained the integrity of his consciousness. You, on the other hand, have maintained the integrity of your body. You exercise your body, but your consciousness atrophies. El Viejo knew the truth for most of his life, and he walked in the snow without leaving tracks. Not literally, my friend, but mythically, poetically."

He placed his hand on my shoulder. "Our brains are not seventy-two-year clocks. We are not connected to this Earth for a finite time between birth and death. And the Divine does not come from somewhere above, it exists beyond time and space, and informs life. The Earth is our home, and once we have transcended the shadow play that we call biological reality and identified ourselves with the Divine force, we realize that we have no choice but to become caretakers of this Earth." He turned and walked ahead.

"Caretakers of the Earth," I said, and caught up to him.

"It is our responsibility. Ours." He spread his arms, gestured toward the land around us. "Honor thy mother and thy father. Mother Earth and Father Sun. The person of knowledge has no choice."

"And the new shamans will come from the West?"

"Of course," he said.

October 20

Last night, after eating, Antonio drew a mimosa seed pod from his little bag.

I looked to the edge of the little pine wood where we were camped and recognized it from my dreams.

Déjà vu.

"You have imagined this?"

I looked at the pod, dried and wrinkled, four inches, curved. "I have dreamed it," I said.

"You have imagined it," he said. "We have imagined it together."

"Dreamed together."

"Where does the imagination come from?" he asked. "Freud and Jung felt that it came from the unconscious, and that the unconscious spoke to us in our dreams. Close your eyes and imagine. Close your eyes and see things. See with your eyes closed. Dream."

"We dreamed together."

He nodded. "A shaman will often begin a lesson on such a fundamental level."

"Consciously?" I asked.

He bowed his head over the object in his hand, and the firelight shone on his silver-gray hair. "That word begins to lose its meaning, does it not?"

I shook my head. "No. I still know when I am conscious. It's the reality of my experience that has lost definition."

"The planes of reality," he said, without lifting his head, "are the levels of the possibly conscious. You can slip between them." He raised his head and looked at me. "Willingly."

He leaned forward and placed the pod on the fire. There was still some moisture in the thing, and as it evaporated in the heat of the fire, it twisted, writhed a half-turn, and its wrinkled surface browned before it caught flame.

"You must go back to the jungle. Complete your work of the West."

"I've finished with the South, haven't I?"

"No. One is never finished. Remember that the medicine wheel is a circle. A great spiral. You have entered the world of myth and have encountered elements of your past. And you have begun to shed the skin of rational thought that you have worn these years. The past has begun to lose its grip on you, and death is stalking you like that cat."

His eyes shifted and I turned to look back, over my shoulder, into the darkness.

"And there is the eagle that is waiting to prey on you. You must return to Ramón, return to that lagoon."

I nodded and Antonio shook his head. "Do not fool yourself," he said. "Do not think that once you have reconciled yourself with your past and freed yourself from death and the fear of the future that you will live the life of a warrior, that you will step fully into your present as a person of power. Do not be trapped by the simplicity of this theory. The present does not last. It is past even as we revel in it. You are still standing in the shadow of the mystery. It is the shadow you cast. Your shadow."

"But the person of power, of knowledge, walks in the snow without leaving tracks. Casts no shadow."

"Many who travel along the Medicine Wheel become seduced by its power. Few complete the circle, commune with the ancient ancestors and their knowledge in the North and overcome their power in the East to become persons of knowledge, children of the Sun." He smiled up at me from across the fire. "And if you wish to take the metaphor literally, consider the one thing that casts no shadow."

"And that is?"

October 21

The Sun is the only thing that casts no shadow.

Are energy and consciousness the same? The energy of the Sun is the energy of all life—all matter, for that matter—an energy that forms all structures as there is a consciousness that informs all life.

We returned to Cuzco and I made a reservation on a morning flight to Pucallpa.

October 24

Came to Peru to experience the *ayahuasca* and was introduced to Death. Came to Peru to find a shaman and found a roomful.

Tomorrow I return to the jungle, return to the garden.

Eighty thousand year ago we acquired a thinking brain, a reasoning machine that set us apart from Nature. In one quantum long-jump, the brain nearly doubled in size. We could evaluate. Reason. Think. And the hand of Nature was joined by the hand of man.

There is a Gideon Bible in the drawer beside the bed in this hotel room. "And Jehovah God went on to say: 'Behold, the man has become like one of us in knowing good and bad, and now that he may not put forth his hand and take fruit also of the tree of life and eat and live to time indefinite—' With that Jehovah God put him out of the garden of Eden to cultivate the ground from which he had been taken."

I return to the garden to put forth my hand and eat of the tree of life everlasting.

Spoke with Stephanie. She sounded long distant. Must return to the States for some last-minute editing for *Realms of Healing,* so I'll recover from the jungle on the plane ride home. Will meet Antonio at the airport in the A.M. to say goodbye. For how long?

Antonio never came.

I telephoned the school, but there was no answer. I waited until the last possible moment, then boarded the twin-engine plane for Pucallpa. I was scheduled to return in five days. I would have a couple of hours in Cuzco before my connection to Lima and home. I could see him then, surely, take a taxi to the school and see him before I left.

Nevertheless, I felt uneasy. Why hadn't he come? There was so much to say.

14

The eyes are not responsible when the mind does the seeing.
　　　　　　　　　　　　　　　　　　　　—*Pubilius Syrus*

I was in time to catch the bus at the Pucallpa airfield. In time to stand in the breeze of the old Westinghouse fan and drink a *cuzceña* at the bar. The barman remembered me.

I got off at kilometer sixty-four and looked for the banana palm that had marked the entrance to the path, but it had grown such that I could not identify it, and I had to guess.

There was something in the air, something that penetrated even the pungent pulpiness of the jungle. Something that had settled in the clearing around Ramón's house. He was there, his back to me, stooped over a thick, twisted tree branch on the sand. He straightened as I emerged from the trees, turned, and I saw that he held a machete in his hand. We stood there, motionless, looking at each other across thirty feet of clearing. I smiled and he squinted at me, then raised his eyes and tilted back his head to look at the sky. There was no sign of recognition or surprise, no friendliness. He sniffed once or twice and lowered his gaze to mine.

"What is it?" I asked.

"Burning," he said. He shook his head and looked at the ground.

October 25

Somewhere to the south, far to the south, thirty or forty kilometers to the south, the jungle is burning. Chains are slung between tractors and the life of the jungle is stripped and burned to create grazing land for cattle. Beef for U.S. food chains. And the waste is precious—exotic hardwoods.

Never a man of many words, Ramón is particularly taciturn. There is a darkness about him. He is alone here and I hesitated to ask after his wife and daughter. When I did, he just nodded. "We need rain," he said, and it is raining now, a torrent in the pitch darkness. An Old Testament kind of rain. To stop the fires? To wash away the white men?

How does he feel? Angry, resentful. I am welcomed begrudgingly. Somewhere the jungle is burning and a white man walks out of it and into his home.

Uneasy. If I feel this way in the morning, I will leave.

I slept too late. It was almost noon when I awoke. The rain had stopped and the jungle was steaming. Something was brewing on the brazier over the fire in the sand and Ramón was gone.

I wandered. To the bend in the little river where I had bathed and written in my journal years before. I followed the little stream, wading where there was no shore, where the jungle had overgrown the mud and sand banks. An hour's wandering, meandering, and there was another bank, a stretch of sand and a path, and I followed it to a clearing a hundred feet into the jungle, where there was a ruin, some sort of building, a small temple perhaps, draped with the ornamentation of the jungle, eight hundred years of growth, vine-worn grooves in smooth granite blocks. The friction of time. A scene from a nineteenth-century explorer's lithograph. There were the remnants of a fire in the center of the clearing, wet with the night's rain. Who came here? Did Ramón?

I started across the clearing, toward the ruin. Suddenly the jungle stopped.

The cicada hiss stopped. The high-pitched cacophony of the birds and the insects, the chatter and hum that fills the heat and throbs in the heavy atmosphere of the Amazon, ceased, suddenly, and the last sound was the squish of my footfall before I stopped, and listened to the silence.

October 26

Sitting on the sand by the lagoon. Late afternoon, watching these two ducks cleave the surface. At the far shore they feed, rolling forward, tail to the sky, then back, shaking the water from their heads, working their bills.

Paradisiacal place. The jungle is simmering all around.

Sh-sh-sh-sh, sssss.

I can close my eyes and lose myself in the sound, open them on this little body of water that has become for me a symbol. I have mythologized this place, sanctified it in my imagination and it has become for me a place of power, somewhat sacred. Magical things have happened here; it exists in my mind—a place to come to in the twilight. A landscape of my imagination, my consciousness? But I am here now. Really here.

A rational construct.

I am here, writing.

A conceptual construct.

But I really am here, now.

As I write this.

I can exist here for a moment, realize that I am here, write that I am here, thus the writing of it represents reality twice removed.

There is a point to be made here and it has something to do with the difference between book-read philosophy that we understand with our thinking minds and applied philosophy—direct experience. The experience of the abstract happens in a different place. Perhaps because experience involves the whole brain, the whole body, the whole consciousness and not just that part, that fraction that we use to think.

So who has the direct experience? The elite? The men and women moved to go forth and touch the mystery become the subject of myth and religion and through them the mass of humanity experiences spirit vicariously. The heros. Difference between experience and faith.

Sure. And, though Buddha and Christ, Mohammed and Black Elk may all have touched the Divine, experienced power and loosed themselves in the stream of consciousness that informs all life, the commonality of their experience has been lost in the telling or, rather, the enforcement of the telling, and experiences and knowledge that should unite all humanity have divided the world because a common experience has been told in different ways.

Sacred places.

There is a place in the jungle. An hour from here. Something chilled me there. Something. . . .

I'll go back there, though the thought scares me. Fear. That's what I've come for. I think I'll

"Have you eaten?"

I had not heard him approach, but he was by my side. He sat beside me in the sand. I closed my journal and said no. He nodded, stared across the lagoon.

"You are welcome here," he said.

"Thank you," I said. "I was not certain. . . ."

He shook his head. "They . . ." he looked to the south, "do not see," he said slowly, "the Nature . . ." he looked into my eyes, ". . . of things."

Later

The *Nature* of *things*.

Ramón is a man of few words.

"There is an eagle following you."

I shifted on the sand, the better to face him.

"Yes," I said, "I . . . am sorry."

He frowned. "Sorry?"

"Your daughter. . . ."

He cocked his head and looked at me sideways. "She was honored," he said. He shook his head and almost smiled.

"Honored? But the eagle . . ." I stood up, my back to the lagoon. "You did not send the eagle?"

"No," he said simply.

"But I have been told, and . . . I *feel* that it is not mine."

"It isn't," he said. "It is from a man of great power. A man to the North. The one you have worked with."

"Antonio?"

He shrugged his shoulders and nodded his head at the simple fact.

"He told me that *you* had sent it!"

Ramón's eyes opened wide. He coughed out a laugh and shook his head as though to shake away the grin that was tugging at his mouth. He stood and walked away toward the brazier. He bent over to stir the embers, and it was the only time I ever saw him laugh. Doubled over, hands on his knees. It may have been the funniest thing he'd ever heard.

I spent the afternoon with Ramón, watching him prepare the *ayahuasca,* cut and mash plants and roots and vines.

"Go back to that place," he said, as the sun began to sink into the jungle.

"What place?"

"Where you were."

"This morning?"

He nodded.

"What do I do there?"

"Sit." He poured the broth from the hanging pot into a wooden bowl, and I followed him to the hollow *chihuahuaco* tree. He placed the yagé inside. "Prepare yourself. Summon your power. We will take the *yagé* tomorrow night. Come back when you are ready."

How vivid are the sensations of that night. Retracing my steps along the river bank and through the water and along the path when the sun had set and the jungle play of shadows had resolved itself into darkness. Eyes adjusting, stepping into that tiny clearing before the ruin, a looming blackness, for the moon was not yet high.

Surrounded by the fear I had felt in the daylight, returning to it in the night. Sixth-sense fear as heavy as the air in which it lived. I remember sniffing the back of my hand, my forearm, its hair matted smooth with sweat. Was I smelling the fear? The jungle noise was its nocturnal self, the sounds distinct, *vibrato, staccato,* the long treble hiss. The only thing between me and the darkness and whatever lived in it were the clothes that I wore.

I lost the fear by giving myself to it, offering myself to it, tearing off my clothes, clumsily, hands shaking, and . . .

What am I doing?

Standing alone and naked in the middle of the Amazon. Trembling in the heat, defenseless in the claustrophobic darkness, the smell of my fear, sweat, stench of mosquito repellent, radiating out from the clearing.

But the foolishness that I felt, that peculiar brand of humiliation, was, I think, a symptom of my fear: something to feel instead. My eyes darted here and there. The moon was on the rise, and I began to see things in the periphery of my vision, different shades of darkness.

I sat on my shirt and closed my eyes and meditated on the sounds, trying to separate the birds from the insects, far-off shrieking from nearby cicadas. . . .

If you stare at a violinist in a symphony orchestra, you can almost separate the sound of that particular instrument from the rest, so I breathed from my stomach and conjured up images, visualizations of the creatures of the jungle, focused on their sounds, the tick-tick-tick of a hard-shelled horned beetle, the chuckle and cluck of a giant macaw somewhere . . . far off . . . and there was the *plap* of a drop of water on a broad, waxy, green, elephant ear palm. . . . Filter out the sounds, hear how the rest dissipate in the darkness . . . silence themselves.

And there was my breathing. The thudding of my heart. Quickening. The passing of leaves, vines, low to the ground.

I was moving. And breathing.

And I could smell myself beyond the moist tangle of the jungle.

Moving like a shadow.

Sitting, sweating, naked in the moonlight.

I slept there that night. Awoke and the memory of the cat, the memory of myself, brought me to my feet. I slipped into my trousers, tied my shirt around my waist, and followed the path to the river.

I cleansed myself in the water, followed the stream like an Ariadne thread, out of the maze of the jungle, back to Ramón's.

It begins with a sound.

I lay back on the sand, on a flat spot near the brazier, twenty feet from the water. The air was warm and moist. Mosquitoes whined near candle flames, the candles stuck in the sand. The smoke from Ramón's pipe hung over me in the humidity. Suffocating smoke married with the moisture in the air. Heavy.

I felt fine. I had spent the day fasting, sitting by the bend in the river, writing, reviewing, reliving the recent past. I had even stripped and cleansed my chakras in the water that flowed through the lagoon and around the bend, rubbed my body with leaves that Ramón said would keep the mosquitoes away.

I had taken stock of my thoughts and feelings. For each of them I had chosen an object: my clinical curiosity—Would this night's ritual replay the events of the first?—this was a triangle of paper torn from a page in my journal; the security I felt, my courage in facing the darkness and the jaguar of the night before, was a sharp sliver of wood; my expectations, my desire for an experience of transcendence, was a braid I fashioned from three strips of palm; my confidence that I would come back, that I would go beyond the moment of near-death and return to life, was a leaf with five points, like a hand. Each of these I placed in the stream, like offerings into a fire. I watched them float away. The open-palmed leaf touched the edge of the bank and turned, rotated a full 360 degrees, before disappearing around the bend.

Now, on the sand, I felt my potency, although my preparedness nagged at me. Must separate my desire to serve this ritual from the experience. Ramón had nodded satisfaction as he handed me the cup of *yagé*, and again as he blew the smoke over me. Had he felt my strength?

Looking up at the stars, I remembered the moment when the light met at the ceiling of Ramón's hut and fell, opening its jaws to me. That was a long time ago. How would this be different?

This? What?

Wait. I am waiting for it. The stars are in their place. The moon, so full, lights the clearing, as it should. Ramón has danced a circle in the sand and cleansed me with tobacco and we have smoked and I have taken the *ayahuasca* and all that I feel is the discomfort of an associative memory: the bitter aftertaste of the *yagé* and the memory of a nausea that I do not feel. This time. Stop comparing. Expecting. Investing the moment with anything but your presence.

Look at you! You're sitting up! Looking at Ramón as if to say, Is everything all right? What's happening to me? Is anything happening to me? Lie down. Lie back down. But Ramón's eyes . . . he is a sorcerer. Look at those eyes! He's not just a shaman, a master of the West, a gardener in this Eden. He is a trickster. He could do anything with me.

Do you know what I am thinking?

He nods, his head inclines forward, not a nod, he's looking. Down. The serpent beside the leg stretched out before me, my leg. The snake, dappled gray in the moonlight, opens its mouth between my legs.

It begins with a sound.

Like a cataract. Water rushing to the Earth. A great falls, roaring, water mistified. . . .

It takes both of my hands to grasp the snake below its jaws, forked tongue in midflick as it opens its pink membranous mouth. I know you.

All throat, all muscle, it works its way through my grip, scales sliding this way and that against my fingers and palms.

"Cannot conquer me the way you conquer women. Cannot subdue me the way you subdue yourself."

Back and forth the great head shifts through my grip. Back and forth to the song Ramón is singing. Snake charmer humming Satchamama, serpent, spirit of Lake Yarinacocha, protector of the garden, giver of the fruit of the tree of knowledge. Archetype, wrapped around my leg, sliding toward me, my trouser leg bunching up, pulled by its scales.

I let go and its head falls with a thud on my stomach, a sickening blow. Pass over me that I may cleanse myself of this foulness in my stomach.

Black-and-white jungle. Film noir. Moonlight wash. Ramón stops me at the edge of the trees.

"No. Here."

Follow the line from his finger to the sand, drop to my knees and vomit, roaring from the bottom of my stomach, a wide-mouth primal sound that echoes back from the wall of foliage, a hundred voices, screaming back at me, Ramón, blowing smoke at me, moving closer and filling me with his strength, body humming from the inside out, like a sonic vibration starting deep within, a green-and-violet hum.

And I stand and the jungle around me wavers wetly, sickeningly. The trees, the brush, the vines, the leaves, green now and luminous, liquify and run in rivulets into the lagoon.

Fluid jungle flowing into the sand, running in rivulets toward the lagoon, and I, standing witness, watching the waters until . . .

There was nothing but the lagoon, the water rising as the jungle ran into it. Water rising, at my ankles, warm and invigorating. I dipped my hand into its phosphorescence, and the water crystallized on my fingertips, sand drops falling, and I walked down, down into the desert beneath the water.

There, beneath the surface, the sky was a web, a holy architecture of stars connected by strands of crystalline light, a star at every crossing, every star an intersection of every strand, every star connected with every other, each a mirror reflecting the whole, the fabric of the universe, a three-dimensional filigree, and I knew that I traveled along that infinite pathway, every juncture an act of power, of choice, leading me to the next . . . all infinite possibilities.

Lost in it. Seduced. By this creature, this holy woman, this essential, sensual Madonna before me, her back to me now, clothed in a mantle of feathers with eyes, a thousand brown feathers, the feathers of an owl, flecked with silver, standing just beyond my reach, facing away, her head turning, slowly, face obscured by a veil made from this fabric in the sky. I reach out to pull it away, but my fingers brush the air an inch from her face.

"How many times must I call you to come to me, my son?"

Move! Nearer. She is still. Another step forward. Reach for it, but no, again, so close to seeing the face behind the veil, a face that is laughing with such sweet music that I am overcome by its joy and fall to my knees in the sand. Back into the sand and the web of the sky is broken, torn to shreds. Something is moving between me and it.

Again, the eagle, wings stretching, shrieking toward me out of the night, blotting out the architecture of the night, but for what? You're not a scavenger and this flesh is dead, cold. Lividity has set in and the blood has stopped flowing and seeks the lowest point, collects in the veins and arteries, and in the capillaries and cavities in my back, lying on my back, flesh mortifying, dead already, food for flies and condors, worms and ants. I'll be dismembered and carried away piece by piece now, so why do you bother and why do you fly away so swiftly?

I see the cat approaching; the eagle soars away, into the blackness.

I can have two thoughts at once, three. I can see an infinity of things concurrently, because time is like that sky, no beginning and no end, and every moment is a reflection of every other. And vision takes no time.

Where is *she*? And what was it that she said . . . ?

Rays of sunlight beam toward me, skewer the darkness, play an every-colored spectrum across the plain of the desert, piercing the night from a tunnel source on the treeless horizon and along their path, within the light, the jaguar walks so perfectly, so resolutely. Poetic fluidity, remorseless motion, so black that I cannot see its contours, its musculature beneath the shadow-black hair, but there! As the sun source at the tunnel's end catches it just right, the black hair glints, golden. Glistens.

She sniffs at me, at the mortified flesh that I am apart from, and, satisfied, turns back toward the light and I follow. We move together like we did before, as one, toward the source of the light. I turn and look back, moving forward, but we are too far along the tunnel, the desert is lost in a play of colors.

I will never return. The light is closing in behind me, and I know that I will never go back, that the moment of death has already passed. Passed without a whisper, never announced itself. Effortless. A revelation. That was death. Somewhere, back there. Did I?

Breathe out?

Die consciously?

Voices.

The chorus swells. It sings to me with one voice. The dead. The familiar. Here humanity speaks with one voice in many tongues.

Welcome.

Bliss.

There, there is the light. Bright, brighter, brightest. Blink? No reflex! That's funny. Not curious, funny. I cannot blink, for I have no eyes, and I would laugh at the thought, but I have no tongue, and my laughter is my last, ever last joy.

An exultation that starts within me and expands away. Fills the universe . . . spreading . . . inclusive of everything that ever . . .

I can see time. I can feel time, follow any pathway, ride the shock waves of this explosion whose center is the light.

Discover that the future is not ahead, and the past not behind. I never knew that. I thought that time. . . .

Was . . . what? Did I ever know?

Can't remember. Memory. Memory?

When was my last breath? When is it?

Lost. I am lost in far-off echoes of light.

Contracting now.

The echoes contract. From there to here. All that expands contracts, collapses.

And the Lady is there, in her mantle of feathers. Her head turns smoothly, a cat, an owl.

I will never forget her face, because I could never remember it afterward.

The eyes behind the veil. Pupils dilating . . . everything that expands . . . contracting, head falling back, open-mouthed in ecstatic birth.

She sighs and my heart aches, chest hurting.

Breathe.

Gasping as my face breaks the surface, lagoon water in my eyes. I inhale a scream. Take my first breath.

I don't remember what happened next.

I heard a scream. I awoke, chilled by the sound, listened to it resolve into a howl, a long howl that echoed distantly. I was in the moment fully. I knew that I had been traveling, that I spent the evening in ritual, and that I was awake, on my back, in the little thatched room where I would recover.

A stillness hung heavily in the night, the moisture suspended there, waiting to rain. Again. Far off. Excruciating. Echoing in the stillness. Beckoning in the dark. The jungle listened with me to the sound, not so very far off as I thought. . . .

I stood, naked, and moved quickly through the house. I went because I had to. I moved without thought, then stopped myself as I felt my toes dig into the sand outside, on the bank of the lagoon. Ramón's machete was in my right hand. That stopped me.

Was I dreaming? No.

There was Ramón, still smoking the pipe. His profile shadowed by a single candle in the sand, he was distantly aware of me.

Standing on the edge of the lagoon, facing the break in the trees that marked the path to the bend in the river. Fully conscious? My God, yes! In the moment and tuned to it. I looked down at my body, already glistening in the liquid air. My chest was heaving.

It was a cat, screaming in the night down that path, at the bend in the river. I knew it. I had known it all along. Then the air moved, shifted toward me in a gentle breeze before the rain, blowing the scent of the animal toward me. I smelled its musk. Sensed its scent and followed it into the jungle.

I moved in a half-crouch, swiftly along the path. Following the scent and the banshee wail. My turn now.

Stalking the cat. Does it know that there is a power stalking it?

Going to meet it. Going to kill it. Maybe. I did not know. I knew that nothing had ever been so important.

And I knew that my scent, the twentieth-century smell of me, was ahead and behind, and I felt the jungle recoil and grow tentative, holding its breath as I moved in something like silence toward the bend in the river.

Almost there, I left the path. The advantage was mine now. I stepped into the river, waded stealthily through the water, leaving no footprints in the silt beneath the surface.

It was there, on the silver sand, screaming, stretching, writhing in an ecstasy of lust, black like ebony, side to side, howling, luxuriating in itself and the sand. Wailing. Moaning. It smelled like sex.

I don't know what it was doing. I know that I stood there, naked, knee deep in the river, Ramón's machete in my hand, heart beating furiously, blood rushing to my head. A cooler breeze brushed my back.

The wind had shifted.

The sky rumbled. Any second now. . . .

The jaguar thrashed on the sand, on its belly, all of a sudden standing, arch-backed, frozen in a low crouch, paws dug in, perfect stillness. Then its long tail twitched. Once. Twice. Reflex. Its eyes were yellow, wide, staring with perfect focus. Fifteen feet apart we stood, locked in each other's stare and reflected in each other's eyes.

I raised my hand, reaching out across the space that separated us. A tremor passed through the cat, rippling its fur from head to hindquarters. Its ears folded back.

Sand skitters across the water. The jaguar leaps, instant acceleration, sideways, pounces through the leaves and into the green darkness of the jungle. Gone.

Wait! Don't go. . . .

The breeze that blew my scent to it carries me through the water to the sand. I drop to my knees and touch the markings, the hollow place where its body was, the long gashes in the sand. Running my finger along the ridges in the sand, tiny grains falling along the slope, pushed along by my finger. Finger to my nose, I can smell it, its primal catness. Lean in, closer. My hands follows the marking, fingers digging deeply into the sand. . . .

The sky rumbles.

Stretch out. Flat on my belly. Lie in it. Roll in it, the sand scrubbing my chest, my loins, my back. I work my legs back and forth through the sand. I breathe in the smell, can't get enough of it. Not smelling, breathing. Fast. Faster. There is a stirring in my belly. Breathing so fast, breaths become short and urgent. Stephanie. . . .

She appears as a thought. I roll onto my back and close my eyes and draw my hands down my body, down the layer of sand sticking to it.

My breathing fills my head, and I am moving through the hallway. The cat, moving purposefully down the short hall, black-and-white night vision. I slink into the room unnoticed, smelling sweat and Stephanie, her short, urgent breaths.

Stephanie and. . . .

Stephanie grunts, sighs from her chest, heaves up against the man. I stop in my tracks, low to the ground, the Persian rug. Up! Silently. Treacherously. Up atop the chest of drawers. Looking down. The peach-colored sheets are twisted and bunched at the foot of the bed, and a pillow has fallen to the floor. Her lover's back is broad and hairless, and his head moves back and forth on a limp neck as he slides himself in and out of her. He is a stranger to me.

The rage surges through me, rage held dormant in my belly, rushes, rising through my chest, filling my head, stomach hollow now, but fluttering with adrenaline, body bristling. Upper lip twitches over teeth. I am deadly.

Kill him.

I can do it. I can gut them both, leave them lying together in each other's blood.

Swallow it. Wait. Down from the chest top to the rug, thudding front feet first on the Persian rug. Move slowly to the bedside.

Will I recognize you? With your face straining, tendons taut, lips drawn back from straight white teeth as you finish on top of her. Hair a mess, matted to the sweat on your forehead, you look stupid.

Will I remember you and the nausea in my belly? The hollowness of the fact of Stephanie's infidelity, the murderous rage that I swallow?

My cry is lost in the thundering rain.

Last image: Stephanie pushing him off her, sitting up in alarm.

"What is it?" he says.

She shakes her head.

"Nothing. It's . . . nothing."

But you know that isn't true.

15

This is an essential experience of any mystical realization. You die to your flesh and are born into your spirit. You identify yourself with the consciousness and life of which your body is but the vehicle. You die to the vehicle and become identified in your consciousness with that of which the vehicle is the carrier. That is the God.

—*Joseph Campbell*

Rain. Pouring into the river, pummeling the broadleafed jungle, cratering the sand with pockmarks. On my hands and knees, the rain beating on me. Sobbing.

There was a stranger in the clearing when I emerged, soaking wet, naked, wide-eyed and trembling. An Indian, a middle-aged man in a short-sleeved shirt and old jeans, a straw hat streaming with water, dragged a litter across the clearing toward the house. He froze at the sight of me, bent at the knees and eased the litter to the sand and crossed himself. The litter was covered with banana palm leaves shining waxy in the rain.

Ramón appeared on the wooden veranda. He looked at me and then stepped down onto the sand and into the rain and went to the man. They spoke for a moment, and Ramón helped him carry the litter inside. At the door he looked back at me, nodded sideways, and I followed, went to my room, put on a pair of shorts.

October 28

It is early morning. Sun's not up, dark gray. The rain has stopped. Ramón has stopped the rain?

Will I believe any of this when I read it?

My head is clear, perceptions sharp-edged. I am sitting on the edge of the veranda, feet on the sand.

I should be asleep. I should be dead, but I have never felt more alive. Tuned to the moment, sensitive to the subtleties of the morning.

I know that I am coming off the *ayahuasca,* know it because nothing that happened last night seems as important as the drama that I am witnessing as I write this.

There is an Indian here with a young boy, I assume his son. Ten years old, I guess. The boy has been bitten by a snake, a jungle viper. He is unconscious and feverish. Ramón has built a fire on the sand and the boy is stretched out, naked on the litter that his father used to get him here from who knows where.

Ramón is working on him, kneeling beside the boy, beside the fire, working on his spirit, working with his hands before him and above the child, lifting the air, disengaging the boy's energy body from the physical, raising it before him.

How do I describe this?

He started with smoke, blowing smoke into the boy's chakras, humming into them, then lifting the spirit from the body. Now he is healing it. I have never seen Ramón like this. His face is drawn and placid. His concentration is trancelike as his hands trace the outline of the spirit body before him.

Now his palm touches the boy's forehead. He makes a fist and draws it down the length of the boy's body. More smoke from the pipe.

He speaks to the father, who stands stupefied and fearful beside him. The anxious parent. Again he says something and his tone is sharp. The man snaps out of his distraction and tries to untie the knot in a dirty cloth drawstring bag. Ramón snatches the bag from him and opens it. He reaches in and withdraws the snake, four feet long and speckled. It is dead. Its head deformed, bloody and torn by repeated blows.

He carries the snake to the edge of the jungle and kneels in the sand, laying the serpent's body out before him. He heals the snake.

Drawing his hands down its length, flicking his wrists toward the trees, making a sharp *whoosh* sound with his mouth. He handles the body with reverence.

A sacred object.

At the boy's side again, Ramón slices off the head of the snake with a long knife. I think I left his machete downriver.

He presses it, the head, to the boy's leg. He binds it there with a strip of palm, a leaf, another strip of palm. He leans close and whispers into the boy's ear and the patient groans.

I am in another world. I have done what I came to do and discovered that there is more to be done. A lifetime's work ahead of me.

I slept that day and through the night. It was the blackest sleep I have ever known. A dreamless void. Curious how I give myself so fearlessly to sleep, free my consciousness from the concerns of living, abandon myself to something like death, allow my body to lay dormant and my mind to wander. In any case I lost a day and a night. I remember nothing but waking.

The boy was recovering. His fever had broken and he was eating. His father told me that the bite was usually fatal, that don Ramón was a sorcerer.

I have every reason to believe that the boy recovered, that he and the creature that had almost killed him had both been healed, that some kind of balance had been effected, that Ramón had set things right with Nature.

But who knows? How can you test such things?

I returned to Cuzco the next day.

October 30
Airborne

Heading for Cuzco. I am seized by the anxiety that comes with discovery. Close to understanding something fundamental, wary of collapsing my *feelings* into an intellectual construct. A neat package.

Looking down from this height at the jungle below, feeling my kinship to this place, to all of it, to the essential power of Nature.

In facing death I know that I experienced the death also of my rational consciousness, the death of ego and logic. Things can never be the same again. . . .

Should I say a few words over this corpse before consigning it to the sea? This body that I left, lying in the sand in that desert at the bottom of the lagoon, covered by a pall woven from a fabric in the sky. Burn it on a funeral pyre, bury it, no matter, nothing will be lost because it's just a form of energy, an interpretation of consciousness that served a purpose for a time. I'm babbling. Don't give a shit, because I'm thrilling with the force of this new awareness. Feel like a child. Dead to the flesh, born into the world of spirit, an infant.

The jungle slides away to the southwest below me. This is where evolution began and begins, a continuum. The Garden was not kicked out from under us. We left it, turned our backs on it. Cut the umbilical cord.

I can't write fast enough.

Organize. Understand as best you can, because what you have experienced must be translated. Made understandable.

Early man. Limbic and reptilian brained, living in an animistic environment, inseparable from the trees, the rocks, the animals, the sunshine. There was no distinction—his brain was *incapable* of *making* a distinction between himself and the rest. There was no duality, no subject/object evaluation. No this and that. The Earth was a garden of timeless unity, because none could *experience* it as otherwise. One with Nature, literally.

Then, the neocortex. Self-reflexive consciousness, the ability to experience awareness itself. Reason. I and thou. Duality comes in, distinctions of this and that, subject, object.

Man could separate himself from Nature, set himself apart from the plants and the animals, evaluate his *experience* of Nature's influence. Self-reflexive.

We ate from the tree of the knowledge of good and bad and went East of Eden. We lost our connection to Nature. Lost a connection to ourselves as an integral part of Nature. Lost our connection with the Divine.

The Cartesian revolution: I think, therefore I am. Awareness shifts from experience to an intellectual construct of experience. Separation. A reasoning brain, a brain of language and definition, defended by thick walls of logic from visions we could not explain. Laws are conceived, written, programmed into the *tabula rasa* of the neocortex, laws to explain what we choose to see, myths and religions to turn to for guidance and answers to the unanswerable.

Did we simply lose our vision? Lose our ability to access the Divine within Nature, within ourselves?

Here we are, Westerners, born with the burden of a disconnection from God, our destiny fixed in an ever-burgeoning quest for facts, answers, a logical framework in which to place them. We have limited the dimensions of what it is to be human.

Yet, Nature abides. Below me, there in the jungle. Within me. I have been there.

If consciousness is energy, and our energy comes from the same source (that which casts no shadow), if we all come from the same biological ground, is it any wonder that there is a level of consciousness that is common to all things? That an individual can learn the skill of accessing these nonconscious realms, enter and engage with reality on a fundamental level?

Disengage the spirit body from the biological, heal it? Tap into the fucking source!

The energy that pours into the Earth from the Sun courses through me like the blood that flows through my veins from my mother and father.

The energy, the consciousness, the Divine.

This is the message of Christian myth.

The Buddhist creed.

The Cabala.

The Upanishads.

The underlying principle of myth and religion. Principles that I once understood, had faith in.

But faith is meaningless and the faces of God stand between us and the experience of the Divine.

I need to see Antonio, for I have begun to understand him.

I never saw Antonio.

It was Friday afternoon, and I was told that he had left early. He wasn't at home and I couldn't wait for him. I had to go back.

I flew to Lima and, as the Miami-bound plane left the runway, I tried to remember our last moment together. Our return from the *altiplano*. In front of my hotel. It was late and I was headed for the reception desk, the phone, to make a reservation on the morning flight to Pucellpa. We were going to meet at the airport. He hadn't come.

In front of the hotel, he'd placed his hand on my shoulder as he had countless times.

And he had said goodbye.

North

16

Can you experience power and not lose yourself in the process?
—Antonio Morales Baca

Years passed. 1975 to 1979.

I stepped back into my world and surrendered myself to its concerns.

Oh yes. Fresh from the jungle I confronted Stephanie with her infidelity and we had a scene. It was more than she could bear. I remember how mystical and self-righteous I was. Her indignant defense was seeded with references to my "psychedelic masturbation."

She moved to Los Angeles. She wrote to me later that year, after the publication of *Realms of Healing*. She congratulated me, suggested we see each other the next time I came south. I wrote back. We corresponded for a time, then lost track.

I understand that she is now practicing psychiatry at a Southern California university.

I received my degree, was able to add a Ph.D. to my last name, and thought I detected something like deference from headwaiters, airline reservation clerks, credit organizations.

Realms of Healing was well reviewed, well received, well read. It went through five or six printings, and shoved me into the limelight of the human potential movement of the late 1970s.

I met my first wife quite by accident. It seems as though serendipity always follows the "once upon a time" that starts the myth of romantic love. She was a psychologist, the author of a best-selling, groundbreaking book on female sexuality. She was beautiful, brilliant, pragmatic, challenged my intellectual and emotional maturity to within an inch of its life, and we stumbled into love with each other.

I fell for her.

We set up house together, a house stuck to the side of a mountain in Marin County, California, across the Golden Gate Bridge from San Francisco.

She wrote another best-seller. I worked at my private practice and accepted all speaking engagements in order to pay back the accumulated student loans that I had been living and traveling on for years.

And I taught, tried to translate what I knew. I accepted a professorship at San Francisco State University, developed a transcultural psychology course, theorized, conceptualized, brought my theories and concepts into the laboratory.

With great success. My classes were eclectic and popular for that reason, at least. The Biological Self-Regulation Laboratory I founded was a testing ground, a brain/body interface playpen.

My experiences "in the field" were essentially visceral. By this I mean that the seat of the experience was deep within me, in my gut, systemic, emotional, rather than intellectual, of the head. And yet upon my return, I found that the experiences that I held so dear, like a pregnant woman holding her belly, rose to my head. What had been a living thing deep within my consciousness lost its life as it became an intellectual construct.

Like Pythagoras.

Let me explain. There is music: deep, vibrant harmonies of Nature. What can it be compared to? Music and its effect on us is, like love, a mystery that collapses once it is solved. In one of the greatest triumphs of neocortical thinking, the Greek philosopher discovered that music contained a structure and form that was perfectly logical and could be described mathematically. Yet his formulas could not move anyone to tears or laughter, stimulate one from within.

And I felt like a hero. The protagonist of myth, returned to fulfill his social responsibility.

Joseph Campbell, preeminent scholar, authority on mythology, once defined the two types of heroic deeds. One, he said, is the physical deed, in which the hero performs a courageous act in battle or saves a life. The other kind is the spiritual deed, in which the hero learns to experience the supernormal range of human life and then comes back with a message

My anxiety to form a message based upon my experiences consumed me.

I used the cutting edge of brain research to slice through my experiences. Nobody tried to stop me.

I began to reason. My reasoning went something like this:

The human mind has the ability to create any imaginable neuroelectrical configuration, yet it does not innately know how to do this. The neocortex is a clean slate, a *tabula rasa*. The skill of programming the thinking brain is not instinctual, it is learned (instinct lives in the limbic and reptilian systems). Biofeedback laboratories have demonstrated that the celebrated feats of yogis, from controlling pain to walking on red hot coals, can be developed in anyone. The self-organizing, self-programming capabilities of the human brain are awe inspiring, and the implications for self-healing and personal transformation are staggering.

Primitive ritual is a formula, a recipe that conveys information to the neocortex, information encoded in symbolic dance, music, visual stimuli, to which the limbic brain responds, information that instructs the regulatory centers of the reptilian brain to accelerate otherwise normal healing processes. The circuitry of the neocortex is thus imprinted with a set of healing instructions that then can be verbally and symbolically communicated to accelerate healing in ourselves and perhaps in others.

Although access to the visionary centers of the limbic brain has been denied by the rational, theoretically oriented neocortex, they can be reached through ritual. The self-reflexive brain, which controls and evaluates waking awareness and limits it to a fraction of what the mind is experiencing at any given moment, can be programmed to access the unconscious. Programmed by experience. Psychotropic substances such as San Pedro and *ayahuasca* provide shortcuts to accessing those centers of consciousness, lay down a pathway that later can be followed in an ordinary waking state. The existence in the brain of biochemical receptor sites for the mescalines, harmalines, and harmolamines, the psychoactive complexes of these plant preparations, can infer that the brain is capable of producing such chemicals naturally *once it is programmed to do so.*

Finally, the frontal lobes of the neocortex have opened up a new faculty of visionary foresight as well as a testing ground for Einsteinian and quantum mechanical concepts of relativistic time and space. Time could be perceived as flexible, and space as something without boundaries. Previously these qualities had developed in rare individuals, spontaneously, often against their wills.

When the neocortically deficient Neanderthals were on their way to extinction 50,000 years ago, *Homo Sapiens* were left to carry the torch of evolution. The neocortex that set them apart from their ancestors would evolve, eventually develop the necessary neural tracks that would allow it to become fully functional and to navigate the course of human events. The individuals that developed such neurological connections, whether by practice or accident, were the oddities and geniuses of their time, the saints and soothsayers, the miracle workers. The experience of the sublime has been the exclusive domain of prophets and mystics, revered and persecuted throughout history.

The neocortex is still evolving, its circuitry is still forming. We must learn to harness its power to create psychosomatic health. And the isolated visionary will become a thing of the past.

I spoke of such things in the classroom, tested trance states in the lab. The cathartic transformations that I had experienced in the context of ritual and altered states, the healings that I had witnessed from Mexico to Brazil and Peru, had far surpassed the end-product expectations of Western psychological therapy and confounded my understanding of medicine. In every case the common denominator was the state of mind, the one mind, of the shaman and the subject, the healer and the patient.

In the classroom I presented the idea of the individual who, through specific training, familiarized himself or herself with the multiple states of consciousness latent in the human mind, learned how to tune these states, to resonate to the harmonies of Nature, to transcend linear time and three-dimensional space, to mobilize the body's self-healing mechanisms and choreograph such states and mechanisms in others.

The process of interpreting these concepts into discursive prose frustrated me. My work in the laboratory, although successful, was met with polite interest. All of it, a curiosity. But that was fine. What wasn't fine was the nature of my preoccupation.

My last experience in the jungle had swept me away, had pulled me under, down into profound depths of perception, the full-body, kinesthetic perceptions of the "man who has already died." I had experienced a full-blown release from the constraints of thought and reason, from the boundaries of my learning. I had gone beyond the limits of precedent, surpassed all previous experience of myself, had identified myself with an energy, a form (cat? nature? body? call it anything but that which I left on that lagoon's desert floor). And in that form I had traveled an odyssey through time and space, had stepped into the light, had even glimpsed the face of the Lady of myth, the "veiled lady" who was said to lead one into the *nagual,* the transcendent.

I had made my way along the Medicine Wheel. I had sloughed off my past, confronted fear and death. I stood fully in my present, full of myself and dreams of the future.

> *March 24, 1976*
> *Home*
>
> The past is not immutable and death is no end, so let us craft our future, forge an image of the new century, visualize, conceptualize, capture its essence, as it were, in a yarn painting, a sand painting, a spirit catcher, an architecture of light.

I was driven. Not by desire or fear, but by responsibility and anxiety. Had Antonio been near me, he would have warned me that, once again, I was premature.

I would conceive and edit a book, *Millennium: Glimpses into the Twenty-First Century,* a view of the future according to eighteen of the world's most imaginative and visionary scientists and philosophers. I would find a curious dissonance between the authors' dreams and their words, between the content of our interviews and the chapters they delivered.

I would become obsessed with translating shamanic myths and models of the mind in the classroom and producing measurable biochemical and physiological responses to heightened states in the laboratory.

> *May 11*
> *Home*
>
> What is the nature of the ecstatic state, the out-of-body state, the healing state? What were the mechanisms that divided our consciousness into a waking state and a dream state separated by the veil of sleep? How did mind evolve? Further, now that I am convinced that we can engage with it consciously, where and how shall we lead ourselves into the future?
>
> We have irrevocably altered the process of natural selection. Survival of the fittest is no longer the rule of evolution for our species. The triumph of rational Western neocortical thought is nowhere

better evidenced than in the achievements of Western medicine. Science has arm wrestled with Nature and . . . won? Well, we've demonstrated that we can conquer infant mortality and support the genetically weak, the disabled and mentally ill, overridden Nature's prime rule of evolution by saving the lives of those who would otherwise perish. And there is no turning back, short of cataclysm.

The human experience is not on a seventy-two-year clock. God, I know that now. Death is no end to individual consciousness, and the species must stop making bottom-line decisions based on a short-term rental of this space. We're shitting in our own nest. If what I know is immortality, then, yes, we have no choice but to become caretakers of the Earth. I understand that now.

Write a book, *Futuremind*. Research origins of mind. Trace evolution of consciousness and extrapolate.

And on. And on.

Yes, when all conceptions of space and time, life and death, are exploded, when the grip of the past and the fear of the future are, themselves, conditions of one's past, then does one live in the present fully.

But I did not know how.

The present is immeasurable, splitting time and space, dividing past and future. And yet I felt as though my present was expanding, and I began to fill it with frustration. I began work on *Futuremind*.

In *Realms of Healing* professional discretion had required me to qualify the experiences I related in support of the concepts presented. I had been cautious in presenting a subjective view of incidents that, according to medical science, were objectively insupportable. In *Futuremind* I wanted to avoid such qualifications by presenting a rational evolutionary model of consciousness and reasonable hypotheses regarding the capabilities and potentialities of the human mind as the species quantum leap-frogged toward the future. I began at the beginning of time and took it step by step. It was an enormous undertaking, a project that could consume its creator, yet at that time it was but another fragment, a shard of incidental experience in an increasingly fractured present. I taught, worked in the laboratory, spoke at conferences, wrote, served on committees, invested in business interests in the name of hobby, tried to remodel the nest I was making with my wife, refused to surrender myself to my love for her, found weakness instead of strength.

Antonio had once told me that I was in a delicate position: trapped between two worlds, teetering on a fulcrum, easily toppled. That, too, I came to understand.

My thinking and activity became increasingly baroque. My wife wrote another best-seller, and I whipped myself into a frenzy of activity. Our home became an office. The distance between us was stretched by financial issues, competition, insecurity, dependency. I began to lose my balance.

November 4, 1977

Second week. Hepatitis. *Hepa:* "liver." *Titis:* "inflamed." Red, swollen, angry. Second week in bed. Second week of feverish exhaustion, bilious nausea, skin like fish fat left in the sun to yellow, orange piss and gray diarrhea. Second week staring out of the window from bed, watching the houseplants grow.

Heal myself? I don't have the energy or inclination.

My dreams are gray too. Gray and undefined. Amorphous shapes that are terrible somehow and move with an intentional lack of purpose. . . .

Adultery is not the only form of infidelity. All adulterers are infidels, but not all infidels are adulterers. I am both. So is she. I love her, but the love ebbs and flows. It's a tidal love. For both of us. Slack water now. I am in agony.

November 7

Dream. Of sand. Dirty sand. Like a high-water mark on a beach, all the refuse combed there. My body, torn and bloated there.

The part of me that is in Peru.

Walking to the bathroom today, stopped by the window and looked across the bay to the city. Place of the thinking mind. The place we built when we left the Garden. The lines are straight, the angles precise. Artificial environment. Second Nature. Where is the power? In money and representations of wealth. Power objects jingling in pockets, loose change. Balance is defined as the amount of money in a savings account.

In Peru I could not move through the jungle without the jungle stopping and listening to me, sensing me and my foreign presence. Alien, because I am a creature of this second Nature. This is where I function and I am not functional even here. Now. Now after all my time seeking knowledge, being used by clever craftsmen of suggestion, hucksters of mysticism.

Was I not the subject of their primitive sorcery? Like the audience member at a magic show? The volunteer who leaves his seat and stands onstage and submits to hypnosis? Bark like a dog. Submit to humiliation, see what I can do to you? I will hypnotize you and, in return, you will leave a morsel of dignity and a chunk of humility on this stage.

What sweet revenge on the white man! You wish to learn our secrets and traditions? You wish to poke and pry and search for whatever you left us from our past? Yes! We will share it with you. We will carve open your vision, show you the folly of your ways, teach you to build a fire that will illuminate the ghosts of your past, show you what death is, and you will leave your body here for us and return to your place, confounded, schizophrenic, because civilization is unable to support a mind free from thought. You cut the umbilical cord to Mother Earth, and it has shriveled and scabbed there in the dry, dusty places you have built. The place where the clock has been ticking for thousands of years, marking the time since you left the garden.

The joke is on me.

I came to believe this. As fervidly as I believed in the validity of my experiences, the traditions that I brought back with me, the love I felt for my wife, I believed that I had been the victim of Maximo's trickery, Anita's self-effacing sensitivity, Ramón's sorcery. Antonio's premeditated friendship.

December 11, 1978

Psychological DTs.

Dream. The Eagle. Older than it was years ago. It soared up, over the crest of a hill, hovered there, wing feathertips fluttering, carried aloft by an updraft, then I remember it above me, legs spread, talons clutching my shoulders left and right, pecking at my head.

The thought of returning to Peru is festering inside of me.

Two faced, twin souled, split apart. Professionally in demand, cannot fulfill demands on myself.

There is a tradition among the practitioners of Quimbanda, the black magicians of Brazil, that one's soul can be captured in a crystal, held there for eternity. I had glimpsed eternity, seen it reflected in the stars on the ceiling of the lagoon, and I knew that a part of me was captive there.

17

It is said that few complete this journey of initiation. . . . Many . . . stop along the way and are content to be healers and medicine people. They become masters of their own direction. And then there are those who become trapped by power. Lost along the way.

—*Antonio Morales Baca*

Professor Antonio Morales Baca had disappeared. Without a trace. Without leaving tracks. He had retired from the university. His old adobe house in the cul-de-sac near the tail of the jaguar that formed the urban plan of Cuzco had been rented by a Chilean businessman. There was no forwarding address. The clerk at the post office squinted at me and waved his hand as if to clear the air of my question. It was at the old Café Roma that I found myself watching the coffee seep crystal by crystal into the mound of sugar on my spoon, and thought of Dr. Barrera.

I found his clinic a short block from the Plaza de Armas, ended up thumbing through a ten-year-old *National Geographic* in his waiting room. It did not matter that I merely wanted a word with him. The Indian woman with the poncho-wrapped infant, the *campesino* with the gauze-covered eye, the varicose-veined Spanish matron, and the little boy with the urine specimen in the jelly jar were there ahead of me. I waited my turn.

"Professor Morales?" The good doctor arched his brows and leaned back in his leather chair. He was heavier than I remembered.

"Yes," I said. "I was a friend of his, as, I recall, were you."

"And I still am," he said. He frowned. "Did we meet? You and I?"

"Not really. We passed each other in his doorway. Years ago."

Barrera reached out and slid a gold pen across his desk and up against the edge of a prescription pad. He folded his arms across his chest, then reached up and ran a thumbnail along his little grizzled pencil mustache.

"He is gone," he said.

I nodded. "Do you know where?"

He shook his head. "I am sad to say, no."

I nodded again, looked down at the floor. "Did he say goodbye?" I lifted my gaze from the black-and-white checkered linoleum. There was a long, considered silence.

"Yes," he said.

And that was all.

January 3, 1979

Son of a bitch if Antonio hasn't died.

That I question his motives, the purity of his purpose and the authenticity of our relationship is bad enough. The thought that I will never know fills me with rage. That I cannot see him again, am cheated out of confronting him—My God! What have I done to myself that my feelings are so self-satisfaction-centered. But it would be like him to leave me with this eagle at my back, a torn heart and agonized conscience. Like the son who never had the chance to . . .

If ever I needed to center myself, realign my Self with my nature, and summon my power to heal myself, it is now. But the poetry has been lost in the prose.

What has happened to me, that I lost my arrogance years ago in the *altiplano*, informed my innocence, exercised my power, and find myself overburdened with knowledge, stuck in this place between two worlds, losing myself in my concerns.

Where did I go wrong? Where did I lose the lightness, the magic?

If you see the Buddha on the road, kill him. For he is not the way. Do not make obeisance to him or what he represents. To bow before him is to lose yourself, to prostrate yourself before a graven image, a mask of God. So if you see the Buddha along the road, kill him.

Antonio. Have you saved me the trouble? Taken yourself away? My despair is perfect.

Am going to see Ramón.

The plane to Pucallpa was delayed. I sat in the airport and allowed the misery to turn in my stomach. I sat with my butt on the tiles and my back to the wall. Sat next to my Brazilian leather duffel bag and my soft cloth, leather-trimmed shoulder bag. There was a man across from me, a thin man with a sunburned, freckled face. He wore cotton pants and a wrinkled safari shirt. Beside him, on the next fiber-plastic chair, was a frame backpack with lots of convenient outer pockets and leather straps. He had been there for an hour, and I had watched him check his ticket and his watch, smoke two cigarettes, crumple up an empty pack, and peel the cellophane from another. For the past half hour he had been writing in a clothbound journal. Writing without thinking too hard, which I appreciated. He clicked back the ballpoint, stuck the pen in one of four shirt pockets, pulled a thick rubber band off his wrist, snapped it around the journal, and harnessed the book under the flap and strap of his pack.

He had a light blue aura. Turquoise, actually.

My eyes snapped back to normal. Why had I looked? I had not thought to. There had been a time when I was accustomed to looking. Once I had even opted to change planes for a psychology conference in Monte Carlo because the passengers' energy was curiously dim, vague, close to their bodies. (The plane developed engine trouble and made an unscheduled landing). So it was curious that I looked now, without meaning to.

He withdrew a pair of rimless glasses from another shirt pocket and looped the loops over his ears and squinted at me for what must have been the fourth or fifth time.

I nodded and squeezed out a smile.

"Pucallpa?" he asked.

"Mmm-hmm."

"Me too."

I looked at his oversized frame pack. "Engineer?" I asked.

He shook his head and grinned.

"Oil," I said.

"Nope."

"You're not a rancher. . . ." The memory of the barman at the Pucallpa airport brought up a laugh. He just looked at me.

"Anthropologist," he said.

I held his gaze for a couple of seconds.

"I know you," he said.

And he did. He had attended a symposium on holistic health at UCLA, where he was on the faculty. I had spoken on shamanism. He knew my work.

"The damnedest thing!" he said. "I've been on the coast, Temple of the Sun. I met Eduardo Calderon."

The name meant nothing to me.

"A shaman/healer in Trujillo," he continued. "An amazing man. I would have spent more time with him, but I wanted to get to the jungle . . ."

"Don Ramón Silva?" I asked.

His blonde eyebrows arched. "Yes!" He frowned. "How did you know?"

I shrugged. Realized that I would not be seeing Ramón now. And that I did not particularly care. . . .

"I think Eduardo's expecting you," he said.

I looked hard at him. Then soft. The blue was bluer, brighter, excited. I sensed something else. It could have been a wolf: fidelity, intelligence . . .

He continued:

"He didn't use your name, just described you to me, asked if I knew such a man. I said no, but seeing you here . . . it must be you. Don't you think?"

I stood. My heart might have been beating a little faster. I don't remember what I felt. I thanked him and we shook hands.

"Say hello to Ramón for me, will you?"

"I thought you were going to . . ."

"So did I," I said. "It's not important."

He looked confused. We had that in common.

"I don't know exactly where . . ."

"Kilometer sixty-four," I said. "Trans-Amazon highway, south. There's a path to the left." I squeezed his hand. "Stay on it," I said, and walked out into the sunshine.

I leaned against the wall for a few minutes, waved off a taxi driver, and breathed from my stomach. Then I went to the Aero Peru ticket window and bought a seat on the next plane to Trujillo.

How appropriate that Antonio had said goodbye, that I was prevented from seeing Ramón by the presence of that young American, that I should travel to the northern shore of Peru, where Eduardo Calderon waited for me.

Yes, the ability to see fate in history is a trick of hindsight, and hindsight is just another form of perception, and perception is the *leitmotiv* of my story. Serendipity, besides being one of the sweetest-sounding words in the English language, is a sign of well-being, an endorsement of the path of true choice.

Yet even though I felt the gentle prodding of the old ungloved hand of Nature, even though that aptitude called precognition played a part in our rendezvous, Eduardo Calderon was surprised to see me. He laughed so heartily as I stepped off the bus in Trujillo that I stood there, gripping my bag and grinning back at his laughter, smiling at the vague dizziness of déjà vu.

"*Compadre*," he said, and took my hand.

There is no word in English equivalent to *compadre* in this context. English is a language that has not yet found expression for intimacy. *Friend* has lost its meaning among so many definitions.

He stepped back from me and we looked at each other. If there is an archetypal shaman, a cross-cultural hybrid of a native healer, I imagine that Eduardo embodies the image. A Buddha's belly and smile, Asian Confucius eyes, a long, full, drooping mustache parted below flaring nostrils, straight black hair tied back with a leather thong and falling to the middle of his back. The laughing shaman.

He stopped laughing and his eyes described a circle around me, from head to foot and back. He shook his head and chuckled.

"You are surprised to see me?" I asked, still confounded by his heartiness.

"Yes!" It sounded like, What did you expect? "I am always surprised when a vision steps into my life. It is a happy thing. And I am surprised that you come with such darkness around you. We must attend to this."

January 5

Last night I submitted myself to don Eduardo's healing.

A circle of yellow cornmeal on the sand, a small pile of hay inside the circle. A sacred circle, the place of ritual and magic. Eduardo laid it out with the concentrated ease of a painter preparing his palette. He set out his *mesa* on a reddish brown woven cloth from the ruins of an Inca *huaca*, a power site. Two conch shells on either side of three fields: *ganadero, justiciero, medio*—dark, light, neutral (balance between light and dark). Stone figures, a deer's hoof, an Inca sling, fetishes, a whistle in the form of a pelican, crystals, ceramics. Two flat seashells. Power staffs stuck in the sand before the *mesa,* short swords, carved hardwood and bone staffs, nine altogether.

The sky was clear. A half-moon over the flat horizon of the Pacific. There was no breeze to disturb the neat little fire that burned in the sand before the *mesa,* but there was a sea air tang.

I stood erect and self-conscious in the circle of cornmeal, shoeless, stripped to the waist. In my left hand I held St. Michael's sword, the sword of fire, held it lightly by my side. Eduardo sat cross-legged behind the mesa. He took up his rattle, a stick with a soiled brown hollow gourd, the Earth spinning on its axis, and he shook it back and forth from the wrist. It sounded like *chee, chee, chee,* and he sang for my spirit to come and be present. He sang to the spirits of the Earth, air, fire, and water, called upon the spirits of the lakes, the lagoons, the mountains, and the forests.

I shifted the sword from left to right, and Eduardo approached the circle, rattle in one hand, a shell of alcohol, tobacco and sweet oils in the other. He drew the shell up my body, front and back, raising it through my energy centers, then lifted it to his nose, rested its lip above his mustache, and tilted back his head, drinking the mixture through his nose. Nasal cavity, proximity to hypothalamus, limbic brain—refills the shell and gives it to me, tells me to raise it along the blade of the sword, sword in my left hand again. My hand, holding the shell, began to tremble and I spilled some of the mixture on the sand, lifted it unsteadily to my nose, threw back my head, and it ran in, back along my cheeks and under my ears, and I felt my glottis close involuntarily as the mixture fired and choked my sinuses, and I opened the back of my throat and felt it go down and in and the feeling I felt had nothing to do with the potion, for it seized me in an instant. The trembling of my hands had worked its way up my arms and filled me from within.

I can recreate the events, document them like the psychojournalist I was once. I cannot write about the pain.

The anguish and rage that welled up and expelled itself in a scream. I fell to my knees in the circle and cried out my fury, struck my head, my forehead, with a white-knuckled fist, and I saw stars. I saw the forces gathered around us, looming just outside the circle of light, saw the form of the jaguar, mine, circling the perimeter, protecting me from . . . what? The negative forces waiting to claim me in my vulnerability? They were nameless, but I knew them somehow, sensed their intent, at one with the malevolence inside of me. On my knees, at their level . . .

Eduardo called my name. He made a fist around the handle of the rattle, and the sudden spasm shook the rattle once. *Poder*. Power. Strength. I stood, drew myself up slowly against the muscles that held me doubled over in the grip of something like tetany. And Eduardo captured my attention with his eyes, wide, peering with something like astonishment into mine. Then he looked to the horizon, and I followed his gaze to the dark line between the night and the sea, saw the plane of the ocean, the rippled surface that stretched from there to here, flash silver as lightning electrified the sky. Single veins of lightning from cloud to sea, and a cloud passed over the moon.

"*¡Fuego!*" Fire! He turned and lifted an ember from the fire and dropped it onto the hay at my feet. It smoldered, filled the circle with smoke, then caught. I remember looking down at my hand, the hand gripping the sword, and seeing the orange light of the fire playing across my skin, wet with sweat or sea air.

I felt the fire fill the circle, fill a space like a bell jar.

I stepped over the burning pyre, crossed it south to north, east to west, and back. I washed my hands and feet in the flames from the fire, cleansing myself in its flames, then barefoot, danced on the fire, crushing the flames that had singed away the darkness that had oozed from my pores. I stood there, staring down at the sand and my feet, blackened with the ashes of the burnt hay. Eduardo sat behind the *mesa,* arms folded. The cloud had passed by, the sky had begun to clear again, even to the horizon. In the light of the half-moon he looked at me, before me, around me.

He said:

That I had held much power.

That I was stuck in a relationship with a woman I did not know how to love.

That power and magic are neither white nor black, good nor bad, it was a question of intent and expression. Unable to express my power, it had turned black within me.

That I had hunted and been hunted by an eagle, and it had fed from me. He saw where it had torn at my liver, bloated with energy turned black.

Hepatitis.

He stood and came to me, took the sword from my hand, and, standing outside of the circle, passed the blade down my body, cutting away the connections to these things past, present no longer.

That I sever my connections with the past that created my ills.

That I may put to rest the spirits of the women in my life so that I need not seek similar relationships to finish the work of the old ones.

That the eagle which came from a powerful source in my past, the eagle that was also the spirit of the East, embrace me and lead me on my journey into the North—into the *feminine,* he said.

Then he held the sword to the sky, filled his mouth with clear water, blew a mouthful along the blade and to the South, then the West, the North and East. Then at me, to purify my cleansed self.

I hope so.

Something has begun. There is something moving inside of me. Moving me. I will follow its lead. For I know that it is I moving myself.

The story of my work with Eduardo has been told in outline many times, repeated symbolically step by step by many people over the past few years. It all began with that healing on the beach near Trujillo, although Eduardo would later claim that it had begun six months before, when he first saw me in a dream, when my presence began to intrude itself on his meditations. We had even traveled together in a dream, he said. We had journeyed to Machu Picchu and stood before the Pachamama stone and he had known then that together we would travel to the sacred places of legend, where the forces of Nature dwelled in the landscape of places sanctified by ritual for thousands of years. We would undertake the journey to the North together, as *compadres*.

Our journey would span years. Years that would see the dissolution of my marriage to my first wife, the abandonment of *Futuremind,* the writing and publication of *Healing States,* the marriages of six of his fourteen children. Years that would see us together in Europe and the United States, experimenting with the translation and transplantation of shamanic concepts into a new "psychology of the sacred."

The Medicine Wheel described to me so long ago by Antonio, embraced by Eduardo as the traditional map and commonsensical approach to the journey of the Four Winds, would be our guide. The sacred places of power that the legends spoke of would be our rest stops, our places of communion.

We would travel to the Giant Candelabra of Paracas, a six-hundred-foot-long, three-pronged tree of life carved into the side of a barren peninsula that rises from the waters of Paracas Bay, three hundred kilometers south of Lima. There, for centuries, shamans and seekers of knowledge had come to meditate for a vision, a transforming vision, to give meaning and purpose to their existence. There the eagle that had stalked me, preyed upon me for years, would fold me in its wings. Eduardo would see a condor, the giant condor that had been the power animal of his teacher, don Florentino Garcia, the keeper of the sacred lagoons of Las Huaringas.

From Paracas we would travel to the *altiplano* at Nazca, the high desert where it never rained, where unknown artists had broken through the reddish upper crust of the plateau to expose the pure white silica sand and thus carved gigantic figures of fish, reptiles, birds, mammals, human figures, and geometric shapes over an area of 350 square kilometers. There on this heavenly mesa, the "place of the power animals," we would take San Pedro, and Eduardo would watch the spirits of my past combust, burst into flame as I disappeared from sight, walking along the edge of a giant spiral in the sand. The work of the South. There we would consign our spirits to each other as *compadres,* as warriors of the heart.

And we would go to Machu Picchu. I would return to the ancient Inca City of Light. Eduardo would enter its gates for the first time. Together we would begin to discover its meaning.

18

The traveler follows the Dragon Path in the North to discover the wisdom of the ancients and to create union with the Divine.

—Antonio Morales Baca

April 29, 1979

The Death Stone. Again. I must commit to paper here the sweetness of a memory.

Have told Eduardo to go to the cave beneath the Temple of the Condor, outside of the ruins, the place where I performed my fire ceremony so many years ago. He is overwhelmed being here. Having visited it in dreams, Machu Picchu stands below and before him now in all its green-gray lichen-and-granite beauty. He is sort of breathless. Not the altitude. There is something ominous in the air. We both feel it and twice Eduardo has looked at me with a conspiratorial, childlike grin. "Do you feel the power, *compadre?*" I love him like a brother. An older brother, sometimes. That's a queer thing, considering that he is the Indian, certainly, a simple shaman/healer working matter of factly in the context of his community, yet with me he has found the opportunity and means to stretch himself, to live the drama of the legends that he learned from.

He has gone to prepare for his work of the West here, at the Death Stone. I need a few moments myself.

Now, sitting on the grass, the Death Stone before me, a perfect squat canoe of granite floating in a sea of grass and yellow wildflowers.

Antonio. A panoramic memory of standing here so many years ago, carrying my hubris, my Western preconceptions, and my skepticism in a backpack. Seeing the ruins of the Inca City of Light for the first time, dusk, like now, the mists of the Urubamba Valley rising up and over the edge of the precipice. Lying on the Death Stone, Antonio chanting over my chakras, his plaintive whistle, the rustling of the grass. It was here that we "put death on the agenda."

He told me that I would return to this place. That I would enter the city and begin to understand its secrets.

Where are you now? I don't feel your presence. And I miss you.

So here I am. I have shed my past anew in Nazca. The South. I will lie on the Death Stone again. The West.

Which way is North?

I closed my journal on my pen and slid it into my shoulder bag, sat there in the grass and wildflowers, breathed from my stomach, let the cool night air soothe my sunburned face.

An hour passed.

Lying in state on the Death Stone. Eduardo is chanting over me. The granite is cold on my bare shoulder blades and the small of my back. I listen as he pays our respects to the Four Winds, asks that my spirit be taken to the West, the regions of silence and death, blown there by the winds of the South, that it may return from the East, where the Sun rises, that I may be born in spirit as a child of the Sun.

He has had his turn here. I let instinct form my incantation, disengaged his chakras, stepped back, and waited. And I thought I saw something vaguely luminous, something that was Eduardo, but thinner, younger perhaps, disengage from his great belly rising and falling with each breath. I told him afterward that he was carrying too much weight, too much softness, with him. I have often sensed that his work of the South is incomplete, that he has reconciled himself with his past, his ancestry, but he is burdened by it still.

He told me that he felt himself going into the stone, felt a powerful fear in his belly, the claustrophobia of premature burial. Then he saw below him a light, far off, growing larger, coming nearer, and as he fell into its whiteness, I brought him back. He is impressed with my skill.

Now he is disengaging my chakras, touching my forehead, my neck, my heart. . . .

And I wonder, What is the difference between birth and death? Death, the light at the end of the tunnel, the birth canal, light at the end, the light of the world into which we are born. Perhaps, I think, the fear of death, beyond the associative fears of pain and loss, is a vestigial memory of the first fear, the fear of birth, the unknown at the end of the tunnel.

Breathing, regular heart rate, meditative. Wind rustling the grass. I open my eyes, smiling, turn my head to look at the figure at my side, standing over me, arms extended, palms down, a gold bracelet from which a feather hangs, an arm band of hammered gold. Breath catches, held high in my chest. The face: Incan, chiseled brown face framed by two feathers, earring ornaments piercing the dead ears of the jaguar headdress that covers his head and shoulders with black-furred catskin. I reach out impulsively to touch him, my hand passes through his arm, and his eyes, too black to see, open, and he turns away as I sit up, hang my legs over the side of the Death Stone, see Eduardo sitting cross-legged in the grass at the base of the stone, the stern end of this granite canoe.

"Eduardo!"

He blinks up at me, and I jerk my head in the direction of the jaguar priest, walking—moving, rather—down the hill toward the Gateway of the Sun, the entrance to the ruins.

It was after midnight when we entered the ruins of Machu Picchu. We lost sight of the apparition as it moved down the hill, and by the time we stood at the Gateway of the Sun, we may have been the only visible presences in the place.

We had specifically planned to spend the night of the full moon there, and its light cast shadows on the courtyards and glinted silver-gray on the edges of the fitted granite block walls.

I led the way to the Temple of the Condor, past tumbled-down walls revealing rooms open to the weed-grown stone pathway, into an open area, where three massive walls and a stone dais are all that is left of the Great Temple.

"There!" Eduardo nodded toward the central wall. "The place of the spirit flight."

We continued on, between the walls of the ball court, descended a short flight of steps to the right, and stood among the ruins of the Temple of the Condor, directly above the cave where I had once performed my work of the South.

There is a flat, smooth, vaguely triangular stone in the ground at our feet. The stone suggests a condor, a fanciful condor, its head turned back on itself, looking within, neck folded back from the collar at its throat, and I know that the ridges along its beak allowed blood to flow from the surface of the stone and into the space within the collar.

In one of the most spontaneous moments of my life, I withdrew a Swiss army knife from my pocket and cut a small slit in the tips of each of my middle fingers.

And I brought my hands together in the position of an inverted prayer, palms together, fingertips touching, pointing down, and the blood dripped from my fingers and onto the granite beak of the condor.

"What are you doing, *compadre?*"

I still don't know. Once a condor had appeared to me on a silver slip of sand by the lagoon behind Ramón's hut. It had surprised me, had surprised Ramón, and it had pecked the pieces of my dripping face from the grains of sand. It had fed on the mask that I had worn. Now, as the blood stained the gray granite beak, I knew that that condor was the same as the eagle that had taunted me for so many years, the spirit of the East, of vision, of Antonio, worrying me, challenging me to complete my journey.

And I realized something else in that moment. I realized that the work of the West is not only about giving yourself to death so that you can be claimed by life, but it is also about your willingness to give your life for something that you believe in.

I staunched the bleeding with my bandanna, and we climbed the steps and walked back into the courtyard where the Great Temple had stood.

"We can fly here," says Eduardo, and climbs up onto the dais, an enormous stone step protruding from the base of the central wall. He sits in an attitude of meditation, an Indian Buddha, head resting back against the water-stained granite blocks of the wall. I sit in the courtyard, facing him. The bleeding has stopped and I watch Eduardo closely, try to will myself into a sympathetic state, abandon the effort, and concentrate instead on centering myself.

Ten minutes pass and Eduardo is down from the stone, whispering to me. He has seen a figure, older than the Incas, a man in ceremonial feathers, a glowing golden breastplate over his heart.

"Here!" He moves to a spot between the wall and the place where I sat. "He stood here and pointed down." Eduardo places a hand on my shoulder. "I saw him from above, *compadre*. There is something buried here, I think it is a room. We must dig to discover what lies below." He taps his forehead.

I take my turn at the Temple of the Spirit Flight, boost myself up onto the stone and lie on the smooth granite bed, and feel Eduardo touch my forehead with his palm.

A sense of peace and relaxation settles over me, from my head down, as though my whole body sighs, oxygenated blood tingling through my veins. I exhale all tension and anxiety. I can lie here for a long time, no matter that I am in my body, that I see nothing but the blackness behind my eyelids, that I do not soar like an eagle, and it takes no effort to stop my mind from even these reflections.

I do not know how much time has passed, but I hear Eduardo.

"Good. Sit up now."

I sit up, step down from the stone, and cross the courtyard to where he stands, smiling, staring still at the dais.

"Well?"

His head turns, face still grinning foolishly, he looks at me and gestures toward the stone. I turn and look at my body, lying still on the stone. My face there smiles.

"Go back now."

And I opened my eyes on the stars, ghosts of clouds passing across the sky, the moonlit granite wall rising above me to the right. I jumped to the ground and Eduardo clapped his hands and our laughter echoed in the spaces between the maze of the walls of the citadel.

In the years that followed we would explore every corner of the Inca City of Light. I would hike the sixty-kilometer Inca Trail from the outskirts of Cuzco to the Gateway of the Sun, come to know the secrets of the Temple of the Waters and the Temple of the Serpents. Every chamber, angle, and nuance of the place would be known to me, and I would understand the Indian legends that speak of Machu Picchu as the doorway between the worlds, where the veil that separates us from our dreams and the stars becomes thinner, diaphanous, easily drawn aside. That night my footsteps led me north through the courtyard, to the edge of the city, where there was a stone rising out of a meadow.

I knew which way was North.

19

*What is god, what is not god, what is between man
and god, who shall say?*

—*Euripides*

The Pachamama Stone stands in a meadow at the edge of the ruins of Machu Picchu. Twenty feet long, ten high, an irregular, curved edge, smooth granite face, like a precision-cut cross-section of a boulder that grew from the soil of the field. Behind it and to the left, Huayna Picchu looms darkly, its peak a thousand feet above the ruins.

The full moon cast a shadow of the stone onto the meadow, a shadow of its other half. We stood in the grass at the edge of the irregular shadow of the stone, and Eduardo told me that there was a legend that told of an old medicine woman who lived within Huayna Picchu. The caretaker of the temple.

"Grandmother peak," I said.

"Yes," he said. "The Temple of the Moon. It is said that there are tunnels and labyrinths inside the mountain. It is the way into the *nagual*, into the North."

I stared at the speckled granite surface of the stone. It could play tricks on you with its gray-and-brown, black-and-white stone face. You could see things in it, but nothing more than you could see in any patterned surface if you looked hard enough.

"No," I said. "The way to the North is here . . . and here." I touched my belly and heart and remembered Anita, sitting across from me at the Café Roma, touching her pregnant belly. "All along, I imagined it was here." I tapped my forehead with the side of my forefinger. "But it's not."

And I realized that that was the trap: that our rationalization of things ephemeral, our intellectual framing of the transcendent, the thinking brain's version of the Divine, was just another mask of God. That all expressions of God, like the word itself, formed in the brain of language, were merely thoughts about that which is beyond thought.

No. *Before* thought.

Before consciousness itself. To speak the name of God is to name the unnameable, to carry a concept of the Divine within our heads is to carry a shield between us and the experience of the Divine. Jehovah. The "I am that I am." It cannot be thought about. All notions of God are blasphemies.

Things that can be known but not told.

April 30

I thought that the *nagual* would look like infinity.

I thought that I would experience the *ayin*, the divine nothingness spoken of in the cabala.

I thought I would look into the eyes of the Lady behind the veil and see the birth and death and destiny of the universe.

I thought there might be a blackness of such infinite hollowness that I might fall into it, into echoing bliss, and I was willing to risk never returning, losing myself in a self-transcendent flame-out (so maybe I *am* beyond fear).

I thought that in a grand way I might experience myself as God. . . .

"We should perform a *mesa*," Eduardo said.

"Later."

I stepped farther into the meadow, nearer the Pachamama, into the shadow, and sat down. I had no purpose. We had taken no San Pedro, had engaged in no ritual, save for those that had evolved spontaneously: the Death Stone, the Temple of the Spirit Flight. There was no anticipation to sensitize me to the moment. I just wanted to be there, at the doorway to the feminine, sit in a meadow that was somehow ideal. Ideal Earth, the gentle Earth, of which we are caretakers, the potential Earth, of which we are at once co-creators and stewards. I wanted to dream there for a time. I could sit there breathing until the Sun came up to wake me.

I open my eyes with that last thought, aroused, suddenly, by something that approaches me from the stone, stepping through every grass blade and weed stalk between me and the Pachamama.

"*Hija de la montaña* . . ." Eduardo, standing by a stone ledge, off to the right, hisses. "Daughter of the mountain . . ." standing over me now, in the moon shadow of the stone. Her eyes shining darkly down at me, a braid of perfectly black hair falling over her shoulder, beside her naked breast. An Indian maiden, her feet bare, sunk into the soil, like a double exposure, like my own legs, crossed before me, under the surface soil, among the roots of grass and weeds. I touch the soil, take a handful, and it sparkles, iridescent, glistening moist, and my loins are aching the dull, engorged ache of arousal.

"*Compadre* . . ."

She touches me with her hand, at my shoulder, pushes me back, on my back, chest deep in the soil of the meadow. She on her knees, over me, stretching out, laying over me, chest to chest, crotch to crotch, thigh to thigh, the Earth rocking gently beneath us, with us, shuddering with us, a series of orgasms, my groans, my sighs lost, muffled as she pulls my head down into the soil, and I understand something about the nature of sex, something of the male perversion of intercourse, of penetration: the gaining of power through conquest, when, in fact, the collapse of the duality of male and female is a doorway, a way back into the Garden. Something like that. And I think she whispers to me, "my son, my child, my lover, my brother."

I give myself to her, surrender myself to the aged crone that she is when she lifts herself from me, eye to eye, her face worn and wrinkled, the thin gray braid: the medicine woman from the *altiplano,* she who held my hand as El Viejo died. Her breasts sag like wrinkled pears, her lips stretch in a yellow-toothed smile, the corners of her glistening black, black eyes wrinkle, and she laughs and I draw her down to me, inside of me.

Strange that I feel no repulsion, stranger that as I surrender myself to her, she is once again blemishless, young and strong, the daughter of the jungle? Breathe in her humid scent, the Amazon?

Lover, sister, mother, crone. What metamorphosis is this? Do I change too? The heartbeat that I feel is within me, not mine, above and below, at once.

As am I. Where is my place? Are there two of me? Here in the meadow and here, beneath the ruins, seeing the city from the bottom up? Cradled by the Earth, the dirt and stone. Three of me, because there must be *another* me, the one thinking this thought.

A shuddering climax in the meadow, she pushes herself up from me and back. Legs straighten and she stands before me, Indian maiden, daughter of the mountain, walks away, toward the stone, stops there. She turns her crooked yellow medicine woman smile to me, a last look, and steps into the stone.

. . . But the North was none of these things that I thought.

Last night I fell into the Earth, returned to it, a prodigal son. I witnessed something that I will try to understand, then leave alone.

Time is not inflected by gravity in the center of the Earth.

Time lapsed.

And there was the I that lay in the meadow, dreaming.

The I that fell into the Earth saw it from the inside out, sensed its fertility, its pregnancy. Floating in space within the Earth, a prebirth experience in a rock-and-crystal–lined amniotic sac, feeling all the while that I knew what it was to be pregnant, to hold life forming within me.

And there were faces there. I saw them on the walls of the space that I inhabited, on the edges of my awareness, in the corners of perception. Faces ancient as the mountains and of the same stuff, earth, rock, volcanic wrinkles, liquid eyes, everywhere I looked, at every moment, within the moment, simultaneous, infinite exposures.

Was this the council of elders? The crystal cave of legend?

Another mind began to assign historical, religious significance to them, the Christ, the Buddha, undreamed-of faces that I knew, recognized, but could not identify. . . . Antonio? Don Jicaram?

"Antonio?"

The word is carried on a wave, a concentric wave, before me, and the rocks shift, the ice melts, water trickling along new crevices, features forming, replacing the old with the new, another face, and no! This mind is stuck in the past. The mind of graven images. I need not will myself to see and understand. Yes, I can see that other mind thinking now, as the shapes shift. Let go. I do not need to identify you to know you. All of you. I need not think here.

There are memories here in these faces, faces of the ancient ancestors. I cannot place them, need not place them, but will I remember?

Meanwhile, there were still stars above. The moon was steady in its orbit, moving across the Machu Picchu sky, the shadows were shifting, Eduardo was approaching, cautiously. . . .

And I wonder if I cannot claim the lineage of these men and women of the past. We are family, of course, because we come from the same place, share a heritage.

The Sun impregnates the Earth, and life is born of that union, the mating of Sun and Earth. The creative principle, single-cell consciousness.

It is the Nature of things.

I awoke this morning, cold and stiff at sunrise. Damp with morning dew soaking my shirt, clinging to the narrow weed stalks of the meadow. I slept in a fetal position, huddled against the cold of the night. Eduardo draped a poncho over me last night. I found Eduardo not far off, asleep in a corner of a thatched-roof stone hut fifty paces from the Pachamama Stone (which looks particularly cold and formidable in the light of day).

Thought awhile before waking him up.

The sun was not yet over the mountains to the east, and there was time to think before waking him, before the first rays of the morning touched the Inti Huatana.

I decided that I had fallen asleep and dreamed. Eleven thousand feet and we had been hiking all day yesterday and I had been overcome by the grandeur of this place and my own physical exhaustion. I decided that I had fallen asleep in the meadow and dreamed the maiden, the descent into the Earth, the walls of the space in the center of the Earth, my fractionated consciousness, my many minds, a kaleidoscope of ecstatic states. . . .

A dream.

And Eduardo had left me to dream, covered me with a poncho and left me there in the meadow, in the playing fields of sleep.

"You've been fucked by God, *compadre*." Eduardo's first words to me on waking.

Eduardo had stood on the edge of the clearing and witnessed my lovemaking with the maiden.

I tested him. The clinician to the last, I said nothing, just listened. His description of the Indian woman was correct to the final detail. He laughed at his own description of me copulating with the crone in the meadow before the stone.

He said that I had appeared to fall into a trance, *un ensueño*. He was afraid to approach, afraid to disturb my state. He sat nearby, on the edge of the clearing, and the night was alive with energies. Luminous figures, many with golden breastplates, hooded figures of men and women, white condors with ruffled necks, spiraling lights. In a reverie he had traveled to the top of Huayna Picchu, where, he said, there was a Temple of the Moon, long ago destroyed, walls, pillars, portals, existing as energy forms etched with geometric figures, and, at the entrance, a Sun framed by two half-moons shaped like cats: the marriage of the Sun and the Moon, masculine and feminine.

He had returned to the meadow, seen that I had fallen asleep, had covered me with a poncho.

We left the Pachamama and crossed the courtyard, climbed the steps to the Inti Huatana, the "hitching post of the Sun," where the Sun was tied by Inca priests on the occasion of the winter solstice.

As the Sun crested the mountains to the east and its first rays touched the stone, so did we touch our foreheads to the cool granite surface. And, in so doing, acknowledged the gifts of this place, made our obeisance to the spirits of those who lived here, died here, and the legacy of insight that these stones represented to those who came with purity of purpose and impeccable intent.

East

20

No theory is good except on condition that one uses it to go beyond.

—*André Gide*

I need not elaborate much on my years of work with Eduardo. As he had foreseen, we traveled together, laughed together, discovered together the places of power and how they lent themselves to the stages of the Medicine Wheel.

Although curiosity about non-Western healing, both physical and psychological, had drawn me to research and document healing traditions in Mexico, Brazil, and Peru, my experience had taught me something of the fundamental concept of shamanism: that changes in health cannot occur without changes in lifestyle. With time my interest in healing became an interest in personal transformation. It had become increasingly clear to me that the journey of the Four Winds, the path of the Medicine Wheel, was a journey into Eros, the feminine, the intuitive mind, the place of myth and dreams. Most of the human species was living under the dictatorship of logos, the patriarchal, rational mind of the last half of the second millennium.

The concept of a psychology of the sacred began to take shape, and, in 1983, I invited twelve individuals from five countries to join Eduardo and me on a journey of initiation, an introduction to the steps of power along the Medicine Wheel. We would travel, as Eduardo and I had, to Paracas Bay, to Nazca, to the Temple of the Sun and the Temple of the Moon near Trujillo, and to Machu Picchu. The extraordinary experiences shared by this cross-cultural "tribe" would form the basis of *Healing States* and a six-hour documentary film of the same name.

There is no specific formula for transformation within the shamanic tradition. There is the concept of the Medicine Wheel, the Journey of the Four Winds; but the lessons learned and skills acquired along the way are not dependent upon specific places of power. Shamanism is not a religion; it is not a regimented system of devotion. Ultimately it is an attitude, a personal discipline, a state of mind. I once asked Antonio if the healing spirit occupied the unconscious mind. He shook his head and replied that spirit is simply mind at its purest. That exchange has always held for me something of the essence of his teaching.

Nevertheless, Eduardo and I had discovered a tightly knit program, a travel itinerary, that served the steps of the Medicine Wheel, and the high plateaus, sacred peaks, and wild jungles of Peru would be my laboratory, my classroom, where I would experiment, teach, and learn.

Perhaps in creating a forum for learning through experience, by leading groups on such expeditions, I began my own work of the East. According to legend, the eagle path in the East is the return to one's tribe. In the East the individual accepts the gift of vision and the task of exercising that vision to create a better world politically, ecologically, and personally, to dream the possible future. Indeed, I had no interest in people seeking a self-serving transcendental experience. Luckily, those who have traveled with me over the years have, by and large, used their experiences as starting points for their journeys, not as the end products.

But although I imagined that I had found the way East, I was only half right. As usual, there were challenges yet ahead, just over the horizon.

Don Florentino Garcia had been Eduardo's teacher, his mentor. I never met the old man, although I would have reason to feel the effect of his death. Don Florentino was the keeper of the sacred lagoons of Las Huaringas, the place where legend held that shamans had come for centuries to receive their initiation as masters. When the old man died one February, it fell to Eduardo to take his place, to journey to the lagoons and claim his stewardship over its waters and initiations. According to untraceable tradition, he had one year from the date of don Florentino's death to assume his responsibility.

But Eduardo, my friend and *compadre,* had begun to fall under the spell of his own power, become seduced by his own persona and the sychophancy of the New Age Europe and United States. He traveled the shamanic circuit, serving the popular folklore. It is the trap that waits for those who identify themselves with their teachings, carve graven images of themselves. We continued to work together, but I soon became sensitized to his growing weakness. He avoided his journey to the lagoons, and the responsibility began to follow him and sap his strength.

As the February approached and, with it, the date that would mark the anniversary of don Florentino's death, I invited a select group of friends and traveling companions to join Eduardo on his pilgrimage, to participate in his ceremony of the redemption of Las Huaringas. It would be a difficult expedition, requiring us to pack into the hills on horseback and on foot, with burros to carry our gear.

When we gathered in Cuzco, Eduardo announced that we would not be going. There had been rains, he said, and the roads and paths had been destroyed. Another time, he said.

We made the best of it. We traveled instead to San Pedro las Castas and the lagoons of Marcahuasi, situated atop a mesa at twelve thousand feet. We descended to the lagoons through ancient ruins to a natural amphitheater surrounded by smooth granite monoliths carved by time and the elements and eerily resembling human faces. There we performed a ceremony of initiation that mimicked that which Eduardo had avoided in Las Huaringas. It was a powerful experience to those who had made the journey, but it was not what we had set out to do, and, watching Eduardo there, I knew that he had failed his challenge. That he had lost an opportunity.

Two events that followed in close succession are worth noting.

The group assembled in Machu Picchu. All those gathered had been there before, and our spirits were high as we entered the ruins at the Gateway of the Sun while Eduardo stood to one side, learning against his carved ceremonial walking staff, and I brought up the rear. I paused before entering and smiled at him. He shook his head and turned to enter the city, planting his staff before him.

Before my eyes, and the disbelieving stares of our group, Eduardo's staff, six feet long hardwood carved in the form of a serpent, leaped from his hands and snapped, fell to the ground in two pieces. He was profoundly shaken by the incident. I suggested to him that this might be an omen, a sign that he, or perhaps we, should not enter the ruins. He waved me off with an impatient gesture, and we crossed the courtyard together.

Ten minutes later, at the Inti Huatana, Eduardo was seized by what I and a medical doctor with the group recognized as an epileptic seizure. He screamed my name and fell face first onto the stones, his eyes crossed hideously in his badly torn face, and, had we not managed to force a bandanna into his mouth, I am sure that he would have bitten through his tongue.

Elliot, the physician, and I carried Eduardo from the ruins, down the hill to the hotel. He recovered physically from his anomalous seizure, although I feel that he is still recovering emotionally, psychologically, spiritually.

Las Huaringas was destroyed later that month, one year to the day after don Florentino's death. The wooden thatched-roof huts that ringed the lagoons were burned; the standing walls of the temples there were knocked down, and the waters were polluted with the charred refuse from the fires. There were shamans in the area who, angered by Eduardo's resolution to share his knowledge with outsiders, disapproving perhaps of his work in Europe and the United States, may have been responsible for the ravaging of this place of legend. We will never know and it is of little consequence. Perhaps someday Eduardo will return to the lagoons and begin to repair the damage. I will be honored to help him.

It was also at this time that an idea that had been struggling to form itself for years began finally to take shape. I cannot identify the moment when it crystallized. It did not spring fully formed and armored like Athena from the head of Zeus, but I was able, one night in Cuzco, to write about it in my current journal.

> *June 21, 1983*
> *Tambo Machay*
>
> Think of Medicine Wheel as a neurological map for overriding the four operative programs of the limbic brain—fear, feeding, fighting, and sex.
>
> Can look at the Medicine Wheel as a simple progression starting in the South: shedding of the past, death, birth, flight.
>
> South, West, North, and East.
>
> Fine. Can we relate the four directions to the four f's?
>
> The mythological themes of the South seem to address the feeding instinct, the "making sure our plate is full," our hunger for love, support, and filling our bellies. Our attachment to the things of the

world. In the South we shed our personal past, shed the self that is an outcast from the Garden and condemned to travel naked, hungry, and unloved by Nature.

And we free the spirits of our personal past, that they may find peace and that they may no longer feed on our present.

Am I grasping for straws, or am I close to something here?

I think I am close, because the South is the Serpent Path, the uruboros, life engaged in the process of eating, life eating life. Feeding.

There is something here, it is metaphorical, mythological. . . .

The West. This is easy. One goes to meet one's death and step beyond fear. By facing death and learning the spirit flight, we identify with the transcendent, immortal Self, we free ourselves from the grip of fear and claim our lives to the fullest, for we can no longer be claimed by death. We face the unknown, that which we fear the most. Fear.

The North. The Feminine. Eros. Where we claim the lineage of men and women of knowledge. The place of the androgynous mind, the creative principle that we personify as God, the union of Sun (masculine) and Earth (feminine), from which all life claims a common ground. Sex. Obviously.

The East. The way of the visionary, whose task is to overcome pride and self-aggrandizement, to envision the possible human. The place of nonviolence in a world divided by struggle. Fighting.

How curious that this ancient formula could relate to the prime functions of a primitive brain, functions that have kept human behavior and consciousness in check for millennia.

Thoughts tumbling over one another: The neocortex developed at a time when primitive man was living under the influence of an absorbed limbic brain, i.e., an animistic environment in which all things in heaven and Earth were visible, living things. The limbic brain was supersaturated with the stimuli of the environment when the neocortex made its appearance, allowing the human to become self-reflexive and distance himself from the environment and its influences by invoking logic and assigning definition to experience—the exodus from the Garden—here man has become as one of us in knowing good and bad. . . .

And, even after the appearance of the thinking brain, the limbic brain continued to drive the neural machinery and steer the course of human history.

Feeding—our oral and anal fixations—our first act as infants, to seek the breast, to continue to associate food with security and satisfaction.

Fear—of conflict, pain, death certainly. The unknown. We will go to any length to avoid the things we fear.

Sex. Need hardly make the point. We are a race driven to distraction by lust, capable of consumption by passion.

Fighting, the violent impulses that we harbor, that can be directed outward toward others, or inward toward ourselves. Suicide is an internalized murder impulse.

Sociological manifestations:

Grain is rotting in silos while millions go hungry at home and abroad.

Billions of dollars are made annually by advertisers targeting our fears.

Sex and violence share equal billing. Violence in the media is graphically unprecedented. New forms of pathological violence are breeding in our cities: the madman with the automatic weapon who massacres schoolchildren, the woman who kills middle-aged men and buries them in her backyard, the pack of teenagers who beat and rape, laughing, sliding on the razor edge between pain and pleasure.

Are we approaching saturation? Again?

Is the ability to override the prime directives of the primitive brain, to step into a new and grander consciousness the next quantum leap in the evolution of this species?

A consummation devoutly to be wished.

A few months later I stood beside the Death Stone, on the little hill overlooking the ruins of Machu Picchu. The group had worked diligently in

Paracas Bay and Nazca. Now we were preparing to engage in the ritual of symbolic death before entering the gates of the city.

The Sun, radiant in the thin Andean air, had broken through the cloud cover of the morning.

"In Nazca," I said, "we discovered that the past that binds us, restricts and guides our behavior, must be captured before it is set free, found before it is lost, worn until it is sloughed off."

I shielded my eyes from the glare of the Sun and happened to glance down to my right. A group of children had entered the ruins. They were headed for the Inti Huatana.

"What we are doing is attempting to enter into a realm of metaphor and myth. With the use of ceremony and ritual, we are engaging with, playing with, the symbols and poetry of a primitive consciousness, bypassing the question-and-answer discourse of our rational minds. There are no hard and fast rules. Our only obligation is to be fully present in the context of these rituals, to free ourselves to whatever we experience. . . ."

That, I believe, was the gist of what I was saying when I glanced again to my right and noticed the figure leading the children. It is some distance from the Death Stone to the Sun Stone, too far to identify an individual, but there was something about the way he moved. A poncho and a wide-brimmed straw hat moved with a familiar stride away from the Sun Stone and disappeared around a corner.

I interrupted myself, excused myself from the group, and trotted down the hill, through the Gateway of the Sun, and across the courtyards of the city. The schoolchildren were not wearing uniforms; they were Indian children, probably from some rural community or village nearby. They sat politely around the Sun Stone, chattering, playing with flutes, whistles, and other such artifacts available at the train station at the base of the mountain.

I hitched up my pants, squatted beside one, a little girl, and asked where her teacher was. She smiled up at me and pointed back toward the Temple of the Spirit Flight. He had gone, she said, to fetch Julio.

There is a room, a chamber behind the Temple of the Spirit Flight. It is an echo room where words whispered reverberate, can be heard even on the other side of the wall, at the dais of the temple. It was there that I found him. He was tying a strip of cloth to Julio's leg. The little boy had wandered away, tripped, and skinned his knee.

"Antonio?"

He looked up from beneath the brim of his straw hat, and the wrinkles of his face creased in a wide grin. His eyes still glistened.

"There!" He held Julio's face in his hand and said, "Run back to the group now. I will be with you in a moment. You be in charge until I return." The little boy smiled and wiped his cheek with a soiled hand and ran off to join his playmates.

21

I can't just suddenly tell you
what I should be telling you,
friend, forgive me; you know
that although you don't hear my words,
I wasn't asleep or in tears,
that I'm with you without seeing you
for a good long time and until the end.

—Pablo Neruda

Antonio had grown old. There was nothing surprising in this, it was only that my assumption of his death had frozen the image I carried of him. But here he was, a handsome old Indian in his mid-seventies, sitting on a lip of granite. He removed his hat and I saw that his hair, once silver-gray, had turned white.

I just stood there, transfixed by his presence.

"Well," he said. He looked me up and down, my trousers, hiking boots, cotton shirt, sunglasses pushed up on my forehead. "I am glad to see that you have not turned into an Indian. Are you hungry?"

He reached under his poncho and produced his little woven pouch.

"Where the hell have you been?" My question bounced off the walls a couple of times, and I moved to a spot I knew would not produce such a raucous echo. Don Jicaram molded a ball of yucca and corn paste.

"I am an old man," he said. "I have returned to my people. When you returned to your home, I realized that my old suits were as unbecoming on me as a poncho and straw hat would be on you." He smiled at this and handed me a portion of food. Our fingers touched and he looked up into my eyes. "It is true that a shaman can leap between the worlds, not only of spirit, but the worlds of culture. You have shown that. So have I. But it was time for me to go home."

"I thought that you had died."

He raised his eyebrows and nodded. "I did," he said. "I died to one of my lives. But you should have known that there was no cause for mourning or anger. Like the jaguar, we have many lives. Part of our task is to learn to leap gracefully from one to the next when one comes to its natural end." He unslung his *bota* from his shoulder and took a drink and handed it to me. "You have been busy," he said. "I am glad."

And I began to tell him of my work, my return to Peru, my meeting Eduardo, my journey North, but I stopped just after I had begun. He knew where I had been. I could see it in his eyes. We grinned at each other. And then he changed the subject on me.

"The thing to understand," he said, "is that the awakening of the ancient memories of the North is not you, the individual, remembering, because you will only remember the events of your life. It is, rather, stepping through the crack between the worlds and taking your place among the twice born, all those who have conquered death. They are those who have done battle with the archetypes and the forces of Nature to become persons of knowledge. They are our ancestors, the trustees of the Earth." He pulled two cinnamon bark sticks from his pouch and handed me one and stuck one in the corner of his mouth.

"The maiden who came to me from the Pachamama . . ."

Antonio laughed with delight. "So! You met the crone, the spirit of the Mother. How did she appear to you?"

And I explained to him how she had stepped out from the Pachamama Stone, maiden and crone, had made love to me, had impregnated me with an awareness of life there, in the meadow.

"She touches us all in different ways," he said. "When I first met her she took me through the labyrinths." He inclined his head in the direction of Huayna Picchu and the Temple of the Moon. "Obviously she used the means that would most capture your attention."

"Did you see the faces?" I asked.

He nodded. "They are the ones who have come before us and who will follow." He removed the cinnamon stick from his mouth and said: "Become them and allow them to become you, and their memories will grow in you, for they are who you are becoming. You must stand on their shoulders, just like Julio and the other little ones will someday stand on yours."

There was a long pause. He stuck the bark back in his mouth. "History trusts us with a responsibility and we abdicate, take refuge in the drama of our personal past. We dishonor history and the lineage of our species when we do not honor our ancestors. We must step outside of ordinary history and go beyond."

"And the Eagle Path?"

"The way of the visionary," he replied. "Where we dream with our eyes open. We all have a future, my friend, but only men and women of knowledge have the possibility of a destiny. In the East the shaman assumes full responsibility for who we are becoming and influences destiny by envisioning the possible."

"There is a popular belief that there are ways of achieving transcendence and gaining control of one's destiny," I said.

He sucked his teeth and shook his head. "Destiny is not something over which you seek to gain control. Control of one's destiny is . . . an oxymoron. But a man or woman of power can *influence* it. Learn to dance with it. Lead it across the dance floor of time."

"Where do you begin?" I asked.

He lifted his brows in a question, looked at me for a long moment, and then nodded. "With the children," he said. He tapped the top of his head with his forefinger and smiled broadly. "The crack between the worlds," he said. "The gap in the skull that we are born with, that closes soon after birth. The seams are still there. They mark the spot." He waved his hand as though to brush away all but this: "We can split atoms and splice genes. The threads of our destiny are in our hands. The task is in braiding them together and leading ourselves into the future."

"And it begins with the children," I said.

He nodded, then stood. "And I must get back to mine."

He slung the *bota* over his shoulder. He placed a hand on my shoulder, as he had done so many times in the past. "Don't stop now, my friend. Stand on our shoulders and look to a distant horizon. We live through you and within you. I see you every month in my full-moon fire." He cleared his throat. "We will meet again," he said. "We have traveled well together, and there are places where I cannot go alone."

He took my hand in his. "It is good to know these things, is it not?"

I squeezed his hand. *"Hasta pronto,"* I said.

"Hasta pronto," he said. And he was gone.

I have not seen him since.

I returned to the group; we completed our work at the Death Stone, entered the ruins, and spent the night there.

The next morning we made our way down the mountain and boarded the train to Cuzco. There are little girls, Indian girls of ten or twelve, who sell trinkets to the tourists, souvenir ceramic beads, necklaces made from old Peruvian coins, flutes and whistles, and such, and over the years I had come to know most of them. As I was boarding the train, one of them, the youngest, called my name. I turned and smiled down at her.

"The old man told me to give you this," she said. She held out her hand, and I took the tiny cloth-wrapped bundle from her palm. I thanked her, bought a couple of simple silver earrings, kidded with her, took my place on the train, and unwrapped the gold owl from don Jicaram's *mesa*. Night vision, forgotten knowledge, the object that I had held the first time I had run, fully conscious, through a forest on the *altiplano*.

22

Between the idea
And the reality
Between the motion
And the act
Falls the Shadow.

—T. S. Eliot

April 5, 1987
Machu Picchu

After hours. Writing by the light of the fire, the best light to write by. This is a unique group. Ten of the eighteen have *not* been inordinately blown away by ritual, have *not* sought instantly to frame their experiences in intricate superstructures of logic and preconception. Their skepticism is healthy, not a thing to fall back on, to find temporary comfort in.

C. is making an issue of keeping me in line. I'm getting sick of her feminism, though. East Coast liberal, stubborn, privileged, Phi Beta Kappa–type, pain in the ass that she is. An M.D. to boot. At least two of the men are in love with her and she remains independent and aloof, her spirit is indomitable. *She* is indomitable, or acts as though she *thinks* she is. We'll see.

"Close your eyes."

"Why?"

Why. We had boarded the train from Machu Picchu to Cuzco. I had purchased the tickets that morning and had doled out a small fortune in *mordida,* money to assure the group of first-class seats on an overbooked train. It had been easy to arrange for us to share a compartment.

"A surprise," I said.

Her eyes, hazel green, searched mine. I raised my eyebrows. "Close them."

She drew a deep breath, exhaled with something just short of a sigh, and closed them. I pulled a grenada fruit from my pocket and split it open with my thumb. She was smiling. The fruit was ripe, juice dripping from my fingertips to the floor of the compartment.

"Well?" she said.

"Open your mouth."

Her smile lifted into a grin, and she leaned her head back and to one side. I looked at her neck. She shook her head.

"Don't you trust me?"

"No."

"Open it," I laughed.

She seemed to make a decision. Her shoulders dropped half an inch, then her lips parted, tongue ready to taste anything. I reached across, hand wavering slightly with the rocking of the train, and placed a wedge of the fruit between her lips. She bit down and the juice ran down her chin. She caught the drop with her forefinger, opened her eyes, and smiled at me with them.

I went to Brazil to write. She returned to New York, then followed. A month later I held a seminar in Germany. She surprised me there. I moved back to Marin County and she gave up a second-year residency at a prestigious hospital to move with me. She applied to three hospitals, was accepted by three, and is currently working at Stanford University Medical Center.

In February of 1988 I led an expedition on a trek along the Inca trail to Machu Picchu, and returned to witness the birth of our son in March.

January 7, 1989
Death Valley

Second day, three-day workshop in the desert. Missing C. terribly. No phone. Spoke with her night before last. Aching for her. Agonizing over whether or not Ian will remember his father after a week's absence. What sweet pain this is.

Midday and the group has scattered, wandered off into the desert. We are fasting and they have left our circle for a day's vision quest. I have built a makeshift signpost of desert driftwood, a red bandanna tied to a long branch like a flag to mark our rendezvous point. I should stay here to maintain a center for them, yet I feel that by-now familiar something moving me.

There is something out there on the eastern horizon. I can see where it is, though there is nothing to see but sand dunes, a mile off.

But I must wait here. It is my responsibility to wait, to hold the center.

Later

Hell with it. This is too strong a pull, and the anxiety is turning my stomach.

I left the circle and headed off over the dunes. January in the desert and the sun was baking the sand and the air that during the night had been near freezing. It was much farther than I had thought, like those dreams where you walk toward a thing on the horizon that keeps receding, because a horizon is relative to you, and you know that you will never reach it, although you feel yourself drawing nearer.

The sand was virgin, soft and deep, and by the time I reached the base of the dune that I sought, my legs were aching, the sweat was dripping down my face, neck, and chest. I had shed my parka and tied it around my waist, peeled off my shirt and tied it around my head. Above me was a lip of sand at the crest of the dune, wind-whipped to a fine edge, and I struggled up the slope, two steps up, one step lost, sliding back in the sand, halfway up, only to slip back to the base, sand sticking to my arms and chest, overheated, panting at the effort.

I turned and looked back in the direction from which I had come, squinted against the reflected sunlight, could not see the bandanna. I checked my watch and realized that I had walked an hour to get to where I was. Three miles? Maybe.

I looked back at the slope, the crest above me, and saw something that I had failed to notice before. To the right, other footprints in the sand, on the slope, leading up, over its edge. The prints were indistinct, dimples in the soft sand, but the spacing was unmistakable. Someone was there, over the crest of the dune. Waiting for me? One of the group? I looked back along the way I had come, at my trail of footprints in the sand, saw that there was another, that I had walked along without realizing that I walked in the footsteps of another.

By now I had caught my breath, although my heart was pounding at the eeriness of it all. Adrenaline rushing, I scrambled up the slope, and, although the crest gave way, a miniature sandslide, I managed to make it over the top.

The footprints were there, on the top of the dune, those that had gone before me, those that I had followed. They ended there. I scanned the horizon, 360 degrees of dazzling bright wind-sculpted dunes. From there I could see the bandanna, a tiny fleck on the horizon, miles away. Then I felt a presence. Felt it between my shoulder blades. Behind me now.

I turn back and the Sun makes me squint, sweat stings my eyes and I blink it away, and there, where the footsteps end, am I. Stripped to the waist, sunburned and sinewy, healthier than I, leaner than I, he sits, cross-legged, wrists resting on knees, eyes closed, head leaning back slightly. His throat is taut, exposed.

It is I, there is no mistake. There are no moon shadows here to play tricks on me.

I have seen so much, encountered so many manifestations of life and spirit in my travels, yet, it is somewhat comforting to know that I can be astonished. As Eduardo said, I am always surprised when a vision steps into my life. It is a happy thing.

And there is a self that clings to semirational consciousness, and I knelt in the sand and touched one of the footprints. Like pinching yourself when you think you might be dreaming.

And as I look across the sand, his eyes open and his face breaks into a grin, and I think, Is this a trap? An hallucination brought on by the Sun?

And I realized that I had a choice.

I could have walked away from the man on the dune. I could have returned to the self that never left the circle, that swallowed the urge to wander off, that waited dutifully for the members of the group to wander back from their day in the desert.

> I have returned, back to the circle. The first back. No one need ever know that I left. . . .

And he laughs, laughs at my foolishness, my self-doubt. And I laugh. I came out of curiosity, no expectations. I came seeking nothing, following an impulse. To find the other. He whom I had left in the jungle.

He told me so.

He unfolded his legs and stood before me and the Sun at my back cast one shadow, mine, across the sand and through him. He spread his arms, palms up.

We embraced.

And I sat in the sand at the crest of the dune, closed my eyes to the Sun, and remembered things that had no business being in my memory.

> There is no such thing as an integrated self, a real you. Antonio's last words begin to make sense. The concept is manifesting itself. . . .

> It is not a question of multiple states of consciousness, but of multiple selves.

> I have met a significant other. The one I left in the jungle, the one who has followed the path of the warrior while I was engaged with my life, searching for destiny, looking to the North. He has been traveling all this time.

I am hard pressed to describe the things I learned. There will be a time and space elsewhere to test, explore, experience the knowledge that settled into my consciousness that afternoon.

I would not relate this particular incident here were it not for its sublime irony in the face of what had come before. After so many years the hunter and the hunted, stalking power and being stalked by it, to come to the top of a simple sand dune and there live an echo of an experience in a clearing before a ruined temple when I had encountered myself in an attitude of meditation, had opened my eyes to stare into the eyes of the jaguar. I had left that self at the bottom of a lagoon, to find him years later at the top of a dune in Death Valley. That the power that I connected with should manifest as myself, should rise from the bottom of a lagoon and walk, casting no shadow, a warrior, an etheric self.

Since writing this I have begun to understand the challenges that lie ahead of me. But, as I have said, these things belong in another space, at another time.

Suffice it here to say that I began to know something of the nature of the Medicine Wheel, the journey of the Four Winds that I had been traveling since I first boarded that jetliner so many Februarys ago.

> I know that the power that one may acquire on the journey of the Four Winds is made of more than knowledge gained, epiphanies of spirit, responsibility felt, and the skills to become a caretaker of the Earth. It is also the acquiring of different lives.
>
> There is an energy body. One acquires this in the South.
>
> There is a Nature body, an etheric body that one acquires in the West. The body of the jaguar. This is the body I found on the dune.
>
> There is an astral body, one that has a lifetime of the stars. This is in the North. The body of the ancient masters. A mystical body. Wisdom of the universe.
>
> There is, I think, a causal body in the East. The thought before the action. That which exists before the fact. Creative principle. The eagle body.
>
> So here I am, knowing that I must continue my journey. There are new questions to be answered. There are experiences yet to be served.

I sat in the sand for a time, and when I stood and walked down the dune, I took care to go by a different route.

I turned at the far base of the dune and looked up and watched the sand sliding down, a crystalline wave, a ripple that swept slowly, slipping along the face of the dune to cover our footprints. And I recalled that the person of knowledge walks without leaving tracks.

Sitting in the living room, before the fire. I went across the street where there is a steep embankment down to a creek that winds through town. There are oak trees and eucalyptus, and I gathered the wood for this fire, made three trips.

This is a fire that cannot be built of store-bought logs.

My lover, my sister, my wife, and friend just returned from thirty-six hours on call. Healing the sick, dispensing care. She walked into the living room, saw me here, came up behind me and touched my shoulder. She said she was going upstairs to see our son, fifteen months old. She sits with him when he sleeps.

She whispered that she loved me and left. She saw the things on the floor, knows what I am doing here. I have an urge to leave the fire and follow her upstairs, to kiss our son and to take her to bed. I feel my love and desire for her glowing, rising from my belly, but I must attend to business.

She saw the journals spread out in a semicircle before me. Volumes of them. Some are cardboard-bound composition books, there is one spiral-bound without a cover. Many have lost their stitching or the glue that holds the pages has decomposed and the pages are loose. There's one that's all taped up, another held together with a rubber band.

Then there is that one, first one, leather bound, the heaviest of them all.

I have been through them all, some for the first time in years. I've made my selections and there is a manuscript on the desk in the office.

This has been my journey East. This book, an attempt to serve the experiences that have changed me. To share them as best I can. But here, before me, all these memories, the experiences, fatuous philosophy and revelations of spring water clarity. Fifteen years of work. A life captured in words.

Experiences that I can serve best by freeing them. Honor them best by giving them to the fire, consigning them all to the flames of this fire. I welcome the spirits that will rise from the fire, bless them and honor them all, free them and free myself, that I may once again step into my present fully. And live every moment as an act of power.

So here I am, a finished book, my work of the East, and I'm already doing the work of the South. Again.

Full circle, like the Medicine Wheel, a circle passing through the cardinal points of the compass, the stages of evolving consciousness, the seasons. Never-ending circle, cycle, uruboros.

And I've learned something else. That of all of my experiences, in all of my travels across the Earth and through it, of all the feelings I have felt, my love for her is the holiest. There is perfect truth in that. Something that can be experienced but not told.

What, after all, have I been searching for? What, after all, is the power that I have acquired in my journeys? I can summon Nature within me, can see things hidden from sight, can soar beyond myself, can teach others such skills, yet the ultimate state of consciousness, the Divine within me is the thing that glows in my belly, rises through my body, illuminates my Self with a healing light when I look at her.

There.

I have found that I need to tear the pages from the bindings, for I do not want anything left readable in the morning.

The older the pages, the faster they burn.

Nevertheless, the fire seems to hesitate, as if the flames are reluctant to touch the last, the oldest, the first.

It must be my imagination.

All that is left is this.

Writing this last sentence before adding it to all the others, hoping that I'll remember what I wrote, because it might, after all, be the best way to close the ceremony, to end the book.

I had every intention of writing a last sentence and placing it in the fire, creating a dramatic moment. But, as Antonio once said, self-conscious ritual is no ritual at all, and as the last page torn from the journal neared the flames, my hand began to tremble.

I was just wondering why when I heard a yawn, and, turning, saw her standing beneath the archway of the living room. Our son was in her arms, his head on her shoulder. Half-asleep, half-awake, between two worlds and in his mother's arms.

I realized that my journey is best marked by beginnings, not endings.

I tossed the page into the fire, stood, slipped the little gold owl into my pocket, and turned to join my family.

BOOKS OF RELATED INTEREST

ISLAND OF THE SUN
Mastering the Inca Medicine Wheel
by Alberto Villoldo and Erik Jendresen

THE WORLD IS AS YOU DREAM IT
Shamanic Teachings from the Amazon and Andes
by John Perkins

SHAPESHIFTING
Shamanic Techniques for Global and Personal Transformation
by John Perkins

PSYCHONAVIGATION
Techniques for Travel Beyond Time
by John Perkins

JAGUAR THAT ROAMS THE MIND
An Amazonian Plant Spirit Odyssey
by Robert Tindall

PLANT SPIRIT SHAMANISM
Traditional Techniques for Healing the Soul
by Ross Heaven and Howard G. Charing
Foreword by Pablo Amaringo

VISIONARY PLANT CONSCIOUSNESS
The Shamanic Teachings of the Plant World
Edited by J. P. Harpignies

RETURN OF THE CHILDREN OF LIGHT
Incan and Mayan Prophecies for a New World
by Judith Bluestone Polich

Inner Traditions • Bear & Company
P.O. Box 388
Rochester, VT 05767
1-800-246-8648
www.InnerTraditions.com

Or contact your local bookseller